S0-AUO-412

COMPUTER WIMP

COMPUTER WIMP

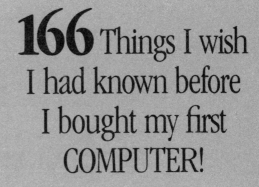

166 Things I wish I had known before I bought my first COMPUTER!

by John Bear, Ph.D.

TEN SPEED PRESS 1️⃣

Book Design and Art Direction: Brenton D. Beck, Fifth Street Design
Illustrations by John Bear, Marina Bear, and Jack Popovich
Illustration on page 50 by Carl Muecke
Book Production by Jack Popovich
Special thanks to Hal Hershey, Jane Rockwell and Jerry Meek

Page 201 reprinted by permission © 1982 Ellis Weiner. Originally in *New Yorker* magazine.

Copyright © 1983 by John Bear
All rights reserved. No part of this book may be reproduced in any form, except for brief reviews, without the written permission of the publisher.

TEN SPEED PRESS
P O Box 7123
Berkeley, California 94707

You may order single copies prepaid direct from the publisher for $9.95 paperbound or $14.95 clothbound + $1.00 for postage and handling (California residents add 6% state sales tax; Bay Area residents add 6-1/2%).

Library of Congress Catalog Number: 81-40024
ISBN: 0-89815-101-5 (paper)
        0-89815-102-3 (cloth)

Printed in the United States of America

10 9 8 7 6 5 4 3

Table of Contents

Table of Contents* v
Dedication and Thanks x

1. **INTRODUCTION** 3
   ***The emperor's new computer: the nature of the
   computer revolution*** 6
   It's just a Medium-Sized Deal
   You mean I really don't have to?
   The effect of the generation gap
   Why they may not be called "computers" in the future
   No one seems to know where we're headed

2. **BUYING COMPUTERS** 11
   Alternatives to buying a computer 13
   Fifty lawn mowers per block
   Time sharing your hardware
   Time sharing your software
   Renting or leasing computers
   Let someone else do it all
   Don't computerize your life
   Psychological aspects of computer buying 17
   Your anguish, despair and frustration quotient
   The Pollyannas
   The Masochists
   The Patners
   Becoming a Former Computer User
   The computer is unlike any other machine 22
   Learnability
   Repairability
   Reliability
   Important issues to consider 25
   Never be the first kid on your block 25
   Bugs in new products
   Plunging prices
   Improving quality
   Disappearing companies
   Resolving the "first kid" problem
   The "But Wait!" syndrome 30
   Dealing with the syndrome
   Why "But Wait!" occurs
   Choose the software before the hardware 35
   Why buy software first
   Shopping for software

---

* Perhaps anyone who requires the Table of Contents to locate the Table of Contents should reconsider getting into computers.

Don't stretch the limits of the equipment 38
   Problems with power
   Problems with time and speed
Never buy anything you can't lift 40
   Moving larger computers
   Moving medium-sized computers
   Moving small computers
Buy stuff for which you have access to duplicates 43
   Longer pre-tests are possible on private equipment
   Diagnosis of problems is easier with two systems
   A back-up machine is available
Why brand-name buying guides are not too helpful 44
The store/dealer experience 48
Technobabble 48
   What to do when they start technobabbling at you
   Hope for the future
Helpfulness survey of 50 computer stores 53
   Choosing the stores
   The questions asked
   What actually happened
   The sad conclusions
Try things out longer than most stores will let you 56
   Usability: will it do what you want?
   Comfort: will you be happy using it?
   The keyboard
   The screen
   Time and motion matters
   The value of a good chair
Don't be snowed by charisma 60
   Some case histories of people who were
   How to avoid making such mistakes
   What you see is not always what you get
Specsmanship 64
   Comparisons among various computers
   Number of bits, speed, instruction set
Bargains 67
Buying computers and software by mail 67
Understanding and dealing with the gray market 69
   Reasons not to deal in the gray market
   Why people deal in the gray market anyway
Buying used equipment 71
   The reasons people sell
   Dealers and brokers
   Checking out a used computer
Buying obsolete equipment 74
   Why computers become obsolete
   Concern about parts and service
Specific hardware issues 78

What memory is, and how much you should have 78
   Necessity factors
   Convenience factors
What modems are, and do you really need one 82
   What modems do
   Problems with modems
   Alternatives to a modem
   How modems get things wrong
Choosing a printer 86
   Appearance of letters
   Cost factors
   Speed factors
   Making your printer decision
Financial matters 91
Price vs. service considerations 91
It's OK to haggle 92
What it really costs to buy a computer 93
   One-time-only start-up costs
   Essential additional hardware
   Non-essential additional hardware
   What software you will need
Financing a computer purchase 100
   Traditional financing
   Lease/purchase plans
   Becoming a dealer or salesperson
   Becoming a demonstration site
   Getting someone else to buy it for you
Warranties 103
Computer warranties are absolutely shameful 103
   The nature of most warranties
   Extended warranties and service contracts
   Negotiated warranties
   If other products were sold like computers
   Independent repair contracts
   The delayed warranty scam

3. USING COMPUTERS
The one single most important thing of all 115
How do you learn more? 122
Computer books and magazines 122
Computer courses 125
   Colleges
   Alternative learning centers
   Proprietary schools
   Courses by mail
   Support groups
Computer shows 127
   Manufacturers' shows
   Dealers' shows
   Consumer shows

Strategies for getting into shows and getting the most out of them
You're smarter than you may have thought (a short pep talk) 134
How computers are used and misused 137
Cataloguing your necktie collection 137
Trivial or unnecessary uses of computers
Educational trivia
Personal finance trivia
Home information trivia
What people really do with their computers 140
About programming 142
What programming is 142
Your right not to be a programmer 144
The five kinds of programming, and who will use them 147
Machine language programming
Programming languages
Program changing
Program adjusting
Program using
Games 152
It's really all right to play games
Games are cheap entertainment
Games do not necessarily develop literacy
Miscellaneous matters 158
What word processing is all about 158
Using word processing
The costs of word processing
Shopping around for supplies 163
Typesetting by computer 165
What it means
Typesetting with your own computer

4. **PROBLEMS WITH COMPUTERS** 169
Sources of problems 171
Computers are more fragile than many people think 171
Problems caused by the environment
Problems caused by mysterious forces
Problems caused by human beings
Mechanical problems
Problems caused by poor disk management
The nature of problems 183
The dreaded 99% factor
Dealing with the 99% factor
The incompatibility problem
What to do about incompatibility
Software failure
How a tiny error can be disastrous
Don't ask why, just keep on going
Psychological problems 196

The causes of anguish 196
    Poor instructions
    Inaccurate instructions
    Equipment failure
Price shock syndrome 198
The Gee Whiz syndrome 200
Dealing with repairs 205
  Finding a support group
  All about Riffims
  Don't (necessarily) do it yourself
  How to talk to a repair person
  Is it a hardware or a software problem
  Repairs by telephone
  Problems with repairs
  Proposal for a telephone repair and counseling service
Two ultimate solutions 225
  Computer consumer karate 225
  Change horses in midstream 229

5.   THE DARK UNDERBELLY OF THE COMPUTER WORLD . . 233
   1,000,000 mistakes per second 235
   Fear of computers 239
     How widespread is this fear
     What is the nature of the fear
     What people do about computer fear
   Health hazards of computers 242
     Physical problems
     Psychological problems
     Spiritual problems
   Deciding whether or not to be a pirate 245
   Stealing computers and computer time 249
     Preventing theft of computers
     Preventing theft of time
   Computer sabotage 252
     Sabotaging a poorly-working machine
     Killing the machine before it kills you
     Dealing with the urge to kill
   Computer crime 254
     How computer crime goes undetected
     Various kinds of computer crimes
     What can be done about crime
   Computers and privacy 258
     How computers destroy privacy
     What can we do about it
   Computers and the economy 260

6.   REFERENCE, ETC. 263
   My computer autobiography 264
   Books you may wish to read 269
   Glossary of relevant terms 273
   Index 284

Dedication

Wait a minute. I know no one reads dedications (except, perhaps, the person being honored) but I wish you'd read this one, because it helps to explain why this book exists, and what's in it for you.

TO THEODORE R. HENDERSHOT, CAPT., U.S.N. (Retd.) for the following reason.

Ted Hendershot runs an art gallery in the little village in which we live. We say 'Hello' to each other outside the post office. One morning, at that very location, Ted stopped me and said,

"Say, *you* know all about computers. Maybe you can give me some advice. We're thinking about getting a little computer for the gallery. You know, perhaps to keep track of inventory, and a customer mailing list. Income taxes, accounts receivable. Things like that. We'd like to have your thoughts on what we might do."

My immediate reaction was to think, "But there's so *much* to say — so many things you need to know — to watch out for — to consider. Good grief, it would take a *book* to say everything that needs to be said."

What I said was, "I'll get back to you."

Sorry it took two years, Ted, but here's my answer, at last.

Very Special Thanks

The only two people I know who are highly fluent in both English and computers have been extremely helpful to me for years, most recently in reading and intelligently commenting on the manuscript for this book. My grateful thanks to Julie Norman and Mike Young.

Thanks

My computer education, such as it is, has come from interactions with a great many people in the industry. As I look back, I realize I have learned the most from Kaye K. Nelson, Marta McKenzie, Bernie Macdonald, Tom Lee, Michael Potts, Swami Ninad, and even David Sexton and Ralph Kling. Thank you all.

PART ONE

INTRODUCTION

The Emperor's New Computer: The
Nature of the Computer Revolution

I always wanted driving a computer to be just like driving a car.

I enjoy driving a car.

I don't mind checking the vital fluids and the tire pressure.

I did change the oil once, but it was no fun, and as long as somebody else is willing to do it in a few minutes for a few dollars, why bother.

Under no circumstances would I ever consider tuning the engine, replacing the alternator, or rebuilding the transmission.

This analogy comes often to mind, as I find myself with telephone handset jammed between shoulder and ear, delicately attempting to plug a 36-pronged chip into what surely must be a 34-hole socket, while an anonymous voice on the manufacturer's Technical Support Hotline in Tulsa, Oklahoma is trying to talk me down.

What has gone wrong?

Why should an intelligent, manually-dextrous, communicationally-proficient human being regularly be turned into a quivering, angry, frustrated, despondent computer wimp, when all he wants to do is drive the damned machine?

There are a lot of books written for the computer beginner. I tried most of them, but the various authors' idea of beginner is not my idea of beginner. And besides, computer people are, by and large, the worst writers in the world, often managing to be both terminally smug and technically incomprehensible at the same time.

Here is an unsolicited testimonial from me. If I had had this book in 1975, before I bought the first of my four computers, I would have saved at least $50,000, thousands of hours of my life, and probably staved off at least four attacks of gout.

If I can spare even one person out there my fate, then I will surely have earned my place in heaven, and a dollar in royalties to boot.

1.

"Driving" a computer should be as easy to learn and do as driving a car — but rarely is.

It is only when they go wrong that machines remind you how powerful they are.

—Clive James

The Emperor's New Computer: The Nature of the Computer Revolution

The medium-sized deal

All right, *something* is going on out there, but it may not be exactly what many of us have thought.

What has happened is that approximately one out of every thousand people on earth has bought a small computer. If the forecasters are right, by the time the 1990s roll around, perhaps four or five people out of every thousand will jump on this particular electronic bandwagon.

In 1983, computer sales in the richest nation on earth will amount to about $35 per person.

The man who wrote *Time* magazine's cover story when they named the computer as "Man of the Year" doesn't particularly like computers. "I've edited on a word processor, and I don't like them," he says.

The man who wrote the book you're reading now *does* like computers, and that is why he used one to write and edit the book.

What a mixed bag of evidence there is, once you get past the popular magazines' cover stories, the 35 computer magazines to be found on any self-respecting newsstand, and the throngs waiting to get into the computer shows, fairs, and festivals. (I've just returned from what the press called "One of the biggest computer shows ever." More than 40,000 came. But more than 3 million living within a 30-mile radius did not.)

Over a thousand computer books are being published each year — but none has yet appeared on a best-seller list along with the diet books and the cat books.

What does it all mean? Clearly, there is *something* important happening out there. Computers have already changed our lives, and will continue to do so. But we must distinguish between *other people's computers* — the big ones that design airplanes, handle our credit card accounts, fight wars, and fill our mailboxes with "junk mail," — and *our own computers* — the IBMs, Apples, Radio Shacks, Osbornes, Timex-Sinclairs, and Sonys that we buy for under $10,000 and set up in our homes or small businesses.

Small computers may, in time, become a really big deal. But for now, they are much more of a medium-sized deal.

Voice recognition is a developing science.

2.
The computer revolution may relate more to other people's bigger computers than to our small personal ones.

You mean I don't have to?

While I was writing this book, I sent letters to the editors of more than 100 daily newspapers, describing what I was doing, and inviting people to write or telephone me and tell me how they felt about small computers. I was deluged by the response. And when I got it all sorted out, the respondents generally fit into these four categories:

About 50% of the people said, in effect, "Do you mean that I really don't *have* to join the computer revolution?" These people expressed a tremendous feeling of relief when I reassured them that they could probably live out their lives in peace and joy without ever setting foot in a computer store.

About 20% of the people told me that they were really interested in taking the plunge, but they were having a lot of trouble finding the diving board. They were almost hopelessly confused by the number of different computers (a new brand came on the market every three days in 1982!); the advertising (who makes a better computer — Charlie Chaplin, Bill Cosby, George Plimpton, or Dick Cavett?); the magazines; the shows; and copious advice and counter-advice from friends and neighbors.

About 20% already *had* small computers and weren't totally thrilled by the experience. They were disappointed by their hardware, their software, or, most commonly, their inability to make the computer a truly important addition to their lives.

The remaining 10% also had small computers, and were so happy with them, they were on the verge of threatening to send goons out to my house to break my typing fingers if I said even one bad word about these fantastic tools.

Of course this isn't even remotely an impartial survey — but I think it does accurately identify the four categories of people who have more than passing interest in small computers.

The generation gap

If we are having a genuine computer revolution, we'll know for sure in about 20 more years. Major changes in society rarely happen all at once to everybody. When huge numbers of people emigrated to America from Germany, Italy and Sweden, the old people never really did learn English well or fit into "the American way of life." The young people learned pretty fast. And the babies born in America grew up utterly American.

3.

Draft dodgers in the computer revolution probably won't be punished.

Just because 'everyone else' is doing it doesn't mean you have to do it too.

However extraordinary computers may be, we are still ahead of them. Man is still the most extraordinary computer of all.

—John F. Kennedy

4.

People who come to computers later in life cannot expect to be as good as children who have grown up with them.

5.

The free-standing computer may fade away as small computers are built into various household tools and appliances.

Date: March 3, 1860
PROJECTED NUMBER
OF HORSES IN
AMERICA, 1860–1980

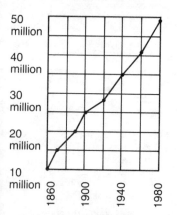

This projection was 25 times too high. Unexpected events play havoc with any long-range forecasting.

So it is with small computers. We middle-aged folks will never, ever feel as comfortable or be as knowledgeable as today's teenagers. My 17-year-old daughter has no particular interest in the computer phenomenon *per se* — but she keeps her diary on the Osborne computer at school, and guards her disk the way the last generation fretted about their secret little books. And *her* children will routinely use computers of all kinds — even though they may call them something else.

What do you mean, they may not call them "computers?"

Therein lies perhaps the best answer to where things are headed.[1] Consider the invention of the modern electric motor by Tesla nearly a century ago. People were fascinated by this development, and many people acquired electric motors simply as a curiosity.

But the *real* growth of electric motors came as they were incorporated into all kinds of other machinery. No one says, "I'm going to buy a vacuum cleaner plus an electric motor" (or a washer or a food processor or a water pump or a typewriter). The motor is taken for granted when we acquire the machine or appliance that it runs.

So it may well be with computers. By the time the millennium rolls around, the "free standing" home computer, sitting there on the kitchen table, may be as rare as a free-standing electric motor is today. But it is more than likely that each home will contain a dozen or more separate computers, built into the television, the burglar alarm, the car, the lighting system, the doorbell, the stove, and almost every other machine or gadget. We may not call them computers any more than we call them "motorized washing machines" today.

However — notice the "weasel words" in that paragraph: "may," "likely," etc. The simple fact is . . .

No one knows where we're headed

In 1948, the founder of IBM predicted that as many as 12 companies might someday have their own computers (an estimate expanded to 50 companies by 1954!). Experts really aren't very good at forecasting the future of technological things.

---

1. I am grateful to Robert Wachtel for the following line of reasoning.

Sometimes, as with the 12-computer prediction, they are incredibly pessimistic. Sometimes, as when AT&T predicted 500,000 homes with picturephones by 1980, the error is on the side of optimism. Banking has been "poised to leap into the cashless, checkless, electronic money world" for a quarter of a century — with *Changing Times* magazine lamenting in 1968 that we would not see the end of checks until the mid-1970s.

Anyone who thinks that *anyone* can predict our technological future with any accuracy is well advised to read back issues of *Popular Science* and comparable magazines. Most enlightening. *Scientific American,* which was intensely interested in the concept of aviation, didn't even *mention* the Wright Brothers flight until nearly three years after it happened!

I enjoy Arthur C. Clarke's hypothesis that about half the great inventions of history were not really big surprises — they had been speculated about for years (airplanes, television, movies); while the other half were complete surprises — utterly unexpected, until they happened (phonograph, nuclear power, lasers).

Will astonishing breakthroughs revolutionize the revolution we've already got going? Or will computers "merely" continue to get smaller, faster, cheaper, and more versatile? Stay tuned.

One last thing, before plunging in

As it happened, I was living in England when that country undertook one of the major social-technical changes of the century: the largest country ever to "go metric."

Years of planning, study, public relations, advertising, and consumer education were undertaken. And then one day I had need of a piece of wood. I studied and rehearsed what I was supposed to say. I headed for the lumberyard, and said to the man in charge,

"I'd like a 5-centimeter by 10-centimeter board, 2 meters long."

Without hesitation, he turned and shouted, "Alvin, get this bloke a 6-foot 2 b' 4."

Somehow, I knew everything was going to be all right.

6.
Experts have been remarkably wrong in predicting where we are headed in our technological revolution.

MARK I

MARK II

MARK III

PART TWO

BUYING COMPUTERS

Alternatives to buying a computer. Psychological aspects of computer buying. The computer is unlike any other machine. Important issues to consider. The store/dealer experience. Bargains. Specific hardware issues. Financial matters. Warranties.

Alternatives to Buying a Computer

Fifty Lawn Mowers Per Block

Once we lived in a fancy Chicago suburb. Every Saturday morning, at about 10:30, a certain ritual began. For as far as the eye could see, up and down Mulberry Lane (and doubtless on all the other streets as well) similarly-attired men went to their garages, fired up their power lawn mowers, and spent the next 20 minutes trimming their one-sixth of an acre of grass.

The thought regularly occurred to me, as I played my role in this pageant, that I was looking at more than $10,000 worth of lawn mowers on my street alone. What would have happened if some enterprising soul had gone 'round to all the houses and said, "Why don't 50 of us chip in $20, and we'll buy one *really* good professional quality lawn mower that each of us can use half an hour a week. Then we can sell the ones we have now, and donate thousands of tax-deductible dollars to worthy charities."

While such a lawn mower entrepreneur may well have been accused of latent socialism and banished from the neighborhood, the philosophy makes sense, and is regularly applied in the computer industry.

In fact, throughout the 1960s and most of the 1970s, most prognosticators were saying that the future of the home and small business computer industry lay in time-sharing: people would have a small terminal of some sort in their homes or offices, connected by telephone lines to a big computer somewhere else.

The development of sophisticated self-contained small computers has vastly changed the future in this regard, but there is *still* a lot to be said for considering possibilities other than "just" your own little machine on your own premises.

7.

It often makes sense to rent time on someone else's computer rather than to buy your own.

It is said that one machine can do the work of fifty ordinary men. No machine, however, can do the work of one extraordinary man.

—Elbert Hubbard

Time sharing your hardware

Think of time sharing this way. Suppose you wanted to own 50,000 books for your business and pleasure reading. The cost is out of the question, so you get thousands of your neighbors to go in with you for a few dollars a year; you buy a building, and fill it with books, to which you and your neighbors have access whenever you want. You might call it "The Public Library." By pooling your resources, all of you can have something that none can have alone.

A similar principle works with computer hardware. You would like to work on a $50,000 machine — so you and lots of other people all agree to pay an hourly or monthly or annual fee, and the money collected enables an entrepreneur to buy the big machine, and make it available to all of you.

"Available" can mean either that you physically go and sit in the place where the big machine is located, or, more commonly, you buy a relatively inexpensive device (a keyboard, a screen, and a telephone connector; probably under $1,000, altogether) that lets you interact with the big machine over the telephone lines.

Time sharing your software

Computer people talk about "accessing a data base." A data base is a place where a lot of information is stored. One data base might contain the contents of all the books in the University of Nebraska library. Another might have all the major league baseball statistics. Another might be all the news stories appearing in the Washington Post last year. Names and addresses of all gynecologists. Three hundred fast-action computer space games. Programs to do income taxes, cash flow projection, and other business behaviors, etc.

With your small computer, you can "access" any or all of this information over your telephone lines. So you, along with hundreds or thousands of other users pay a low hourly rate instead of having to make the very large investment to acquire all that information in the first place.

Is it better to time share, or to buy your own equipment or software?[1] There is no simple answer. You will find advocates of both — and of doing some of each. Using other people's hardware

---

1. Most new words are explained in the Glossary, page 273.

"Time Sharing"

or software certainly increases your repertoire of available programs. Your start-up costs are lower, although you may end up over the years, for instance, spending $7 an hour for 100 hours' use of a general ledger program that costs $350 to buy for your very own. And while time-sharing companies theoretically work extra hard to keep their programs running well, there is no guarantee of this—and you are at the mercy of the telephone company, your own "modem" device that connects your computer into the phone lines—and of the phone lines themselves, which are not always 100% reliable in transmitting electronic information.

It costs so little to try out various aspects of time sharing, it seems to me a better risk to hook into some time sharing and then abandon it, than to buy a lot of equipment for a self-contained system, and then wish you had decided to time share.

Renting or leasing computers

Renting the actual computer equipment that sits in your home or office, whether or not it is to be hooked into some time sharing system, is the least risky way of finding out if you really want to get involved.

In most larger, and some smaller cities, there are companies that rent small computers, printers, and other equipment on a month-to-month basis, often with only a one or two month minimum. Even though you may be paying between 5% and 10% of the cost of the equipment each month, renting gives you an unparalleled opportunity to find out, on your own premises and with your own data and your own needs, whether (1) you wish to computerize at all, and (2) whether this particular equipment is good for you.

Some rental companies will apply a percentage (often 50%) of rental fees to the purchase price, should you decide to buy that

8.
Rent and try out expensive programs over the telephone lines before you buy them.

9.
Rent or lease a computer (or additional equipment) to audition it before you buy.

which you are renting. Software or program rental, formerly restricted either to very large, complex and expensive programs, or to inexpensive "dollar a day" type computer games is becoming available for a wide variety of programs. Some rental companies do rent package deals, such as a computer plus a word or number processing program.

Let someone else do it all

Hanging on the wall at the famous little advertising agency that gave me my first real job were the agency's two mottoes. One was, "Never do anything that someone else can do better."[2] This philosophy is especially important for people considering computerizing their lives or their businesses. There is something psychologically satisfying about having all your possessions within arm's length, as it were, instead of worrying about your precious words and numbers stored in someone *else's* computer, perhaps many miles away.

Also, some people find it very difficult to delegate responsibility, and they fear that some data-keeper — some hired hand — can never treat *my* data with as much loving care as *I* would.

Still, there is a great deal to be said for considering the use of a Computer Service Bureau. These are businesses that have their own computers, and do all the (relevant) work for you. They punch your words and numbers into their machines, using their personnel. Then they crank up their computers, and supply you with your payroll, your reports, your mailing labels, or whatever may be covered by your agreement with them.

You have none of the fears of machines failing (most service bureaus have agreements with other users of identical machinery, to share in case of disaster), programming errors, etc. It's like taking your clothes into a Laundry Service Bureau: you don't really care what equipment they use, who services it, or what brand of soap they use. You just want your clothes back nice and clean.

Don't do it at all

One of the serious options to consider as an alternative to buying a computer is not to computerize your life at all. It is surprising how many people fail to consider this alternative, which is discussed in some detail on page 139.

---

2. The other motto probably has a great deal of relevance for some computer enthusiasts: "Anything worth doing is worth overdoing."

10.
Computer service bureaus are a valid alternative to having your own computer.

Please Patronize
LES & DICK'S
COMPUTER
SERVICE BUREAU
★ ★ ★ ★ ★ ★ ★
PROMPT
ACCURATE
FRIENDLY

11.
Not computerizing at all is a valid alternative to having your own computer.

Psychological Aspects of Computer Buying

Consider Your Own Anguish, Despair, or Frustration Quotient

We humans respond in many different ways in times of stress. A child is hit by a car. While one witness may go into hysterics or stand around in shock, another will rush up to administer first aid, while a third may already be formulating plans to start a citizen's group against drunk driving.

It is most emphatically the case that the process of learning to use a computer will produce a large number of moments that may range from mild frustration to severe anguish to black soul-shattering despair — quite frequently all in the same afternoon.

The *causes* of anguish, despair, and/or frustration are considered on page 171. Here, I wish to look at the four basic ways that people deal with their computer problems. The better prepared you are to understand this matter of dealing with problems, the less likely computers are to be, quite literally, hazardous to your mental health.

I think of the four categories of people as *Pollyannas, Masochists, Patners,* and *Former Computer Users.* The four are not mutually exclusive; you may have some elements of each at any given time, or move from one to another with the passage of time.

The Pollyannas

The original Pollyanna always saw the bright side of everything, and no matter what misfortunes befell her, she just knew that everything was going to turn out all right in the end.

We are all Pollyannas when we buy our first computer. Oh, sure, we're vaguely aware that some people have had some problems, but we've read the glossy brochures and the friendly, well-written advertisements (if only the ad writers and the instruction manual writers changed jobs!), and if Charlie Chaplin and Bill

"Frustration."

12.

We are all Pollyannas when we get our first computer. The feeling doesn't, however, last long.

"Anguish."

Cosby and all those legions of bright nine-year-olds are getting along so well, surely an intelligent, motivated grown-up can (etc. etc.).

And then things start to go wrong. Maybe little things, like a bad cable connection or a flickering screen or an "e" key that types out "eee" everytime you hit "e" or a printer with a funny squeaking noise (to name four things that happened to me so far this month). Maybe big things, confusing things, or mysterious things.

With the first problem comes the quite reasonable attitude, "It must be something minor, and it is undoubtedly my fault for not reading the instructions properly." To be sure, sometimes this *is* the case. (See page 206, on "Riffims.") Often, unbeknownst to the new user, it is not. Some small sores *are* incipient cancers.

With problems 2 through, let's say, 20 or 30, Pollyannaism persists. At this point, anywhere from a few hours to a few months into the computer experience, most users start moving, sometimes slowly, often abruptly, into one of the other three categories.

The category chosen (or evolved into) will determine the level of success or failure in your relationship with computers for years to come.

Masochists

Some people, for whatever reason, seem to enjoy pain. To their "traditional" arsenal of whips, chains, drinking to excess, various drugs, lusting after unattainable love objects, supporting fringe political parties, and/or flying regularly on certain midwestern commuter airlines, can be added a new masochistic diversion, "getting into computers."

It truly surprises me how many people there are — I have spoken to scores of them — who have had the most devastating problems, over and over again, and keep coming back for more.

This dialogue occurs, in one form or another, time after time:

FRIEND: "But why? You have had satisfactory use of your equipment for less than 30 days in the last year. It has been in the shop nine times. Your business is suffering. Why do you persist?"

WIMP: "Well, they said if I bought this new RAM card, and had my connections re-plated in gold, that should take care of the problems."

FRIEND: "Yes, but didn't they tell you a month ago that your problem was dirty disks and a too-slow baud rate on your printer?"

Men have become the tools of their tools.

— Henry David Thoreau

WIMP: "Admittedly—and before that, it was the wrong software, and that I didn't love Jesus. But don't you see, eventually it *will* all be solved."

Unlikely, at least in the way the poor soul thinks. He or she may well go on suffering forever while awaiting computer perfection, or, dare we hope, may move on to one of the other two categories of computer users.

The computer is a hammer. It has its uses, but you don't have to go and hammer something just to prove you're alive.

—Marina Bear

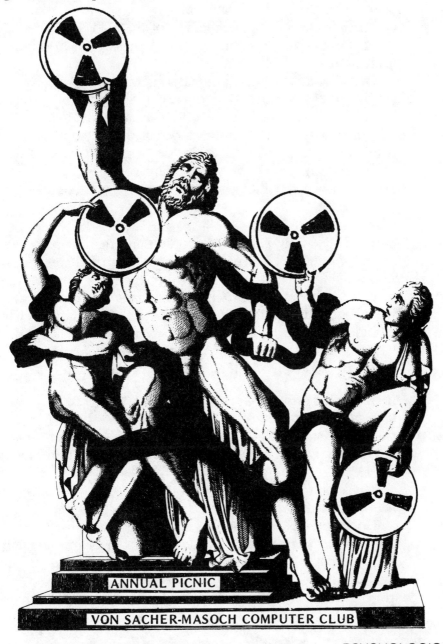

ANNUAL PICNIC

VON SACHER-MASOCH COMPUTER CLUB

13.

Prolonged computer
happiness is more a
matter of personality
than of hardware and
software.

Patners

Long ago, in Chicago, I had a friend named Marshall Patner, who was a very active and very dedicated public interest lawyer. There is a great deal for a public interest lawyer to do in Chicago, and Marshall, it seemed, was trying to do it all: filing suits and counter-suits, seeking injunctions, and otherwise trying to deal with corruption and evil-doing in government, law enforcement agencies, and huge corporations.

An extremely high percentage of the things he tried to do failed. Cases were lost on appeal. Witnesses disappeared. The political machine rolled on.

One day, following a particularly devastating courtroom defeat, I asked Patner how he could go on tilting at this unfair world of windmills. A big smile came onto his face, and he said,

"Ah, but you must understand that the personal satisfaction from each victory overcomes the despair of a thousand defeats. And with each victory, the world improves just a little. Even with nine steps backward for every ten forward, you eventually reach your goal."

A thousand defeats? Well, for me, more like three. But the Patner philosophy is often the only thing that keeps me going. Once I spent the better part of a day trying to alphabetize a list of names using my computer's alphabetizing program. It came out scrambled. It came out backwards. It came out alphabetized by the second letter of the first name. I could have done it by hand in half an hour. But the feeling of joy when it finally did work right was so strong, so sustaining, that it gave me nourishment to survive the next dozen problems in good mental health.

14.

There are two kinds of
errors in getting into
computers: stopping
too soon when you
should have gone on,
and going on too long
when you should have
stopped.

Former Computer Users

Of course there are quite a few people whose anguish, despair, or frustration quotient is exceeded often enough, or powerfully enough, so that their solution is to become a Former Computer User.

There is nothing wrong with this; indeed, it is a subject I treat briefly on page 231.

However, it is sad to see it happen, because quite often, there might have been satisfactory alternatives involving keeping the computer, had there been sufficient understanding or proper counseling.

A man who has been "done wrong" by 16 consecutive women can be excused for giving up and joining the nearest monastery. But number 17 (or indeed one of the earlier ones, with proper counseling) might have been a perfect life mate.

In life and in computers, as in statistics, there are two kinds of errors: stopping too soon when it would have gotten better, and continuing too long when you should have stopped sooner, thereby making it worse.

Whether one goes on suffering, looks for the silver lining, or gives up entirely is, in large measure, a matter of personality. The better this is understood before taking the initial plunge, the better the likelihood of surviving nicely as a Patner, and that is not only the best for which one can hope, it's actually not bad at all.

Giving up entirely is a valid alternative.

Job was visited with a series of tests from the Lord: his children were murdered, his sheep and camels killed, and he was covered with running sores from head to foot. He shaved his head, rent his cloak, yet kept his faith in God. Cyber-Bible scholars have recently determined that, had Job been visited with mis-aligned disk drives, he most assuredly would have torn out his hair, rent his apartment, and whether or not he actually ended up in the lower circles of Hell, it surely would have felt that way.

The Computer Is Unlike Any Other
Machine You Have Dealt With

15.

Learning to use a computer is the most complex mental activity most people will engage in between school and death.

As we go through life buying machinery — cars, lawn mowers, refrigerators, television sets, washing machines, and the like — we have developed certain expectations about what it is like to deal with a new machine in our lives.

These expectations relate to:

— its learnability: how long will it take before the machine is up and running, and how long will it take to learn everything there is to know about it;

— its reliability: how often can we expect things to go wrong; and

— its repairability: what happens when things do go wrong.

In all these respects, dealing with a computer is quite different from any machinery experience most people have ever had before. Understanding and acknowledging these differences can greatly reduce the frequency and the duration of the periods of distress and anguish that inevitably will occur. Consider:

Learnability

If you are all through with school, and unlikely to take up brain surgery or differential calculus as a hobby in your later years, learning to use a computer is probably going to be the most complex and difficult mental activity you will experience between now and the end of your life.

Our machines are so complicated, the human element doesn't enter into them.

—IBM spokesman, quoted by the New Yorker, 1946

There is nothing wrong with this — indeed, for some people, the intellectual challenge is more stimulating and satisfying than the end result. But for people who have grown accustomed to plugging in a refrigerator and immediately filling it with food; or buying a new car and spending at best a quarter hour with the owner's manual to learn how to work the radio, air conditioning, and six-way power seat, there is a rude awakening in the realization that it will be many hours, probably days, perhaps weeks or months, before one can drive the computer slowly around the block.

Another factor to consider — more psychological than educational — is the fact that no matter how hard you try, you will probably never be as skilled in using a computer as thousands and thousands of teenagers are right now. For people who are accustomed to becoming quite good at things they do, the feeling can be quite debilitating: "If I'm never going to do it well, then I don't want to do it at all."

(A foreign language teacher once told me that he no longer brings in small native children to speak to the class. When a person who has been struggling for five years to speak Japanese suddenly realizes that she will never speak it as well as that five-year-old child, a pall of gloom descends over the learning process.)

Reliability

As buyers of machinery of all kinds, from can openers to pick-up trucks, we have come to expect a certain level of performance, and we have developed a set of behaviors to deal with unsatisfactorily performing machinery.

In fact, the State actually intervenes in certain common machinery-failure situations, as in the so-called "Lemon Laws" that require a car dealer (in California, at least) to replace or refund the purchase price on a new car that needs repairs four times for the same problem.

For many people in many situations, these expectations simply do not apply to the computer experience. Whether the failing is in the machinery, the programs, the instruction manuals, or the human being using the equipment, the number of actual failures (that is, situations in which something, or perhaps everything, works incorrectly) will be vastly higher than with any other kind of machinery.

To be sure, "failures" will range from 15-minute stoppages while you try to figure out what the manual is attempting to say, to two-month delays while a part is returned to Korea for adjustment. But it is the sheer number of events that cause some users to throw in the towel. This matter is discussed further on page 18.

BOEING 717

There are three roads to ruin: women, gambling, and technicians. The most pleasant is with women, the quickest is with gambling, but the surest is with technicians.

—Georges Pompidou

Repairability

Once again, we mortals who never quite understood why refrigerators get cold, or whether the toast in the toaster rises due to magnetism, levitation, or a catapult of some sort, have grown accustomed to a certain procedure in getting machinery repaired. If it's heavy, someone comes to the house and fixes it. If it's light, we take it in somewhere (or, perhaps, mail it in somewhere) to be fixed.

The small computer industry is still much too new to have established standard procedures for getting stuff repaired. I have been told a great many stories of complex and distressing problems people had while trying to get repairs done, not the least of which is figuring out which part is defective to begin with (when each of six different parts might be sent to six different places for appropriate treatment).

This matter is discussed in some detail on page 220.

Important Issues to Consider

Never Be the First Kid on Your Block to Buy Anything New

If my publisher told me that, due to a cost overrun problem, this book would have to be re-subtitled, "Two Things I Wish I Had Known Before Buying My First Computer," this definitely would be one of them. (The other is described on page 115.)

The First Kid On His Block

The temptation is often almost overwhelming to buy the newest, the latest, the most clever computer or electronic gadget, machine, or program. As one who has long subscribed to the "He who hesitates is lost" school of life (as opposed to the "Look before you leap" school), I have, time after time, acted quickly (detractors might say "impulsively"), buying some computer-related wonder, and been very sorry for it, anywhere from nine seconds to a few months later.

There are four good reasons to resist this sort of temptation. The first is by far the most important, but the others bear consideration as well.

1. Bugs

New technology, whether hardware or software, is almost certain to have bugs, or flaws, or problems. Because of the difficulty in detecting all the problems at the factory and because of considerable pressure from the marketing and the financial departments to get the item out on the market before someone else comes along with something similar (or better or cheaper), it is quite common for flawed or defective computers and computer programs to be offered for sale.

16.
Never be the first on your block to buy anything new.

17.
Manufacturers often rush products onto the market before they're ready.

Sometimes the manufacturer knows *specifically* what is wrong, and hopes that it is not wrong enough to cause most buyers to return it. Much more often, however, the manufacturer can be pretty sure that *something* (or, more likely, *many* things) are wrong—and he is going to let the early customers be the guinea pigs, to find and report the flaws.

Once, a remarkably candid service department manager, who was checking my machine in for the fifth time for the same problem (disk drives that were supposed to be double-sided—i.e., able to read *both* sides of a two-sided disk, but could only read one side) said, "You know, when they came up with these double-sided drives, they figured it would take six months to a year of testing them to be sure they had it right. Rather than deprive the public of them for so long, they decided to release[1] them at once, and let the early customers do the testing for them."

Gee, that's great. I was a guinea pig, and didn't even know it. Howzabout an ethical marketing department saying, "We're looking for 500 customers to try out our new Whatever for six months. We'll sell it to you at 30% off, and give you a year's free service for your help." Sounds great, but the Vice President for Ethics would be overruled by the Vice President for Marketing: "We can't do that. We know that three of our competitors are about to release similar products, and *they* aren't going to wait to get all the bugs out."

Alas.

2. Plunging prices

When you are first on the market with something wonderful that everyone wants, you get to set your own price. In the fall of 1972, I paid $350 for a one-function digital watch, complete with batteries that lasted about six weeks. It didn't even work that well. It has been on my mind to go back to Tiffany's and ask for a refund, but since comparable watches are now selling for $3.95, they are unlikely to treat me seriously unless they covet one for their museum of historical curios.

Computer prices have fallen quite incredibly since the days, a generation ago, when a million dollars bought a room-sized machine that literally was able to do less than the $39 Casio calcu-

18.

The price of new products often drops dramatically soon after they come on the market.

---

1. "Release" is the word computer marketers use for putting things out on the marketplace, as if they are setting them free from cages.

Relevant antiques

lator watch on my wrist. Computer people are fond of pointing out that if automobiles had followed the same pattern, we could now buy a 400-miles-per-gallon Rolls Royce for 25 cents.

So, even if you were convinced (or could rationalize away your concerns) that a new product was genuinely bug-free, it might make good financial sense to wait, at least a little while, to see if the laws of the marketplace (competition, supply and demand) will work to bring the price down quickly and dramatically.

With my first (and largest) computer, I paid about $7,500 for a mailing list storage and maintenance program that required hundreds of hours to write from scratch. With my second computer, I bought, off the shelf, a mailing list program for $750 that was more sophisticated and versatile than the first. With my fourth (and current) computer, I bought a $150 mailing list program that does far more than either of the first two. And lately I have seen some intriguing ads for $50 to $75 programs that do the same thing, perhaps better.

> The future appears to be pretty much like the past: a lot of hype, products released before they are fully developed, and big promises that are never kept.
>
> —Charles Chickadel, computer consultant

3. Improving quality

As price comes down after the introduction of a new product, very often the quality (sophistication, reliability, cleverness, speed) goes up, as competitors vie with each other for the share of the market carved out by the original innovation.

The Osborne computer was first shown to the world in the spring of 1980. It represented several major breakthroughs, offering for under $1,800 a combination of hardware and software that would have cost at least $3,000 elsewhere—and doing it in a single transportable[2] unit.

---

2. Osborne's term, "portable," is a little too optimistic for a 28-pound device— nearly double that with its optional battery pack. Perhaps "carryable" (but not from the check-in counter to Gate 4,387 at O'Hare).

Everyone is claiming to be the most "user-friendly" while no one but an expert can even begin to fully utilize the products that are so billed.

—Charles Chickadel, computer consultant

19.

Hundreds of computer companies fail every year, leaving their customers in a precarious situation.

There is always a place for a bright young inventor.

Within a year or so, there was the almost-identical-appearing Kay-Pro, but with a larger screen, more software, the same price, and available with more memory capacity.

And at the national computer show exactly 21 months after the Osborne was first shown, I counted 23 direct competitors, each one with lower price, more features, and/or smaller size. Needless to say, Osborne is also coming out with revised models.

This is very typical of the way things happen. Forty percent of the delegates to the national convention were also exhibitors — 20,000 of them! — and you can bet they were filling their shopping bags with their competitors' literature, and planning for next year's show even before this year's closed.

4. Disappearing companies

What a blow it is to write or telephone the manufacturer of your computer or program, and learn that it no longer exists. But it happens all the time — to big companies and small. Not only did Joe's Backyard Computer Company[3] go out of the computer business, so did RCA, General Electric, Singer, and Xerox (although Xerox later came back in).

Companies don't necessarily disappear because their products are poor or faulty. More often, it is their finances that are one or the other. Here is an all-too-typical scenario of events that transpire, leaving a bunch of wimps holding a bunch of bags:

a. A home workshop tinkerer comes up with a really good idea. To take an actual example, exhibited at a recent dealers-only computer show, consider an attache-case-sized portable box. Into the top is built a large one-inch-thick television screen, using the latest plasma gas technology, whatever that may be. An innovative sliding disk system allows five disks to occupy little more than the space of one ordinary disk. There is a full-sized typewriter keyboard *and* a clever built-in printer.

b. The home tinkerer rents a booth at a big computer show, offering his product at a price based on how much it would cost to make 10,000 of them, not a few dozen. (The clever device just described was priced at a surprisingly low $4,000 — even though

---

3. Of course it would never be called this. There seems to be a rule that company name is inversely proportional to size of company. Wang and Digital and Tandy are billion-dollar companies. The probability is high that International Cosmotronic Industries is run from someone's back bedroom.

it might well cost $10,000 or more to make each one in small quantities.) The hope is that sales will mushroom, big distributors will start buying them by the carload, and the manufacturing price will come down from $10,000 to perhaps $2,000 before the money runs out.

c. The money runs out.

d. The "first kids on the block" are now like the legendary art collector for whom Picasso drew a picture in the sand at low tide. They have something quite wonderful right now, but they know its days are numbered. When the tide comes in — when the first major repair is needed — they may have themselves a $4,000 bookend.

Resolving the problem

What, then, does the sensible consumer do? You don't want to be the last kid on the block, either. It's one thing to be cautious; it's another thing to drive your horse and buggy down the interstate freeway.

There is a sensible path to be steered between "first kid-ism" and the "But wait" syndrome described on page 30, in which people never buy *any*thing because something better is just about to be released.

Some guidelines:

☐ Wait. If you see something wonderful that you must have, but can live without for a short while, promise it to yourself in, say, 120 days — and during that time, watch the literature, talk to people who did buy one, try to get a feel for how it is going.

☐ Search for equivalents. The wonderful new "X" may be one company's answer to the more tried and proven "Y" that has been on the market long enough to get the early bugs out. (A local friend, enchanted with the Osborne, was one of the first to buy a new imitator of the Osborne — just about the time Osborne had gotten some of their earlier bugs out. Said friend is, sadly, having great miseries with his first-on-the-block model.)

☐ Work on overcoming that quite normal feeling that there must be something wrong with going along with the pack. Save your uniqueness for the way you look, dress, invest, etc. There is nothing wrong (and a lot that is right) with being Apple, TRS-80, IBM or Northstar owner number 10,000 or 100,000 or 1,000,000. But there could be a lot wrong with being number one.

As autos boomed into a mass market, the Peerless, the Hupmobile . . . and many other early starters fell by the wayside. . . . Nothing is more uncertain than the early days of a giant market.

—Kathleen K. Wiegner

Dealing with the "But Wait!" Syndrome

20.

Many people put off buying in the expectation that better, more versatile, or cheaper things will be available shortly.

Even though small computers are being sold by the millions, I am convinced that sales would be double or triple their present level were it not for the "But wait!" syndrome.

The number of people frozen into total immobility by the serpent-haired Medusa has nothing on the vast legions who are paralyzed each month upon picking up the latest issue of their favorite computer magazine.

Here is how it works—an actual case history, chosen from scores that I have observed:

Four years ago, my friend Frank decided that he needed a small computer. Frank is a writer, and thought he would like to use a word processing program. He is also an investor, and believed a computer would be desirable for tracking stocks, performing various calculations, and perhaps doing his taxes.

Frank figured he was probably going to get either a TRS-80 Model I or an Apple II. As he was reflecting on the relative merits of these two systems, someone said to him,

"But wait! Radio Shack is coming out with the Model III in a month or two, and it's a far superior piece of machinery." Frank waited.

Just about the time the Model III was coming into the stores, Frank read an article that said, in effect,

"But wait! Sony has just announced the portable battery-powered Type-Corder computer, for delivery next March." Frank put off the writing project he was about to begin, and waited. After

21.

The "But wait!" attitude can become truly debilitating, as even *better*-sounding products are announced before the one you were waiting for becomes available.

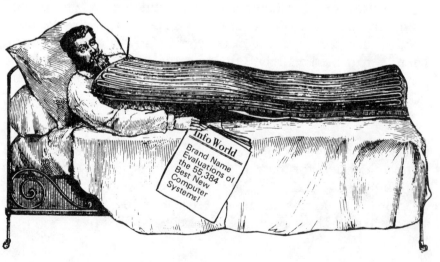

all, it would be pointless to write a book on an old-fashioned typing machine.

Well, the Sony came out, only a few months behind schedule, and all Frank had to do was walk into the store and buy one. But the devil in disguise said to him,

"*But wait!* I know a man in Michigan who can get it for you wholesale. You'll save $400!" Frank delayed starting his next novel one more time. The deal in Michigan dragged on and on, and while it was dragging,

"*But wait!* Teleram is coming out with a battery-powered unit with an 80-column screen and a huge built-in memory." (But when it was introduced, it came with a hefty price tag that put it out of Frank's reach, and besides, the screen may have been 80 columns wide, but it was only two lines high.)

"*But wait!* The Osborne computer is going to be available soon. It is far more sophisticated than the Sony, for only a few hundred dollars more. Deliveries will start next September."

"*But wait!* The Osborne screen is so small. Kay-Pro has announced they are coming out with a similar computer but with a large screen."

"*But wait!* Jonos has just exhibited a smaller unit with even more storage using hard disks!"

"*But wait!* Look at this Epson HX-10 brochure. Smaller. Fancier. Cheaper. And deliveries next March!"

Frank set his heart on that little Epson, which finally did arrive in November, although the software was not expected for a few months more. He even went as far as placing an order for an Epson—

"*But wait!* Epson has announced an even *better* HX-40 model coming along 'later this year.' And Radio Shack has just announced an even more sophisticated portable computer for delivery 'in a few months,' and the rumor mills are buzzing about what Apple has up its sleeve, and there is the forthcoming tiny IBM 'Peanut' that is getting lots of publicity, and surely Sony is going to do something clever, and there's the snazzy new version of the Timex-Sinclair, and what about bubble memories and there was that article about protein memories, and prices are falling and and and and and. . . ."

Poor Frank. It has been four years since he decided to buy his first computer. He actually sold his old IBM typewriter somewhere along the way, and he has not written a thing—except

DON'T BUY A THING . . .

UNTIL YOU'VE SEEN THE NEW AMAZING

STETSONTRONIC COMPUTER IN A HAT!!!

COMING SOON FROM

TEXAS HATS & INSTRUMENTS

GREATER PEORIA
COMPUTER SHOW
AND HOG CALLING FESTIVAL
Booth 134
BACKYARD MEGATRONICS

Dr. Spock's Book of
Baby & Computer Care

GOD IS MY
CO-PROGRAMMER

InfoWorld

CompuLove

Master Your Computer
in Less Than Thirty Years!

BYTE MAGAZINE

How to Win Friends
and Influence Computers

Osborne Vol. -1

Rod McKuen's Favorite
Computer Ballads

When Bad Things Happen
to Good Computers

The Personal Computer Book

letters to computer companies asking when such-and-such a model, rumored to have been shown at the South Korean Computer Fest, will be available. It's really painful to see Frank cycling home from the post office with his daily fix of computer magazines, newspapers, and newsletters, ready to absorb information about at least a dozen new "But waits."

Why "But wait!" occurs

The computer world probably has more new products, new services, new technology in a shorter period of time than any field of endeavor since the industrial revolution began. The reasons for this are that it takes very little time and/or very little money to come up with a major breakthrough.

Unlike designing and then manufacturing a revolutionary kind of automobile, airplane, or paper clip, which can require very expensive machinery and/or years of planning, any bright kid with a $99 Timex (or even a 10-cent pencil) can sit down and write a brilliant new program that will truly revolutionize a certain aspect of the computer world.

Then, "going into production" means running off copies of a disk or tape at $2 each, taking a booth at the next computer show, and off we go.

Other bright folks can buy a basket full of spare parts and a few $10 chips and create a splendid new kind of hardware in a matter of days, and have it on the market in a matter of months.

So this really *is* a time of vast and rapid change. If you don't see what you want, wait a month or two and it may well be along. If you *do* see what you want but can't afford it, wait till next week and it may cost half as much.

But what are you going to do during those weeks or months that you're waiting for the next wonder to come down the pike? *That* is the crucial issue. If you are going to be frozen into immobility, setting aside work you should be doing and fun you could be having, in the hope of something a little better (or even a lot better), my message is this:

Get what you want *now*. And if and when something even nicer comes on the market tomorrow morning or is announced for "probable release in June," don't worry too much about it. You've got what you wanted. And the new "wonder" probably won't be available for many months, probably won't work well at first, and probably won't be all that different, anyway.

And finally, don't be taken in by false "But wait!" reports. A common marketing ploy is to announce the imminent arrival of

Sirs, I have tested your machine. It adds a new terror to life, and makes death a long-felt want.

— Sir Herbert Beerbohm Tree, when asked to write a testimonial for the new gramophone

22.
It is easier to produce and market a new computer program than any other complex product in history.

23.
Buy what you want now if it is both available and affordable. You are not locked into a lifetime contract; you can always replace it later — but at least you can get going now.

24.

Computer companies often test the marketing waters by announcing a new product before they decide whether or not to manufacture it.

something that is but a gleam in a designer's eye, to see how the marketplace will react.

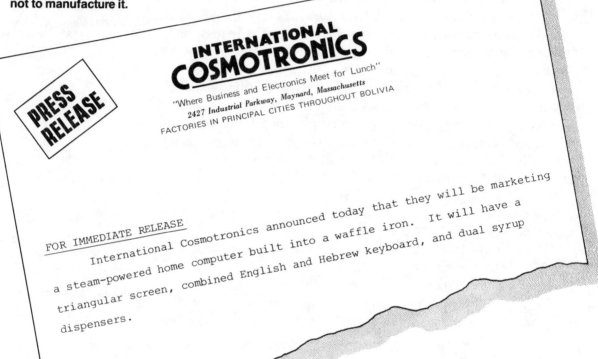

PRESS RELEASE

INTERNATIONAL
COSMOTRONICS
"Where Business and Electronics Meet for Lunch"
2427 Industrial Parkway, Maynard, Massachusetts
FACTORIES IN PRINCIPAL CITIES THROUGHOUT BOLIVIA

FOR IMMEDIATE RELEASE

International Cosmotronics announced today that they will be marketing a steam-powered home computer built into a waffle iron. It will have a triangular screen, combined English and Hebrew keyboard, and dual syrup dispensers.

The announcement is sent to hundreds of magazines and newspapers. If extreme interest is shown, advance orders placed, switchboards flooded, then the company *might* consider going into production. If not, they will quietly abandon the whole idea, and the only memory of it will lie with the Franks of the world, who will go about telling their friends,

"*But wait!* Don't you know that International Cosmotronics is just about to. . . ."

Choose the Software Before
the Hardware

I once met a man who lived in the remote Canadian wilderness. He drove a Mercedes with a diesel engine. The only gas station within a hundred miles of his home did not sell diesel fuel. When I asked him why a diesel car, his lame response was, "Well, the Mercedes advertising was so persuasive. I just didn't think it through."

Many people regularly make the same mistake in buying their computer and their programs, and for just the same reason: they don't think it through.

It is a case of the hardware manufacturers doing a great deal more advertising than software makers. How many ads have you seen for IBM or Apple? How many for the WordStar word processing program (the most popular one)? For VisiCalc (one of the best-selling software programs ever)?

So people rush out and buy themselves an IBM PC or an Apple IIe or a Radio Shack or a Texas Instruments or whatever — and *then* start thinking about which programs they are going to require. And that's when some people find themselves with a diesel-powered computer surrounded by unleaded software stations.

Of course this isn't a problem for those people who buy their first computer without knowing exactly (or even vaguely) what they are going to do with it. Unless they buy some obsolete Hungarian machine at a flea market, there will always be plenty of software of *some* sort for virtually any machine on the market.

But there are many buyers who know what their *primary* use is going to be: word processing, financial planning, tax preparation, mailing lists, game playing, learning programming, or whatever. Since there are immense differences among programs in the same general category, it is often wise to shop around for the perfect program, and then consider the computer or computers that it will run on.

Two examples should suffice to explain this.

The purpose of word processing is to make writing and editing easier. But some people write mostly business letters, some write novels, some write scholarly papers with footnotes, some write non-fiction books requiring an index or two, some write

25.
Choose the software first; then buy a computer that runs it.

many copies of the same letter (sales, fund raising, etc.) but with different names in the text ("Just imagine, Sister Louisa, this brand new Porsche Turbo parked outside Little Sisters of the Poor Convent . . .") etc.

No two word processing programs are alike. And many programs will run only on certain specific computers. So if you want a program that can automatically produce up to four separate indices and a table of contents, and you have a Radio Shack computer you're out of luck. If you want to use the popular Wordstar program and you have an Apple, you'll have to buy hundreds of dollars worth of gadgetry to install in the Apple to make the Apple behave like a machine that can run Wordstar. If you wish to do <u>underlining</u>, or elaborate mathematical formulas or **bold face lettering** or ~~strike out type~~, or Scandinavian Ø's and Å's, or any number of other things *possible* but not *universal* in word processing, it behooves you to select your software first, and *then* shop around from among the different computers that can run the software you select.

To take a somewhat more esoteric example, I have corresponded with a designer of small boats. He told me of his quest for a program (or, more accurately, an entire family of programs) to assist him in all phases of his work: graph plotting, buoyancy calculations, pricing and materials selection, drafting, and much more. And he needed it to run on the Texas Instruments computer he already had bought.

After months of frustrated searching, he made use of one of the firms that find software for people — operating like rare book finding companies. They found him the perfect program — but not only was it unavailable for his TI computer (sorry, Dr. Cosby), but it was, in fact, specifically made for a certain Dutch computer, and apparently would run on nothing else. He had the instruction manual translated into English and became even more convinced that this was what he needed. He thought his only options were trying to convert the program to run on an American machine (see page 183 for reasons why this is not a great idea), or figuring out how to import the Dutch computer (and, one would strongly recommend, a Dutch repairman as well). Then a perfect answer came, almost miraculously, at a "swap meet."

At such an event, this man found a recently-arrived Dutchman looking to trade his Dutch computer for a 110-volt and more readily repairable American machine. An even trade was made, and this particular problem of buying hardware before software was effectively solved.

Shopping for software

Software is harder to buy than hardware for these four reasons:

1. There is so much more of it. While there are "only" hundreds of computer manufacturers, there are thousands of software manufacturers, ranging from huge companies to one-person cottage industries.

2. Some software companies sell only by mail, and some advertise sparsely if at all.

3. It is not easy to browse through software the way you can browse through a museum and gravitate toward those things you wish to spend more time with. It may take many minutes, perhaps hours, to determine whether any given program is seriously worth considering.

4. Because of the very small profit made in selling most software, sales people in computer stores are unwilling (and often unable) to spend the time needed fully to explain how a program works, especially if they perceive that you are shopping only for software, not hardware.

There are five things that can be done independent of computer store personnel:

1. Consult books about programs. There are quite a few very fat books describing and evaluating many of the available programs for the more popular brands of computers.

2. Read magazines. More than a dozen major computer magazines contain articles, reviews, and advertising relevant to programs of all kinds. Often there will be survey-type articles, such as "General Ledger programs available for your IBM PC."

3. Go to computer shows. Often, there are a great many booths run by manufacturers or distributors, displaying and demonstrating their different programs.

4. Look into user groups and computer clubs. Within these organizations can often be found people who have been through the particular mill you are just entering. You *may* be the first person in history to want to calculate boomerang trajectories with your computer, but the odds are that there is someone some-

26.

Buying software is harder and more complicated than buying hardware.

27.
There are software
search firms that match
people with programs.

where who has already done it, and will be willing to tell you how.

5. Consult software search firms. Some enterprising companies have collected descriptions of tens of thousands of available software programs, and will sell you their findings at prices that may seem high at first—but not when you consider how long it would take you to do the same research. The largest such firm, SofSearch of San Antonio, Texas charges between $25 and $50 per search, and what you get is the particulars on everything available in that category, whether it is one program or one hundred.

Don't Stretch the Limits of the Equipment

Elevators generally have notices in them giving their maximum capacity. Of course this doesn't mean the elevator will fall if it goes one pound over the limit—but I would not be overjoyed to be a passenger in one near the limit if a 300-pound person was about to leap on.

Whether it is airplanes, kitchen mixers, lawn mowers, or computers, machinery is less reliable and more likely to fail or cause other problems when operating at or near the limits of its specifications.

With computers, the problems are generally those either of power or time.

Power problems

Theoretically, there is no upper limit to the number of peripherals, or additional things, that can be hooked into even a small home computer. Many computers have "slots" into which the additional electronics needed to run several printers, monitors, voice synthesizers, disk drives, hard disks, and so forth, can be plugged.

This is similar to plugging more and more appliances into the same wall socket. They will all work, up to a point. They may all work at reduced power or efficiency. Then they may all fail at once.

Some small manufacturers make devices which make it easier to overload the system. These electronic equivalents of the extension cord permit even more extra units to be plugged into the computer than the computer maker intended.

There is some dispute as to whether the computer can actually be *damaged* by this strain, or whether it just means that the peripheral devices may just not work well, or at all. The dispute sounds exactly like the one we found ourselves involved in when we tried to find out if we would damage our Volkswagen by using it to pull a trailer. Some experts said no, we would just lose speed and power and efficiency. Others said yes, we would probably ruin the engine.

(Almost everyone agrees, however, that the more stuff you pack into a computer, the more heat is generated, and the more desirable it is to add a cooling fan, if one is not part of the basic equipment.)

Time problems

The time a computer requires to do some things is disproportional to the size of the job. For instance, if a certain sorting program takes 10 seconds to sort 50 names into alphabetical order, it may take longer than 100 seconds to sort 500 names, and vastly longer than 1000 seconds to sort 5,000 names.

Consider the old-fashioned (pre-computer) approach, which has many similarities. Let's say you have 50 envelopes to sort into Zip code order. No big deal. Probably two or three minutes of sorting. Now, with 500 envelopes, you might want to deal them into 10 piles, one for each starting number. Then each pile is sorted and put into the main pile. This still might take no more than 10 times longer than the 50 cards. Now say you have 50,000 envelopes. You might begin with 100 piles, or perhaps 1,000 — placing them all over the house, and some in the garage. Now each time you pick up a new envelope, you may have to walk around looking for the right pile to put it on. When you've gone through it the first time, you'll *still* have 100 or 1,000 separate piles to be individually sorted and then combined together with the other piles. And 50,000 envelopes will inevitably take over 1,000 times longer than 50 envelopes.

The same sort of thing happens when you try to use a computer program at or beyond its limits. The sorting analogy holds here, too. My mailing list program is claimed to have "unlimited capacity." True, since the names and addresses are stored about

28.
Computers are less reliable when operating near their capacity.

Moving disks back and forth can be a tedious process.

29.
Never buy anything you can't lift.

1,000 to a disk, and there is no limit to how many disks I can use.

But let's see what happens when I want to sort my list into Zip code order. Say I have 50 disks full of names. I can sort the records on each individual disk in about 10 minutes. (Some programs do it a lot faster, but that's what mine takes). Now I have 50 separate mini-lists, each in Zip code order. Now I can electronically take all the records with Zips from 00000 to 02000 of *each* of the 50 disks and store them, combined, onto a new disk. That will involve a lot of manual switching back and forth, and take about half an hour for 00000 to 02000; another half hour for 02001 to 04000, and so on. A total of 50 half hours. Finally, each of my 50 new combined[1] disks must be sorted into Zip code order—another 500 minutes.

The total process, then, will require between 40 and 50 hours—because my system will really be running at its outer limits. I could speed things up by adding more disk drives, perhaps a hard disk, perhaps a more sophisticated sorting program. But as I do, I move more and more into the position of the Volkswagen pulling an ever-larger trailer.

A large "mainframe" computer could probably do the whole thing in well under an hour, probably in a few minutes.

There are no simple solutions to these problems after they arise. Bigger equipment means more expense, more expensive repairs, more complex operation. The only satisfactory solution is the retroactive one: anticipate needs in advance, and, most relevantly, choose the software before choosing the hardware (as discussed on page 35).

Never Buy Anything You Can't Lift

The title says it all . . . but a little background and further information can do no harm.

On page 171, I make the point that computers are much more fragile than most manufacturers pretend. In the best of all worlds, *no* computer would ever have to be moved—even the small ones that are called "portable." Far more things can happen to *any* computer in motion than can happen while it is stationary.

---

1. The technical term for combining of files is "concatenation," should it ever arise in a crossword puzzle.

It is extremely rare (but not totally unheard of) for soldered connections to come undone, mechanical parts to become bent, disk drives to go out of alignment, chips to become defective, etc., when a machine is sitting still in a friendly environment.

Moving larger computers

The larger and heavier a piece of computer machinery is, the more difficult it is to move safely. Even a move from one side of a room to another can be dangerous to its health.

And the temptation to bring computer equipment in for repairs, rather than have a $50- to $75-an-hour repairperson come to you, is great indeed. But the very *act* of bringing it in—getting it into a car, out of a car, etc., without proper equipment, dollies, trolleys, padding, and so forth, might wreak more havoc than the original problem calling for the move.

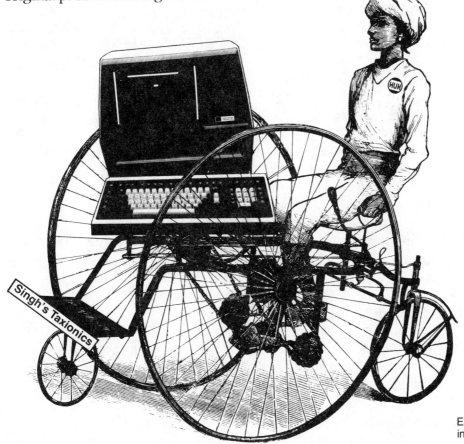

Extreme care must be taken in moving larger computers.

30.
Move all computers, including so-called portable ones, with great care.

A few years ago, when people thought about household computers at all, they thought of some small, inexpensive individual unit that would keep track of the family checking account . . . Now we know it won't be like that at all. It will be far cheaper to build one monster computer with thousands or even millions of customers hooked to it, than to have small individual machines in individual homes.

—Popular Science, 1967

One pen-pal told me the following wonderful story. When his engineering firm was planning its move to a new building, there was some question whether their large free-standing Digital computer would fit through the door at the new premises.

The partners were afraid that if it was a really tight fit, the computer might be damaged by tilting it or forcing it through. Careful measuring showed it would be a matter of a fraction of an inch one way or the other.

Their brilliant solution was to have a carpenter build an exact duplicate of the computer out of wood, and they would try moving *that* through the doorway at various angles. At no small expense they commissioned the duplicate to be built. And when it was done . . . it was too large to fit out through the door of the carpentry shop.

Moving medium-sized computers

In some respects, moving a computer in the 50- to 100-pound range may be the most hazardous of all. It is small enough that users may feel funny about calling in computer-moving experts — and yet it is unwieldy enough that an inexperienced person (or team of people) can get into real trouble attempting tricky maneuvers, especially in confined spaces.

Elsewhere, I recount my experience staggering up the stairs to the repair facility with my 50- or 60-pound Micromation computer. One of the saddest tales recounted to me was that of an accounting firm in Florida that was expanding its office space to several adjoining rooms. They put their $10,000 Lanier word processing computer on the little cart the secretaries used to bring coffee around to the partners. Halfway through its 30-foot journey, the cart collapsed, and the Lanier literally fell to pieces on the tile floor.

Moving small computers

Some computers are designed, according to the manufacturers, to be moved about regularly. That's why they have handles on them. Advertising for the Osborne, the Kay-Pro, and other machines in the 25- to 30-pound range show slender people strolling along with them, deftly sliding them under airplane seats, etc.

A number of repairpeople have told me, however, that it is the very *smallness* of such machines that result in behaviors causing damage. People are used to swinging their briefcases or attache cases around, setting them down without great care, and lobbing them onto luggage racks or into car trunks. You just can't do that with a small computer and expect it to last.

Also, a corollary to the title of this section might be: Never plan to carry anything that weighs 10% or more of what *you* weigh for a distance greater than 100 meters. Quite a few people have a terrible time attempting to carry a 28-pound "portable" computer from the check-in counter to one of the remote gates at O'Hare Airport. However, even that is probably better than the alternative of checking it in, and having it carried in the baggage compartment of the plane.

There are virtually no limits to miniaturization.

Buy Stuff for Which You Have Access to Exact Duplicates

In the complex and convoluted process of trying to decide which computer and which programs to buy, an important consideration — quite possibly *the* most important consideration — is whether or not any local people own exact duplicates of the hardware and software in question. There are three good reasons for this:

1. Pre-testing
If you can use the actual programs on the actual machine for a significant period of time — not the few minutes generally available in the computer store — you will have a much better idea of whether they are right for you. (See page 56.)

2. Diagnosis
If you have access to an identical system, when problems arise, you can substitute each component into the duplicate system to see if it works.

For example, one time when my system simply was not working at all, all I knew was that I had a problem with (a) my computer, (b) my disk drive, (c) my printer, or (d) my software. Because my neighbor John Fremont has a matching system (we planned it that way!), we set them side by side, and substituted parts one at a time. None of them seemed to work. Then we made the clever discovery that we hadn't substituted (e) the cable con-

31.
Often the best reason to make a purchase is because a friend or neighbor has the same equipment.

necting the computer and the printer, and there, indeed, was the problem—solved promptly with a few dollars worth of wire, instead of a long delay and perhaps a big repair bill.

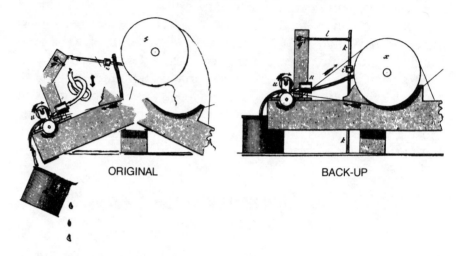

ORIGINAL   BACK-UP

3. A back-up machine

Ultimately, (if not regularly), breakdowns will occur which will mean you will be without your equipment for anywhere from a few days to a few weeks or more. At such times, it is highly reassuring to have worked out a sharing arrangement with one or more local people with identical equipment. Not many enthusiasts use their computers all 168 hours of the week, and so, even if it means coming in nights or weekends, at least you will get your necessary work (or necessary games) done.

Everything else being equal—or even not-quite-equal, I would use the criterion of access to duplicates as the major factor in deciding what to buy.

Why Brand Name Buying Guides Are Not Too Helpful

Some "how to" computer books prominently feature, or even consist entirely of, a "brand name buying guide." Such guides have two possible values, but I am not convinced of the merits of either one, hence the absence of such a guide in this book.

One possible virtue is a comparative chart. Is this model faster than that one; which has larger memories; which languages do they operate with; etc. The main problem with this is that things change in the computer field much faster than they change in the book field.

Even if you buy a book the day it hits the bookstores, it is almost certain to be at least six months removed from the author's pen (or word processor). In that length of time old models will disappear or be modified, new models will appear, new companies will introduce equipment, and so on.

Many philosophers or prognosticators in the technical fields have been predicting that small computers will follow the same marketing pattern seen with calculators, digital watches, CB radios, and other "high tech" small items: a tremendous proliferation of manufacturers, continuing decline in prices, and ultimately a relatively small number of manufacturers surviving and prospering.

In fact, a study by prestigious SRI International predicted that by the turn of the millennium, only three computer manufacturers would be dominant: IBM, Sony, and Apple.

I have the feeling that this may not be the case, or at least not for a long, long while. Computers may be the most versatile piece of technology to come down the pike since the wheel. There is a limit to how innovative one can get with a CB radio. You just make 'em like everybody else's, and hope they will somehow get distribution and sales. But computers, as I postulated earlier, *are* likely to appear in our lives in more and more ways, if not necessarily in the free-standing units now accounting for most small computer sales.

The other possible value of a brand name guide is that it conveys the author's feelings about various models, both by what he or she says, and by which models are included and which are left out.

The problem with this is that it takes time to develop a certain rapport with a reviewer, whether of restaurants, movies, or computers. If you try that wonderful new bistro that some new food critic went into raptures about and you think it was dreadful, you've only wasted an hour or two and a few dollars. But if you follow a critic's recommendation in buying a small computer and discover *it* is dreadful for you, matters are far more serious.

Unless you have money to burn, buying a computer system is

32.
Brand name buying guides have very limited value.

33.
Product reviews are only useful insofar as you have rapport with the reviewer.

too serious a matter to follow just the recommendation of one person, no matter who it may be. Like the old psychiatrist joke ("Get married, settle down, raise a family. If that doesn't work, we'll try something else.") the steps you take are, if not irreversible, at least major. Collect opinions where you can, but make your own decision.

BRAND NAME BUYING GUIDE
Computers Worth Considering

IBM	Apple	Radio Shack
Xerox	Digital	Osborne
Kay-Pro	Epson	Wang
Toshiba	Jonos	Franklin
Attache	Hewlett-Packard	Atari
Sharp	Seiko	Burroughs
Eagle	Sony	Cromemco
Tele-Video	NEC	Casio
	and 135 others	

Computers Not Worth Considering

Ilyushin 44-W Motorized Slide Rule from the People's Compute and Steam Propelled Piroshki Manufactory of Vladivostok

The Treadlemaster SV-200 data processor with dual foot controllers and a hinged lockule (see illustration).

Atahualpa Marco IV from IncaTech Industries (a 44-mile-long piece of knotted string)

The Fred-One All-in-One Home Computer, Ravioli Press, and Handcuff Demagnetizer, from Fred's Machine Shop, Ozone Park, N.J.

Apple imitators include the 'Orange,' the 'Pineapple,' and, inevitably, the 'Turkey.'

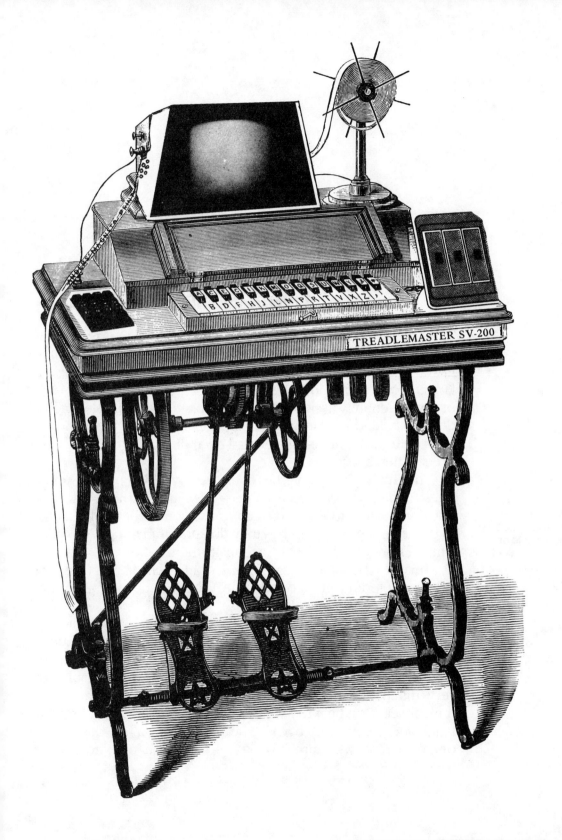

The Store/Dealer Experience

Technobabble

The only course I came close to flunking in college was calculus. Then I happened upon a wonderful book entitled *Calculus Made Easy*.[1] The author begins with a splendid essay on how Vocabulary is the most precious weapon in the arsenal of the high priests of any scientific discipline. He goes on to give simple English definitions and explanations of all the concepts I was failing to comprehend. It was as if a veil had been lifted, and calculus was a breeze thereafter.

34.
Many computer people are either unable or unwilling to speak in comprehensible English.

The high priests of the computer world—programmers, salespeople, writers, consultants—also guard their language. They not only refuse and disdain to use comprehensible English to describe the simple things they do, they grab things out of our simple, non-technical world, and make them their own.

This fact becomes clear from the moment you activate the exterior/interior interface module (door) and enter your first computer sales parlor.

Elsewhere (page 273), I have endeavored to explain, in language that even *I* can understand, just what many of the most common computer-related words and phrases actually mean. But it hardly seems fair to make fun of this rampant technobabble. It is very much like making fun of Quasimodo because he was a hunchback. Don't get me wrong. It would be perfectly all *right* to laugh and point at him because he was wearing a hideous necktie or got a Mohawk haircut or voted for Nixon or played Barry

---

1. By Silvanus Thompson; republished by St. Martin's Press in 1965.

Manilow records all day long. But not because of his physical defect.

I mean, can one feel anything but pity for the person who penned these words in sales literature for a brochure for a very simple product designed to let a non-expert connect a computer to an ordinary electric typewriter . . .

"In the first mode, the cable can be plugged into the controller port and the unit addressed either with the usual PR#N commands with N a nonexistant [sic] slot, or with a subroutine call. The handler is automatically loaded with the system. The same cable can be plugged into the XBOOT card which is then plugged into an Apple slot for use as a standard Apple peripheral. This card has an electrically alterable PROM to allow user modification of controller functions without a software handler."

When I was ready to buy my second computer system, I decided that the most important factor for me (at that time) was neither the hardware nor the software, but being able to deal with a human being who understood computers well, and who could speak to me in my own native language (simple English).

This was not easy. A formidable number of salesmen and women throughout northern California lost the commission on a more-than-$10,000 sale because they could not or would not speak to me in English.

It was a little like questing after the Holy Grail. ("No, not in here." "How about over there?" "No, not over there either." "Oh, well, then, on to the next town.") In dealership after dealership, what I heard was, "Do you require single-density or double-density disks?" "You'll be wanting a high kilobaud rate, won't you?" "This CPU has four index buffers under direct command." "You can address three peripherals simultaneously." No I can't. But I *can* utilize the interior/exterior interface module and move on to another store.

So that's why I bought Computer #2 in a tiny store in the tiny town of Yountville, 150 miles from my home. I am "led" to computer stores the way other addicts are led to garage sales, taverns, or other relevant sources of concern. Wandered in while there as a tourist. Kaye K. Nelson, proprietress of the establishment, was the first computer-selling person who spoke to me in simple English. (I have subsequently met a few others, but they are a rare breed.) Because I *did* understand, and liked what I heard, I spent a lot of money there.

Grant, O God, that we may always be right, for thou knowest we will never change our minds.

— Old Scottish prayer

35.
If someone cannot or will not speak to you in simple English, you are entirely justified in asking for someone who can, or in leaving.

What, then, do you do when they start technobabbling at you?

Two options come to mind. One is to leave. There are many more computer stores/dealers/salespeople in the world. Keep looking until you find one you can talk to, and who can talk to you. This card may help.

Does anyone here speak English?

Or you can hand the technobabbler a copy of *this* card and then leave:

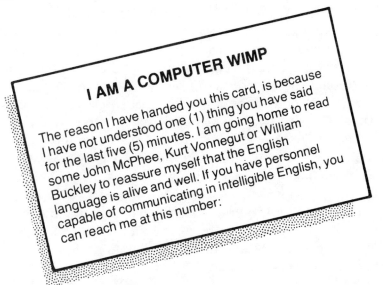

I AM A COMPUTER WIMP

The reason I have handed you this card, is because I have not understood one (1) thing you have said for the last five (5) minutes. I am going home to read some John McPhee, Kurt Vonnegut or William Buckley to reassure myself that the English language is alive and well. If you have personnel capable of communicating in intelligible English, you can reach me at this number:

Hope for the future

In 1983, two major companies introduced computers that were designed specifically to be as easy to learn to use as possible. Sensibly, they were using the computer itself as a teaching tool to teach users how to use it. Both companies claim that it is genuinely possible to be using their computer meaningfully within half an hour of unpacking the box.

So far, many reviews and comments on both have been wildly enthusiastic. There is *still* the problem of learning enough to decide if you want to *buy* either, and if so, which. And that means either interacting with potentially difficult humans, or reading the descriptive literature. The latter has proven an interesting exercise.

Normally, if you want to sell something, the sales tools should relate to the thing being sold. A printer wants to have beautifully-printed brochures. A health club doesn't want a flabby salesman. And an incredibly easy to use computer wants to have incredibly easy to understand literature.

Consider the opening lines of the introductory advertisements for the two machines in question:

THE APPLE LISA: "The hardware is awesome — MC68000 32/16-bit processor, 1-Megabyte RAM, 364X720 bit-map display, dual 860K disk drives, 5-Megabyte Pro-File hard disk."

THE EPSON QX-10: "It won't make you any smarter. It'll just make you feel that way. That, of course, was the promise nearly all computer manufacturers made to us. But along the way, the promise was unfulfilled. People found out that even the simplest computer languages were as troublesome and time-consuming as high school French — fine if you like that sort of challenge, but a real barrier if what you want to do is *use* a computer, as opposed to *learning* to use a computer. A lot of people found they could live their whole lives without ever knowing what GOSUB, LOGIN, or MID$ meant."

They are probably both wonderful machines. But the Apple ad made me say, "Phooey, more of the same." And the Epson ad made me say, "Where can I see a demonstration?"

Technobabblers take note.

36.

Computers are ever-so-slowly growing more "user friendly" — meaning beginners can use them successfully without books or humans to help.

"Helpfulness Survey" of 50 Computer Stores

In order to find out how ordinary retail computer stores treat the intelligent-but-uninformed public, I conducted the following experiment:

During the month of March, 1983, I telephoned 50 computer stores all over the country. I informed them that I had two questions to ask about my computer needs — questions that might result in purchases.

The results were just as depressing as I feared they would be. Only one of the 50 "experts" to whom I spoke answered both questions correctly. I was given dozens of wrong answers, including some that might have damaged my equipment, had I followed the advice.

Here's what happened.

Choosing the stores

Using the yellow pages of the phone books from Indianapolis, Chicago, Boston, Atlanta, St. Louis, Dallas, New York, Columbus, Minneapolis, Portland (Oregon), and Honolulu, I selected four to six stores in each city, primarily based on the size and the content of their advertisements.

I figured the general public would be more likely to answer the larger ads, and especially those that stressed their knowledge ("We know Apple to the core") and helpfulness ("Plain English spoken here").

They included, among others, Computer Shop, Computer-Land, Computer Room, Computer City, ComputerMat, Computer Mart, Computer Center, Computer Shack, Computer Station, Computer Country, Computer Trend, Computer Factory, Computer Depot, Computer Junction, Computer Parlor, and Honest Bob's Silicon Toy Store.

Seven of the 60 stores I tried to call were no longer in business (this seems quite a high percentage), and three put me on hold for so long, I finally hung up. So I ended up speaking to exactly 50 stores.

I had carefully formulated two questions that a beginner might ask: one simple, and one simple-sounding, but actually quite complex.

The presence of humans in a system containing high-speed electronic computers and high speed, accurate communications, is quite inhibiting. Every means possible should be employed to eliminate humans in the data-processing chain.

—Stuart Seaton, 1958

The questions

Question 1: "I have an Apple II+ computer, and I have a chance to buy a good used Qume Sprint 5 printer. (This is a very common brand.) Will the Apple be able to 'drive' the Qume, and if so, what additional hardware or software am I going to need to make this happen?"

The correct answer is, Yes, the Apple *can* operate the printer. One must know if the printer is a "serial" or a "parallel" printer (two different kinds of wiring that are used). On learning that it is serial, one simply buys an Apple Super Serial card (or equivalent), which plugs into the Apple, plus a cable. Total cost: about $250.

Question 2: "I have an Apple II computer. My business associate in Chicago has an IBM Personal Computer. We want to be able to transfer files and information back and forth over the telephone lines. Is this going to be possible?"

The correct answer is that there are several methods that *may* theoretically work, such as sending the raw data over telephone modems from one computer to the other, or using the intermediary of a large computer service (such as The Source), which allows users to store information in an "electronic mail box" from which another user can retrieve it (with the proper code). However these methods are not reliable, and when they work at all, are very much prone to the "dreaded 99% factor" described on page 183. There is one method that *will* work. An ingenious company called Alpha Software has marketed something called "The Apple-IBM Connection," whose sole purpose in life is to transfer files back and forth between the Apple and the IBM. Anyone with my "problem" can order the necessary stuff through most computer stores, and be off and running.

37.

Many computer stores dispense unreliable or inaccurate information.

What actually happened

What happened at Computer City in Boston is that I was given precisely the right answers immediately by the friendly lady who answered the phone.

What happened at the other 49 stores was a mixed bag of correct, partially correct, and totally wrong information, blended in with a fair amount of "You'll have to come in and talk to us; we don't give information by telephone" and more than a few "I don't knows."

Of the 50 stores, 34 were able to tell me on the phone that the

Apple would indeed operate the Qume. Of those 34, 23 knew that a Super Serial Card (or equivalent) was needed. Sixteen of them mentioned the cable, although 3 said (incorrectly) that there were no commercially available cables, and they would have to be made to order.

Eleven people either seemed unaware of the two kinds of printer or were certain that Qume printers *all* were parallel (they are not). Three pressured to send me out the *wrong* interface card by United Parcel. Use of it might have damaged my equipment.

Of the remaining 16 stores, 4 had no one there capable of answering, 7 said I would have to come in, and 5 said that they were pretty sure (or certain) that the Apple could *not* operate the printer (3 of these then told me about printers they were selling).

The results were even less promising with regard to the second question. (The question, by the way, is entirely reasonable. With hundreds of thousands of each brand of computer in use, there are undoubtedly many situations in which the user of one could benefit from communicating with the user of another).

As I said, only *one* of the 50 stores gave me the correct answer. A second was familiar with the Alpha product, but assured me that it only worked one way: Apple to IBM but not back again. (He was so certain, I actually called the Alpha factory to make sure he was wrong. He was.)

Nearly half—22 of the 48 remaining stores—told me that what I wanted was impossible. (A few qualified that with "as far as I know"). Fifteen people said they simply didn't know, nor did anyone else there, nor could they suggest how I might find out.

Of the remaining 11 stores, 3 gave me information that I believe to be totally wrong: "If your Apple is equipped with a Z80 Softcard, it will play IBM disks." And 8 suggested methods that at least have a chance of working, although not with 100% reliability: using modems, and using an intermediary large computer.

38.

Get a second and a third opinion on all important computer questions no matter how confident the first person sounds.

Conclusions

These findings are not very reassuring, but neither are they especially surprising. They might be displayed thus:

	Easy question	Hard question
Right answer	Many	Very few
Wrong answer	Some	Some
Don't know	Very few	Many

What to do about all this

Weep. Wring hands. Bewail fate. And, most importantly, *always* seek at *least* a second opinon, and, better still, a third. If all three agree, you're probably in good shape. If they don't, it is up to you to find out why. You must say to Information Purveyor #1, "Hey, but the people over at Computer Seraglio told me that . . ." And then go to or call the second place and say, "Hey, but the people back at Computer Gazebo said . . ." With persistence, a correct and usable answer may emerge.

You Should Try Things Out Longer than Many Stores Will Let You

In 1970, I was in charge of marketing for the world's first water bed company. We found a great deal of sales resistance. Most people were fascinated by the concept, but after a bounce or two, followed by a smirk or two, the typical customer said, "Thank you very much; I'll think it over," and was never seen again.

At the other end of the scale, and equally a problem, were those people who *did* buy one after the two-bounce test, and then returned sadly (or angrily) a few days later, to report that they simply couldn't sleep (or do whatever else they had expected to do) on their water bed.

The obvious answer (we eventually came to realize) was that there are some things that require more than a two-bounce test. (Our solution, which may be the reason you can find water beds in Sears, Macy's, and other formerly-sneering retail stores today, was 1. to install as many water beds as possible in hotels and motels, and 2. to offer a 30-day free home trial.)

39.

Few dealers will let you try things out as long as you should before buying.

There are close parallels between small computers and water beds (in terms of marketing, that is. Not many people report that their sleep or their love life improves after buying a computer). Specifically, the amount of time you have to try things out in the store may not be nearly enough, and yet many retailers are not prepared to offer satisfactory alternatives.

There are two kinds of reasons to thoroughly test out computers: one set related to usability; the other related to comfort.

Usability

Will a computer (or a new program, for that matter) do what

you want it to do, in your home, your business, your life? Buying equipment on the basis of reviews, hearsay, and the manufacturer's literature is very much like going to a movie on the basis of reviews. Sometimes you will be delighted; sometimes you will be extremely disappointed. But if you don't like the movie, you're out five bucks and a few hours of your life. An unhappy computer experience can multiply both figures by a factor of hundreds or thousands.

Realistically, however, you can't expect to sit in a computer store for many hours, entering data in a machine, to see how it performs in ways you will actually use it (rather than in flashy demonstration programs prepared by the manufacturers to show off their equipment at its best). Some enlightened stores, or dealers, *will* permit this, and even encourage you to bring in your own personal or business data, but they are rare.

Some defects or deficiencies can, of course, be seen during a short demonstration. I once bought a learn-to-type program for my daughter, without trying it, and when I got it home, discovered it ignored lower case letters; it was an upper case course only (because many Apple computers do not *have* lower case letters available). Perhaps it could be used training telegram typists for Western Union.

Other defects may take months to become apparent. I had a name-and-address sorting program that was able to sort the records into Zip code order. It worked fine when I only had a few hundred names. But after I had entered several thousand names, I found that this program took something like half an hour to do the sorting that other, better programs might do in two minutes.

There is no simple solution to these kinds of problems. They can, however, be minimized in these ways:

Homework. Learn all you can about any given hard- or software before you visit a dealer. Read reviews in the various computer magazines. (Many rate products, as in *Consumer Reports.*) Ask the dealer for the names of other local people who are using similar equipment, and talk to them.

Investigate the possibility of renting the equipment. There are companies that rent small computers on a short-term basis. And there is a promising new trend toward software rental as well: one company is currently marketing an ingenious package, in which you can buy several thousand dollars worth of software

Recommending the right computer is a little like recommending the "right" religion. People tend to like the system they've ended up with. The most important point about computers, more so than about religions, is that the difference between a good one and a bad one is tiny compared with the difference between having one and not.

—James Fallows

(word processing, bookkeeping, etc.) for about $50. The clever gimmick is that, while the programs can go through all their paces, no data can be saved permanently. Thus you can become familiar with the way the programs work, in your home or office. If you don't like them, then you're out $50. And if you *do*, you return to the dealer, pay the full price (for those programs you want), and the dealer will electronically "unlock" the storage portion of the program, so you can use it for your own words and numbers.

Ask for return privileges. If you can (honestly) convince a dealer that you almost surely want certain equipment, but need to put it to a longer test, you may be able to work out a deal enabling you to return unsatisfactory hardware and/or software for a full, or nearly-full refund. It is certainly worth even a 10% penalty fee to be able to get rid of thousands of dollars worth of unsatisfactory equipment.

Comfort

Getting accustomed to using a new computer, or even a new program, is very much like buying shoes. A pair that feels fine in the store may be causing great miseries a few weeks later. Or a borderline pair that you bought anyway may evolve, with time, into your most beloved and comfortable footwear.

There are three kinds of comfort that are important for me in considering new equipment:

1. *The keyboard.* "Keyboard action" is an extremely personal thing. People talk about the "great feel" of a certain keyboard, the "action," the "response," etc. All that can really be said is that keyboard action differs greatly from brand to brand, and if you are going to be typing a lot, you will want to spend as much time trying it out as possible before you buy.

(When Sony came out with their portable Type-Corder computer a few years ago, I decided I had to have one. My five-minute tryout at the Sony "toy store" reinforced this feeling. Boy, am I glad that my order was goofed up [computer error!] and never delivered—because I have subsequently had the opportunity to type for about an hour into someone else's Type-Corder, and I grew to dislike the keyboard feel considerably.)

2. *The screen.* You will spend a great deal of time staring at the

40.
Free or low-cost home trials can be negotiated with some dealers.

41.
A keyboard and a screen that seem all right at first may become much less satisfactory with extensive use.

"TV" screen, or monitor. Is it big enough? (Some transportable computers have tiny tiny screens.) What about the color? (Many offer white letters on black; some have black on white; some have either green or orange filters; some have non-glare glass; and so on.) Does the screen show all the work? (Some small screens act like a "window" on the work, in which you can only see the left half, for instance, at any one time. Of course you can move the window up and down, left and right, by pushing buttons, to see all the work, but some people find that a nuisance.)

3. *Time and motion.* What, actually, are you doing with your hands to make the equipment work, and how long does it take? For example, I once had a word processing program that worked in the following way: First, I put in a disk and typed a special code to turn my printer on. Then I put in a second disk, which made my Apple "think" that it was an older-model Apple (because the program had been devised for the older model). Then I replaced the second disk with a third, which contained the actual program. And finally, I replaced the third with a fourth, on which I stored my own words.

Although this did not seem unduly complex in the store, I grew to resent having to do all that stuff—and not just at the start of my working day, but also once or twice an hour, when, due to some defect in the program or in my equipment, I was suddenly cast back to square one.

For that, and other reasons, I bought a new word processing program. Now I put in one disk, push a button, and off I go. (Of course there *is* a 15 to 20 second delay after pushing the button. At this moment, I can live with that — but what if I learn about some other model that comes to life in three seconds . . . ?)

Finally, a few lines about sitting down. I am baffled by the extremely common practice in which people spend thousands of dollars for equipment at which they will be sitting for literally thousands of hours (if it and they survive), and then they end up doing that sitting on a cast-off dining room chair, a thrift shop wonder, or some other object condemned by the American Spine Association. This is one case where an extra hundred bucks for a really good chair can immeasurably increase the pleasure (or, more accurately, the absence of pain) you will get from your computer.

42.
Computers and programs that seem fast enough when new may feel annoyingly slow after you become more adept at their use.

43.
It's amazing how many people ruin their backs by sitting endlessly at their $3,000 computer in a $3 chair.

Don't Be Snowed by Charisma

44.

Some computer salespeople have a great deal more charisma and selling skills than computer knowledge.

My mother, whose only nautical experience was a trip on the Staten Island ferry, once bought a five-year subscription to *Popular Boating* magazine. Her helpless explanation was that "the young man at the door seemed so pitiful, and he said he just needed this one subscription to win a trip to Disneyland . . ."

People often buy things, including computers, for all the wrong reasons. The advertising genius, Howard Gossage, put it this way: "You should never confuse the thing *promoted* with the thing *itself.*" In other words, the buyer thinks that he is buying a macho image; a rugged, masculine bit of the old west; a piece of history; something that makes him a real man. The outside observer sees that he is buying a tube of dried, shredded tobacco leaves. (Does anyone else remember when Marlboros had red tips, so ladies, virtually 100% of Marlboro smokers, wouldn't leave ugly lipstick stains on their cigarette butts?)

The only computer "expert" a lot of computer buyers ever talk to is the salesperson in the computer store. Who is this "expert?" For one thing, he or she is likely to be a salesperson on commission, who only earns a decent living if sales are made. A good many skilled salespeople have moved from commodities futures, desert land sales, and life insurance into computers. Some will conscientiously learn all they can about their product. Many, however, know nothing more than the superficial promotional materials reveal. And some, like the clerks in our local supermarket, which sells Commodore and Timex home computers, know literally nothing about the product, other than the price.

45.

Most computer salespeople work on commission. If so, it is not in their best interest to suggest that you go elsewhere for a more appropriate purchase.

In some ways, the knowledgeable salesperson may be more of a hazard to your computer happiness. It is a rare salesperson, indeed, who will say, "Chevrolet doesn't have anything that suits your needs. Why don't you try the Ford dealership across town?"

If the seller perceives that he or she knows more about computers than you do, then it is clearly desirable to try to sell you something from their inventory. The more skilled they are at their craft, the more likely it is that the novice buyer will believe the "We have exactly what you need" pitch.

To be sure, sometimes it *is* exactly what is needed, or comes pretty close. And sometimes the charm, charisma, and influence of the salesperson results in the naive buyer getting something that is utterly wrong for his or her needs. The error, not surprisingly, is generally in the direction of buying something much more elaborate than is required.

Two elderly sisters told me that they were considering a computer to do some of their genealogy and family history work, such as storing family tree information. They shopped around a bit, and found an ever-so-helpful young man. And what did they buy? A Radio Shack Model II with four 8″ disk drives! The same sweet young man could probably have sold them a Maserati, sky diving lessons, and a double lifetime ballroom dance course.

A small-town businessman told me of *his* shopping expedition. His requirements: a small computer on which to keep inventory records for his feed and grain warehouse. He had been using 3×5 cards with considerable success, but felt that somehow he wasn't being a good businessman unless he computerized. The salesman at his local computer store persuaded him that he should purchase equipment with a hard disk, giving huge memory storage capacity, so that if his business expanded dramatically, he wouldn't be "caught short." This is like buying a thousand rolls of toilet paper, just in case all the factories should burn down. Memory can always be added to a computer system, and there's enough silicon on earth to last for at least the next 40 million years.

A small private school in Missouri wanted to keep track of student records. A persuasive sales team sold them an IBM Personal Computer (this is quite a reasonable choice)—and *then* talked them into paying thousands of dollars more to have special programs written specifically for their needs, when no more than $200 worth of "off the shelf" software would have served their needs perfectly well.

How does one avoid making mistakes like this? It is essential to remember that the salesperson is very likely someone you never will see again. And so, no matter how charming and helpful they are, it is the *machine* you are buying, not a friend. ("Just 50 more sales and I win a trip to Armonk, New York . . .")

Even if the salesperson assures you that he or she will be there to answer all your questions, they offer no guarantees. That kind of reassurance was a factor at the little store at which I bought my Apple—and the extremely knowledgeable, helpful, and nice lady from whom I bought it was gone a few weeks later, never to be replaced by anyone nearly as helpful, and the store itself eventu-

"Would I lie to you?"

46.
It's OK to anticipate your needs, but not for the next 400 years. You can always expand the system later or get a new one.

ally went out of business.

If after-the-sale advice and consultation is an important factor, then it would be appropriate to select a vendor that has enough employees so if your contact leaves, there will be others available.

If you are going to seek before-the-sale advice on what to buy, it is wise to choose a salesroom that represents a wide range of computers. If, on the other hand, you have pretty well made up your mind before you go out to buy, then it is simply a matter of shopping around for the best deal.

And if you take the middle ground suggested on page 35 and determine the software you think you need (after testing it thoroughly), then your hardware shopping goal is narrowed to finding the most economical equipment that will reliably run that software.

Whatever your approach, it is important to bear in mind throughout the transaction that what you are doing is buying a computer, not developing a lasting relationship.

47.

Unless you know exactly what you want, it is wise to visit a dealer that represents a wide range of manufacturers and suppliers.

Is What You See What You Get?

Often. Not always.

Once, long ago, I was hired by the Pacific Area Travel Association to write travel brochures for all 36 country members. "Great," I said, "I figure about one week in each place would be about right." "We need it in two weeks," they said, "and there's no money in the budget for travel."

Oh. Well, there are certain problems inherent in having someone who has never seen something write about same. I don't think I want to reveal the details at this time, for fear that some of the folks who went to Fiji or Guam or Singapore with those brochures in hand may wish to, um, pay me a visit.

48.

Sales literature is written by marketing experts who may never have seen, much less used, the goods being described.

That's one kind of reason that I worry just a little about computer literature. It is always possible that the person who wrote it has never seen or used one, but is assembling bits and pieces from different sources to produce something of a Russian road map.[2] Another concern is that because of the rapid growth and change in the industry, the product described in the literature (or

2. We discovered, driving through Russia, that our official road map bore little relation to the actual location of roads and cities. It was well designed and very pretty to look at, but we got lost a lot.

in a review) may be different from what you buy. To be sure, much of the time it probably won't matter (but tell that to those thousands of Buick owners who were presumably happy with their cars until they learned they had Chevrolet engines in them).

Still, a significant theme in many of the letters I have gotten from less-than-happy computer users involves cases in which literature and reviews had either gotten ahead or, behind, or totally removed from what was *really* going on. For instance, Sony literature described a portable battery-powered printer to go with their Type-Corder, but by the time it reached the stores, it had a 110-volt cord dangling out the back; the batteries presumably had proven unsatisfactory. For instance, one man ordered an IBM Personal Computer in large measure because it came with a word processing program he happened to like. But by the time he took delivery, IBM had switched to a different program.

Many computer brochures contain a line like this one: "Manufacturer reserves the right to make changes and improvements in the product described at any time, without prior notice, and without liability." Well, that's fine (since many of the changes *will* be for the better), as long as the customer reserves the right to say "No thanks," and not accept the changed or improved product, if he or she chooses, without liability.

49.

Because of product changes, brochures may be out of date even as they are printed.

"Manufacturer reserves the right to make changes and improvements in the product at any time, without prior notice and without liability."

Specsmanship

Some people pay close attention to the printed specifications when they buy machinery of various kinds. In particular, they use this information to compare two or more competing brands. This stereo has 100 watts of power per channel, and 10-inch speakers. That one has only 80 watts per channel but 12-inch speakers. This car has a four-barrel carburetor, digital speedometer, and a six-way seat; that one has two barrels, an analog speedometer[3] and a four-way seat. And so on.

The problem with this method of comparing and buying is that there is sometimes little relationship between the specifications and what the thing is actually like. That's why most people *listen* to stereos and *drive* cars before buying. (Sometime, let me tell you about the Model A "replica" car I once bought solely because of its glorious brochure, full of utterly misleading specifications.)

With computers, matters are more complicated. Not only is "test driving" a great deal harder, especially for the beginner, but the specifications writers seem, sometimes, to be quite carried away with enthusiasm. As Mark Garetz, the president of a large and reliable computer company, CompuPro says, it is "possible to buy really bad machines with specs that sound really good. The 'specsmanship' that people play in this business is really incredible."

A simple example of this is described on page 89. One printer may have specifications claiming it prints at 80 characters per second, another at 60. But the first machine may be capable of occasional *bursts* of the 80 character speed while overall it averages 50. The second printer may chug along at a steady 60, and therefore be a faster machine, even though specifications indicate it is slower.

A much more complex example deals with the "instruction set" of a given computer. The instruction set is the internal logic that, in effect, tells each microprocessor chip how to operate. Some computer reviews go on at some length about the "power" of this instruction set as compared with that one. From the little I know, I am strongly inclined to agree with Owen Davies, writing

50.

Printed specifications for a computer or other equipment, while technically accurate, may not correspond to actual performance under normal conditions. This is especially true of the speed of computers and printers.

---

3. This is what one car brochure actually called the old needle-swinging-past-the-numbers type of speedometer.

in *Omni* (March 1983), who has this to say about an instruction set:

"Ignore it. Promotional fliers often babble about the powerful instruction set of the chip used . . . In general it's true that a large, well-thought-out instruction set makes for a more powerful processor, while a limited one makes it difficult to write versatile, easy-to-use programs. *But only a skilled programmer will ever notice its existence.*"

Two other things that specifications comparers worry about are a computer's speed and the number of bits that it can process at once.

Speed. Most small computers work at a speed of somewhere between 1 million and 10 million cycles per second. One simple operation is performed with each on-off cycle.

For many users, the difference between a 3 million cycle per second machine and a twice-as-fast 6 million cycle per second machine is very much like the difference between a Chevrolet that can go 90 miles an hour and a Maserati that can go 180 miles an hour, when what you mostly do with your car is pick the kids up after school.

The performance quality of a "slow" computer that can perform 45,000 complicated calculations per second and a "fast" one that can do 60,000 or 90,000 calculations per second is not anything that most users need to worry about.

Sometimes excessive speed doesn't help, and may even hurt.

(Incidentally, on specification sheets, speed is usually given in megaHertz. One megaHertz, or mHz, is 1 million cycles per second. One megaAvis is presumably a little slower.)

Number of bits. A "bit" is a single unit of information—a single "off-on" switch in the computer's memory. (Bits and bytes are explained on page 86.) Old-fashioned small computers (1982 and earlier) were able to deal with 8 bits at a time. Some newer models can handle 16 or even 32 bits at a time. The literature for computers with 16-bit processors leads one to believe that using an 8-bit processor is the equivalent of driving a horse and buggy down the freeway. Not so. It is, perhaps, closer to driving a Ford Pinto car down the freeway, instead of a Cadillac. It may not be as fast or as powerful, but it will probably get you there nearly as well. (Alternative image: a 16-bit ladle may empty the soup pot faster, but an 8-bit ladle will get the job done.)

The main advantage of a 16-bit machine is in situations involv-

51.

A computer should not be bought primarily on the basis of its specifications.

ing extensive use of large numbers, since a 16-bit processor can work with numbers 250 times larger than an 8-bit. Still, as Mr. Garetz of CompuPro says, "A poorly-designed 16-bit machine is not likely to perform as well as a well-designed 8-bit computer. And software that's inefficient or hard to use can undermine the best computer equipment."

In summary, then, computers should not be bought primarily on the basis of comparison of specifications. Let the specs be taken into account, if it seems appropriate, perhaps to narrow a choice down to a smaller number of possibilities. But many other factors are far more likely to be significant in making the final choice.

Bargains

Buying Computers and Software by Mail

Even worse than the dreaded "RIFFIMS" (see page 206) in the eyes of computer dealers are what some of them call "SHABES." SHABE (rhymes with "babe") stands for Shop Here and Buy Elsewhere.

This is perceived as a major problem in some retail establishments, and may account for the less-than-thrilling service given to *all* their potential customers. It can take a long time to discuss a customer's needs and then give a complete demonstration of one or more computer systems. If the person then says, "Thank you very much. I'll think it over," the salesperson probably thinks, "There goes a Shabe."

And why not? Mail order computer and software sellers generally offer prices from 15% to 25% lower than retail stores, plus the fact that you don't have to pay sales tax if you buy from out of state. On a $3,000 system, that's significant.

Why are mail order sellers cheaper? When they are part of the "gray market" (see page 69), they can get goods at a price much lower than most retail stores. In any event, they don't have to worry about a fancy retail establishment, and can operate out of more austere quarters in the low rent district. They don't have to support a staff of demonstrators and customer's hand-holders. They don't really care too much about satisfied customers or repeat sales. Most significantly, they don't have to worry about Shabes!

Is it ethical to shop around locally, then buy by mail from a discounter? That's a decision you'll have to make for yourself. Some people won't do it. Others do it but feel guilty. And many do it without regrets, believing it to be a logical extension of our free enterprise system.

Some people feel that it is OK to buy computers by mail, but

> If there is a technological advance without social advance, there is, almost automatically, an increase in human misery.
>
> —Michael Harrington

the software is better bought locally. The logic here is that there aren't really *that* many choices in computers, but it is really important to be able to try out software before paying for it, hence the local purchase. The flaw in this is that most computer dealers are familiar with only a fraction of the software programs they sell, and may be quite unwilling to let a potential customer (and potential Shabe) break open the box and try out something new.

Other people tell me it is crazy to buy software at retail, since discounts go as high as 50% on mail order programs, and it is the manufacturer, not the local dealer, who will service it if something goes wrong.

My preference is to be as honest as possible with the local store. I will ask either for them to match the available mail order price, or, when relevant, suggest that I may pay retail if they can assure me of outstanding or special service. This doesn't work so well for me, but other, perhaps more persuasive, folks tell me they do it all the time with good results.

About "$CALL"

In many discounters' advertisements and catalogues, you will see listings like this:

Commodore 64 . . . . $595
Timex TS1000 . . . . $74.95
Epson MX80 . . . . $CALL
Atari 400 . . . . $197.95
Osborne 1 . . . . $CALL

How much is $CALL? This designation is reserved for items that are heavily discounted, highly competitive, and/or filling up the warehouse. The price can vary from hour to hour, or even during the course of the phone call. (On one "$CALL" I made, the chap on the phone said, "Make me an offer." I did. "You gotta be kidding," he said.)

Understanding and Dealing with the Gray Market

Paradox:

IBM and Apple will not sell their computers to unauthorized dealers.

52.

The main reason to buy by mail is price. The main reason to buy locally is service. In some situations one is better, in some, the other.

53.

Most dealers are familiar with only a fraction of the software programs they sell.

IBM and Apple do not allow their dealers to resell their computers to other dealers, or to sell computers by mail.

Probably the largest single seller of Apples and IBMs in the United States is an unauthorized dealer, 47th Street Photo of New York, which singlehandedly accounts for almost one percent of the entire multi-billion dollar small computer market — and most of it is done by mail.[1]

How can this be?

The answer lies in understanding the nature of the so-called "gray market" — an important consideration for anyone thinking of buying a computer by mail, or over the counter from a discount house.

The major small computer makers — Apple, IBM, Osborne, Hewlett-Packard, and the rest — generally do not allow their products to be sold through discount houses. Cheapens the image, they say. To reinforce this policy, they require all their dealers to sign a pledge that they will not resell their own stock to a discount house.

The dealers smilingly sign this pledge — and then ignore it.

Consider a typical dealer for a major brand. If he or she buys 5 or 10 or 20 computers from the manufacturer, the discount will be around 30%. But if the order is for 80 or more computers, the discount drops to around 40%.

Thus dealers all over the country are buying far more computers than they can possibly sell, in order to get the big discount, and then shipping most of their order out the back door to 47th Street Photo, or any of the other hundred-or-so mail order or discount house computer dealers.

Often they make no profit whatever — sometimes even take a loss, in order to get needed cash, or to avoid the carrying costs for their excess inventory. And then the discounter turns right around and sells the computers at a 15% to 30% discount to the public.

It appears to be perfectly legal for the general public to buy from these discounters. The only irregularity in the system appears to be that the authorized dealers are violating their agreements with the manufacturers by selling to the discounters. But

> As the eagle was killed by the arrow winged with his own feather, so the hand of the world is wounded by its own skill.
>
> —Helen Keller

---

1. They are also among the more interesting of America's businesses. Probably the only $100 million business run from premises upstairs over a delicatessen, the core of the business is a room in which dozens of Hassidic Jews, equipped with yarmulkes, side curls, and long distance telephones, take orders for electronic gadgetry from all over the world.

the nature of the contract allegedly being violated has never been tested in a court of law, and is believed by many dealers to be unenforceable.

Reasons not to deal in the gray market

1. Lack of technical expertise and advice before purchase. The mail order sellers may not have the time, inclination, or knowledge to counsel customers as to which machine is best, or which additional equipment they might want.

2. Lack of service. Although some mail order houses also offer mail order service, most do not. Computers can always be brought into an authorized dealer for repair, whether or not under warranty. But many dealers (even the ones who sell to the discounters in the first place!) are reluctant to service machines bought on the gray market, and some downright refuse to.

3. Lack of advice and assistance after the sale. If you are having problems understanding how to use the equipment, you are unlikely to get help on the phone or by mail from a discount house.

Reasons people deal in the gray market

1. Low prices. They will generally run from at least 15% to 30% (or more on special sales) less than the prices for identical equipment from authorized dealers.

2. Greater availability. Because a giant discounter may do 500 times more business than a little local store, their inventory at any given time is likely to be vastly larger as well. And, if they don't have something you want in stock, there is a good chance (not unlike the car theft rings that will steal a certain make and model to order) they can encourage one of their secret suppliers to order the goods and ship them on.

So, after all this, what do I recommend? There is no one solution right for everyone. Please see page 91 for my recommended strategy for buying new computer equipment.

What About Buying Used Equipment?

Buying used computer equipment involves taking something of a risk — but, all things considered, it may be not too much greater a risk than buying new equipment, and the cost savings can be

54.

There is a huge and apparently completely legal computer "gray market" — legal, inexpensive, and offering a wide selection, but with limited advice and service.

immense. The crucial factor to know, or to attempt to ferret out, is why the original owner of the equipment chose to sell it. There are, logically, only four reasons why computer equipment would find its way onto the used machinery market:

Previous owner upgraded

If a computer user is happy with his or her equipment, but decides it would be nicer or necessary to have something faster or more powerful or with greater memory storage capacity, then that person's old equipment is well worth considering seriously. A happy and satisfied user is more likely to have taken good care of the equipment, and treated it well. Indeed, a number of the used-computer-for-sale ads I see in the classified section do specify "owner upgrading."

One of the most common "upgradings" is replacing a "dot matrix" printer (the kind that looks like computer printing) with a typewriter-quality printer.

Previous owner fed up

When I telephoned a lot of people who advertised computers for sale, I found quite a few who simply had given up, and decided *not* to computerize their businesses, homes, or lives after all. Some of the prices quoted by these people seemed remarkably low. When I remarked on this, one man replied, "It's an albatross around my neck. I just want the damned thing out of here by Saturday, regardless of price." (This may be the computer equivalent of throwing your golf clubs in the water hazard. You may well regret it a few minutes or a few hours later.)

If the nature of being fed up is genuinely an inability to learn how to use the computer properly, and not a problem with the machinery itself, then here, too, may be some very good buys. A non-profit organization I spoke to was selling a $10,000 computer for $5,000 — and they had literally never even turned it on. It was given to them by a foundation, as a charitable gift, and they had neither interest nor inclination to figure out how to use it.

It really is a lemon

Some people give up and sell their computers because they are genuine certified lemons. Sometimes they mention that they have "had a few problems," and sometimes they don't. There are

55.
Buying used equipment makes sense if the seller is upgrading his equipment or giving up on computers. Often, however, the reason is that it is a lemon.

some deceitful computer-selling practices, akin to unscrupulous used-car dealers putting diesel oil in the crankcase to make a miserable engine sound OK—for about 300 miles.

Happily, most pieces of computer equipment are relatively simple to check out, if the checker-outer has the right equipment. (More on this in a moment.) Unhappily, not too many buyers of used equipment do this. They either are too trusting, or are dazzled by a few simple tricks they see the computer do; they take it home only to discover they have indeed bought a lemon.

It's being sold by a dealer or broker

Quite a few computers, large and small, are "sold" to insurance companies. Once the insurer has paid off on a claim, they often are eager to dispose of the stuff as quickly as possible, generally to dealers. The two main categories of events leading up to this are (a) computers stolen, and recovered after the claim was paid and the owner had presumably bought new equipment; and (b) computers damaged in a fire or other disaster.

(One used computer dealer told me that she often picks up computers that were sprayed by fire extinguishers, and look pretty awful—but more often than not, when she cleans them up, she finds they work fine, and she can sell them for five to ten times her "fire sale" purchase price from the insurance company.)

Dealers and brokers do essentially the same thing. The main difference is that brokers don't actually own the equipment in question; they are acting as a middleman between the seller and the potential buyer. As such, brokers are likely to represent larger, more expensive computers, but not always. For instance, one recent ad had a broker selling the remains of a bankrupt company, including 36 desktop computers, purchasable in minimum lots of two. (Bring a friend.)

Although you will pay more than you would if you bought from a private party, you may have the advantage of at least *some* kind of warranty on the equipment. Some dealers offer anywhere from a 15- to a 90-day warranty on what they sell. The question, of course, is where the dealer got the computer.

Checking out a used computer

Without question, this should be done to the best of your ability. There exist "diagnostics" for most kinds of computer

Be suspicious of used computers for sale.

56.

There are ways that unscrupulous sellers can make mostly-defective used equipment perform satisfactorily for a short demonstration.

equipment, including computers, disk drives, and printers.

A diagnostic test might consist of putting a special disk into the system. The disk, which takes anywhere from a few minutes to an hour or more to run through its paces, "exercises" every component of a system, and reports on its condition. (Just as a four-

57.
There are self-diagnosis programs that should be run, preferably by a repair service, before buying used equipment.

engine jet can fly on three or maybe two engines, some computers can do a lot of impressive things, even though a good deal is wrong with them. The diagnostic tests should find any inactive bad parts, however.)

Although sometimes the diagnostics are built into a system, often it requires one or more special disks, not widely sold, and often quite expensive. (I did buy one once, for over $100, but it was invaluable in identifying just which tiny parts of the system were malfunctioning, probably saving hours of detective work by an expensive repair person.)

Some computer repair facilities will have the diagnostics for popular makes and models. But the computer repair industry is still in its infancy, and you may not find satisfactory ways and means of getting something checked out.

The next best thing is to observe the equipment in operation for as long as possible — with the seller's own programs and data, or, better still, your own, if you either have compatible programs, or can figure out how to enter and process your own data.

You may wish to try to negotiate a conditional purchase (3-day return privilege) or a short warranty from a private seller — but unless the seller is truly desperate, this is unlikely to be granted.

What About Buying Obsolete Equipment?

From a marketing standpoint, computers become obsolete amazingly fast. On the day the new Model 12 with Enhanced Thises, Thatses and The Otherses is introduced, that whole warehouse full of Model 11s suddenly becomes a drug on the market, and a lot of people who own the "good ol' faithful 11" are going to have a lot more trouble selling it.

There is certainly nothing wrong with buying and using obsolete computer equipment — as long as you understand *why* it is obsolete, and can live with that, as well as the shame of having your friends know you have last year's (or last month's or yesterday afternoon's) equipment.

As an example, in 1983, Apple came out with something called the Apple IIe, thereby making the Apple II+ (which I, and several hundred thousand others, have been using) obsolete. As best I can understand it, the main differences between the splendid new

One of the new computers in the billing department had gone berserk, possibly from the strain of replacing five elderly bookkeepers, and a hundred thousand dollars' worth of credit had been erroneously issued to delinquent charge-account customers before anyone caught it.

— Lois Gould,
Necessary Objects

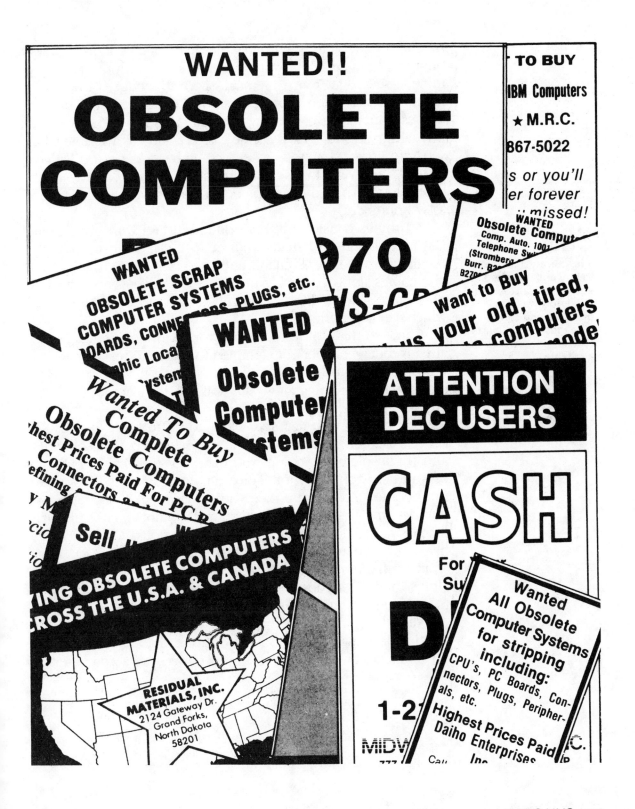

IIe and my obsolete II+ are that the IIe has a little more memory built in (I can get along without that—or add more memory to mine—see page 79 on memory size); it produces lower case letters on the screen without additional gadgetry (a pleasant but non-essential feature, and anyway many II+ owners have already invested in an add-on lower case gadget); and it is available with a separate array of buttons to enter numbers, as on a calculator, instead of having to use the numbers on the top row of the typewriter keyboard (perhaps desirable for people who type in lots of numbers).

All things considered, I am quite satisfied with my obsolete II+ model, and so I shall continue to use it until (a) parts and repairs are no longer available and I need some, or (b) something else comes along that makes the Apple *so* obsolete (not just a little obsolete, as now) that I cannot live without the newer model, whichever comes first.

Come to think of it, there *are* wonderful new things around already, but whenever I am tempted to acquire one, I go back and read page 25 on the disadvantages of being the first kid on the block with something new, dust off the iron Apple[2], and start enjoying it anew.[3]

The people who are *least* likely to be troubled by obsolescence, whether in what they already own, or in buying something already obsolete, are those who plan to use their computer for one and only one function. For example, I have talked to quite a few people who treasure their Radio Shack TRS-80 Model 1 computers—the first mass-marketed small computer, not manufactured since 1980, but with hundreds of thousands in use, and prices on the used market remaining fairly high. One might almost call them the Model T of computers, even though they are almost hopelessly obsolete in terms of the speed and power of today's equipment.

Nonetheless, I spoke to people who have been doing their word processing with a Model 1 for five or more years, and have no intention of changing. (I am part-owner of a computerized

58.

It is entirely reasonable to buy and use obsolete equipment, as long as you know *why* it is obsolete and can live with that—and if parts and service are available.

---

2. This is an obscure but rather clever literary allusion, which I mention so theater people will know I didn't say it by accident and others will be impressed (or annoyed) by my erudition.

3. This is not really an endorsement of Apple. Sometimes I *really* wish I had an Osborne or a Kay-Pro or an Epson HX-20 or a Teleram, but I don't wish it enough to make the changeover now. The Apple is not sufficiently obsolete.

typesetting business, and the whole system is based on the Model 1. The lack of versatility is more than made up for by its workhorse dedication to a single purpose.)

Concern about parts and service

An important consideration in buying an older or obsolete piece of equipment is whether or not it can be serviced and whether parts are still being made.

This is a minor concern with popular brand names, because even if the manufacturers stop supporting their own babies (which often happens after ten years), or go bankrupt (which has happened to a great many computer companies), some other enterprising company will generally start manufacturing the necessary parts, which many independent service people can diagnose and install.

This happened, for instance, with our Compugraphic computer-driven typesetting machine. The Compugraphic company said, "Sorry folks, no more parts after next year." And within the year, there were two good-sized companies going, whose primary business was supplying parts they manufactured to the tens of thousands of us Compugraphic orphans.

However, this could be a real problem with small or unknown brands. As recounted elsewhere, a great many companies get into computer or computer component manufacturing — and a great many fail. If a non-standard gear or wheel or chip has to be manufactured from scratch, a 50 cent part (if mass manufactured) could end up costing hundreds of dollars.

I once bought a used disk drive for what seemed like an amazing bargain price of $50. It has been sitting on the shelf for three years, now, because no one in the world seems to know what happened to the Houston Microtechnologies Corp., and no one seems to know how to repair their product.

After growing wildly for years, the field of computing now appears to be approaching its infancy.

—Opening line,
President's Science
Advisory Committee on
Computers, 1967

Specific Hardware Issues

What "Memory" Is, and How to Decide How Much You Want or Need

One of the more important variables in selecting a small computer is the amount of memory it has built in. I have heard apparently intelligent and undoubtedly humorless salespeople in computer stores say to sincere but clearly unknowledgeable potential customers, right off the bat, "How many kilobytes of RAM did you have in mind?" This is like asking the little old lady who wanders into the new car showroom how many cubic centimeters of cylinder displacement she requires in her new sedan.

All computers have a built-in memory of some sort. The memory is the place where the computer remembers, electronically, and temporarily, what you have typed into it, or otherwise fed into it. "Temporarily" means that when you turn the computer off, the contents of the memory disappear, just as the picture on a television screen disappears when the power is turned off. (And just as you can save television pictures forever on tape on a videocassette, you can, if you wish, save the contents of your computer memory on a tape cassette or a disk.)

This temporary memory is generally called RAM, which stands for Random Access Memory.[1]

The amount of memory in a computer is measured by the number of characters (letters, numbers, or special instructions like "Start a new paragraph") it can hold. Since computers wouldn't be as mysterious or special if they didn't have their own

---

1. Computer people talk about the "RAM and ROM" of a computer. You really don't ever need to know about ROM, the "Read Only Memory" which is the permanent memory built into the computer, storing the permanent instructions that tell it how to operate.

words for everything, each character is called a "byte."[2] From metric usage, the prefix "kilo" means 1,000, and so a "kilobyte" means 1,000 letters or numbers, etc. (One also sees the prefix "mega," meaning 1 million, so a "megabyte" means 1 million bytes, or 1 million characters, or about 200,000 words, or the length of a James Michener novel.)[3]

There are two kinds of things to consider when it comes time to worry about what size RAM, or memory, to get with your computer: necessity and convenience.

Necessity

The programs necessary to make your computer do things are also made up of letters, numbers, and other instructions. A simple program, perhaps to calculate a mortgage payment or play a game of hangman with you, might require a few hundred to a few thousand characters, or bytes. A complicated word processing program, or bookkeeping program might require 40,000, 50,000, or more characters.

These programs are permanently stored on tapes or disks, and when you want to use them, the computer electronically transfers the program into its own memory—*if there is room*. If your computer can only hold 16,000 characters, clearly there is no way it can transfer in a program containing 24,000 characters.

The most important consideration, then, is whether or not the computer has at least as much memory as that of the largest program you will ever run. How can you possibly know that? Fortunately, virtually all programs say, on the box or in the catalogue description, how many bytes (or kilobytes) it contains.

For example, typical word processing programs will contain somewhere between 24,000 and 64,000 bytes. (The longer the programs, the more complex or sophisticated they will be.) If you

59.
In choosing memory size, the most important consideration is which programs are going to be run.

---

2. Another word you do *not* need to know, but which keeps cropping up in books and discussions about computers, is "bit." A bit is one of the electronic units that makes, in effect, a *part* of each given letter or number or other character. It always takes eight of these electronic signals to make a complete letter or number. Hence eight bits equal one byte. Now forget this.

3. Actually, to computer people, but to no one else in the world, a "kilo" is actually 1,024. Thus "16K" is *not* 16,000 but actually 16,384. Don't worry about this. It makes no difference to you.

Bubble memory is one of the new technologies now showing up in some small computers. This photomicrograph, magnified at least 4×, helps explain how it works.

decide to use a program that is 32,000 bytes long, then you will need a memory, or RAM, of at least 32 kilobytes.

What looks like the same computer can come with a wide range of memory size, just as a variety of engines can be put in the same model of car. Unlike a car, more memory can be added to a computer, even after purchase, by buying additional snap-in memory units. So, with almost all small computers, even if you don't get enough memory at the start, you can always add from 16,000 to over 100,000 more bytes later, at a cost of roughly 1/4 cent to 1 cent per byte.

Thus if you get 48,000 bytes to start with (a fairly common amount), and then a terrific new adventure game comes on the market, requiring 64,000 bytes to play, you'll have to decide if it is worth investing the $50 to $100 probably necessary to add 16,000 more bytes to your computer.

Convenience

Because millions of small computers have been sold with 48,000 or fewer bytes of memory, thousands and thousands of programs have been written to run on 48,000 or fewer bytes — even though many of them might run better if there were more bytes available.

As an example, the word processing program I am using to write these words requires a computer with 48,000 bytes of memory — just the number mine has. But the *disk* on which the program came has about 64,000 bytes. Thus I cannot use all the program at one time. When I want to go from one part of the program to another (say, from the part where I edit to the part where I print things out), I have to stop, remove the editing portion of the program (perhaps 40,000 characters) from the memory, and transfer in the printing portion (perhaps 24,000 characters).

This process is simple, but requires about 30 seconds. If I had 64,000 bytes of memory, then the entire program could be stored in the memory at once, and I would be spared all those 30 secondses.

The decision I am faced with is typical: is it worth the $100 that the additional memory would cost me, to save perhaps four minutes a day? Well, that's about 20 hours a year, and 100 hours over the next five years. Is my time worth $1.00 an hour? I'd like to think so, so I'll probably spring for the additional memory unit pretty soon.

Another financial factor to consider: every time a computer loads or unloads a program, it works a little. Parts wear out, and disks wear out, just as phonograph records do from frequent playing. Each time I have to go back and forth from one part of a program to another, because my memory isn't large enough for the whole thing, I am probably shortening the life of my computer's disk drives, and the disks themselves, by a wee bit. And that, too, can mount up. Yes, I'm quite sure I'll have to get those 16,000 extra bytes.

Let us return, then, to that incomprehensible question posed by the computer salesman back in the first paragraph of this

60.

It is almost always possible to add more memory to a computer after the purchase, if there turns out not to be enough.

section: "How many kilobytes of RAM did you have in mind?"

Although the proper answer might be, "Please speak to me in English, young man," another answer is, "Let me first consider which programs I am likely to be using, and how much memory they require."

Virtually all small computer programs require 64,000 or fewer, and the vast majority 48,000 or fewer. The 2,000 bytes of the Timex-Sinclair is almost certainly too small for all but the simplest uses. The 1 million bytes (1 megabyte) of the Apple Lisa is almost certainly more than small computer users will ever require. Somewhere in this huge range lies the perfect answer for each user.

What Are Modems, and Do You Really Need One?

The word "MODEM" used to be a contraction of "*Modulator/Demodulator*" (just as "RADAR" used to be a contraction of "*Radio Detection and Ranging*") but both have evolved into words in their own right. A modem (pronounced MOE-dumb) is a device that converts computer output into a form that can be sent over ordinary telephone lines.

Using a modem is, in theory, quite simple. You plug it into a small computer, dial the required telephone number, set your telephone handset on the modem, turn your computer on, and (assuming the person or machine at the other end has done the same), the two machines can interact, whether they are across the room or across the world from each other.

There are two general categories of reasons to consider investing the $100 to $400 that a modem costs:

1. *Access to some very large computers.* On a grand scale, there are several large companies that operate huge computers which they make available to subscribers on an hourly basis. Once you subscribe to The Source, CompuServe, or similar services, you can establish contact through a modem and tap into any of the offerings available: stock market prices, newspaper stories (old or new), sports scores, games, word processing or mathematical programs, bulletin board services (you can leave messages which other subscribers can read), and so forth. You pay anywhere from $2 to $20 an hour (depending on the time of day and the service used) plus the cost of the telephone call.

A very small minority of small computer people use and are wildly enthusiastic about these services (surely fewer than 5%). Most people either haven't felt the need, don't want the expense, or (in the eyes of the enthusiasts) haven't yet come to appreciate the value of these services.

2. *Interaction between small computers.* When two parties who have compatible computers and modems wish to send words back and forth — more words than can conveniently be spoken into your terec (*te*lephone *rec*eiver), and the need is faster than services offered by the pooff (*po*st *off*ice) — it can be convenient to send them over the telephone lines. Or it can be inconvenient or downright frustrating.

Some problems with modems

Consider two people standing on opposite sides of the Grand Canyon wishing to communicate. A loud yell can be faintly heard at the other side. So here I am shouting an important message to you on the other side. If I yell slowly and clearly, all the words might get through to your ears. But if I yell rapidly and shrilly, some words might be lost. If a motorcycle goes past you ("noise in the system"), even more words may be lost.

So it is with modems. They often have different rates of transmission. Transmission rates are measured in a unit called "baud" (rhymes with "fraud"; stands for "Big Al's Universal Delivery," or possibly something else). "Standard" baud rates range from 300 to 1200, and translate roughly into that many words per minute (even though baud measures something else entirely).

1. *Speed problems.* Imagine the task of pouring milk from a large jug into lots of tiny bottles as fast as you can. The faster you go, the more you get into the little bottles — but the more you spill. So it is with words and numbers. The faster you send them, the more you spill. The slower you go, the less you spill (but the more time you spend).

2. *Noise problems.* Just as that motorcycle that went by as I was yelling to you across the Grand Canyon caused you to "lose" some correctly transmitted words, so, too, does noise on the telephone line cause some information to be lost, or, more devastatingly in some cases, to be altered. (How meanings can be changed is not as essential to understand, but is of interest to some people, and thus is explained on page 85.)

So every time there is a faint crackle or bit of static on the

61.
Small computers can "do business" over the telephone lines, but the cost is high and information can get garbled if there is noise on the lines.

line — one which might not even be noticed by the human ear — the more sensitive modem can't "hear" what came through at that exact 1/38 of a second (which is how long it takes to send one letter of the alphabet), and either gets it wrong, or leaves it out altogether.

Ordinary phone lines are pretty good. But they vary in quality from place to place, depending on the phone company's equipment. Where I live, the lines are only fair, and one local accountant told me he has stopped sending accounting data by modem because there were too many alteration errors.

Some businesses and other users will string up "dedicated" or private lines between computers, to decrease the chances for error. And some will opt for other alternatives.

Alternatives to a modem

A modem is the *only* way to tap into the giant computers of The Source, CompuServe, and other information services. So there are no alternatives. But you don't need a $50 million computer to determine Snuffy Stirnweiss' batting average for the Yankees in 1947.[4] Five minutes at, or a phone call to, a public library might do just as well. This notion is explored further on page 137 (Cataloguing Your Necktie Collection).

The other way to get your data (letters, numbers) from your computer to someone else's, or vice versa, is, obviously, to cause the tape or disk physically to move. A hefty percentage of goods traveling hither and yon by Express Mail and the various parcel delivery services consist of computer disks and tapes. The only problem is speed. Overnight isn't as fast as instantaneous, but it's often more reliable.

There *are* other alternatives, but none in widespread use. For example, the Lockheed company regularly needed to send information 30 miles across the mountains from Sunnyvale to the Felton Air Force Base. A dedicated line for computer-to-computer interaction was too expensive. The solution: carrier pigeons. (I asked the military man who told me of this if they were worried about the pigeons being intercepted by trained Communist eagles. I think he took me seriously. So if you see a pigeon with a tiny briefcase being escorted by a jet fighter . . .)

62.
There are much less expensive alternatives to telephone "modems" when speed is not a major factor.

Trained Communist eagle.

---

4. .256

How modems get things wrong

To understand how modems can fail, it is necessary to understand a tiny bit about *how* computers work. This information is by no means essential to understanding anything else in the world, or to achieving computer happiness.

All computers can do is transmit electricity. At any given time and place in the computer, there either *is* or *is not* electricity present. A switch is either on or off. Arbitrarily, it has been

Hats can become cats when electrical impulses get interfered with.

decided that when it is *off* it has the value "0" and when it is *on* it has the value "1." All that computers can handle, at the most elementary level then, are zeroes and ones. Offs and ons.

Each letter and number is described by a series of eight zeroes and ones, or eight offs and ons. When a computer "sees" eight switches in a row, and they are off-on-off-off-off-off-off-on, that is declared to be an "A." Every instance of off-on-off-off-on-off-off-off is declared to be an "H." And so on. (Each "off" or "on" is called a "bit" of information, and the eight bits that go to make up a letter, number or other character, are called a "byte.")

So if, for some peculiar reason, I wish to send the letter "H" by telephone to my friend Jim in Birmingham, I must telephone him, and then ask my computer to transmit that particular series of eight "electricity on" or "electricity off" impulses into the modem. I do this by striking the key labelled "H" on the computer keyboard. If all eight bits of information arrive safely over the phone lines, *my* letter "H" will appear on *his* screen or printer.

If, however, one of those "ons" gets hit by a crackle in the line over Houston and becomes an "off" then a different letter entirely will appear on his screen. I might end up asking him to send me his cat instead of his hat.

Choosing a Printer

Even "complete" computer systems rarely come with a printer, simply because there are so many kinds of them, and so many uses to which they can be put, that it really makes good sense to select your printer independently of whatever else you may be buying.

Printers range in cost from under $400 to over $4,000. They range in speed from about 100 words per minute to thousands of words per minute. And they range in quality from barely legible to professional typesetting quality.

The best way to think about what you can get is this:

1. GOOD APPEARANCE OF LETTERS
2. LOW COST   } CHOOSE ANY TWO
3. HIGH SPEED

Let's consider each of the variables:

No machines will increase the possibilities of life. They only increase the possibilities of idleness.

—John Ruskin

63.
When buying a printer, from the options of low cost, high speed, and good appearance, you can choose any two.

1. Good appearance

There are two kinds of technologies used in the majority of printers to get letters onto the paper.

One involves what is essentially "old fashioned" typewriter technology. A typewriter key, "golfball" typing element, or "daisy wheel" petal strikes the paper through an inked ribbon, putting the letter onto the page.

The other, called "dot matrix" printing, uses the same idea that makes letters light up on scoreboards. There is an array of tiny little wires, packed into rectangular shape—at least 5 across and 7 down. To produce a "G", for example, 14 of the little wires are thrust forward, pushing through the ribbon to the paper, to make a pattern of dots on the page that resembles a "G."

The amazing thing to me is how fast *both* of these systems work.

The "daisy wheel" is spun into the correct position, a little hammer comes forward to hit it a sharp blow, and the mechanism moves one unit to the right—and it can do this at the rate of anywhere from 10 to 50 times per *second*. And the "dot matrix" system is a good deal faster.

The main advantage of "typewriter quality" is, of course, that it looks better. Some "dot matrix" printers have more dots than others (for example, an array of 7 by 10 instead of 5 by 7, so the letters look a little better. (With fewer dots, also, letters that normally descend below the line have to be put above the line, which I think looks quite dreadful.)

```
This is High Speed (160 cps) print style...
```

Also, some dot printers offer the option of "multi-strike" in which a letter is struck, then the paper is moved a tiny bit up or down and the letter is struck again, thus putting dots between other dots. The small improvement in quality is offset by the slower speed.

```
This is High Quality (78 cps) print style...
```

There do exist much more expensive printers that offer the option of one, two, three, or four passes of the dot matrix printing head. By the time you've done it four times, it looks almost (but still not quite) as good as typewriter quality.

64.
"Dot" printers are much more versatile than "typewriter" printers, for doing charts, graphs, pictures, and different alphabets. The major drawback is the appearance of the letters.

With such a printer, you can use the high-speed low-quality mode for rough drafts, and the low-speed higher-quality mode for final copies. However such printers generally cost more than the combined price of a dot matrix printer plus a typewriter quality printer, so if the dual functions interest you, consider having two printers rather than one hybrid.

Dots have two main advantages over typewriter quality: cost and versatility. The cheapest dot printer is about half the price of the cheapest typewriter-quality printer. (I have seen them on sale under $300.) And, because the dots can be configured in *any* shape, dot printers (with the appropriate software or programs coming from the computer) can print in English, Hebrew, Japanese, or any other alphabet, or print various shapes that can be combined to produce pictures, charts, graphs, and designs. Some dot printers also offer the option of regular size, extra-wide, or extra-narrow letters. I have found extra-narrow a valuable feature when trying to get as many words as possible into a given space (such as a mailing label)

Typewriter-quality printers have two main advantages over dot matrix: the quality is superior (even approaching typesetting quality with certain configurations). And a typewriter-quality printer with a keyboard (an optional extra) can double as an "ordinary" typewriter if you wish.

2. Low cost.

Printer costs have come down in recent years, but not nearly as rapidly as computer prices, largely because printers have many more mechanical (as contrasted with electronic) parts in them.

Cost is also linked to durability. If all other factors are equal, a more expensive printer may be (*should* be) more rugged, thus more desirable for situations where it is likely to be running all day, cranking out reports and letters. Small dot printers cost between $300 and $700, while typewriter-quality printers begin around $700 and go as high as $3,000.

Two kinds of gadgets are on the market that allow people who already have an electric typewriter to use it as a computer-controlled printer. One is electronic; the other is mechanical.

The electronic device can be wired into certain models of ordinary office typewriters (for instance the IBM Selectric or Olivetti Praxis), permitting the computer to send the typewriter the same signal that pressing a typewriter key sends to the print

Educators . . . may be uncomfortable with the crisp-looking results of computer-generated manuscripts. So the graduate students are purposely not using their computers' capacity for justifying right-hand margins. The trick, says one, is to use word processing without making it appear that you have done so.

—Chronicle of Higher Education

65.

Almost all electric typewriters can be converted into computer-driven printers, for less than the cost of buying a new printer.

mechanism (such as, "Now's the time for a 'G'.") The sellers of these devices, which run from $300 to $500, claim that anyone can install them, but I'd sure negotiate to have the dealer or a knowledgeable sort do it for me.

The mechanical gadget is one of those things that some archaeologist is going to find in 100 years and set off 10 years of debate on what it possibly could have been used for. It is an array of about 40 plungers, that rests right on any typewriter keyboard. *Now* when you want that "G" the computer instructs the plunger over the "G" key to descend, and so it does, striking the key just the way your finger would have done. Keyboards do vary slightly, and the plungers can be adjusted accordingly. Their speed can be adjusted to match the maximum of which your typewriter is capable.

These "keyboard actuators" have the advantage of being usable on *any* electric typewriter — and of being plonked on or whisked off in about two seconds, so the machine can be used with brain-directed plungers (fingers) as well. Their price is also in the $300 to $500 range.

Keyboard Actuator

3. Speed

Printer speeds are generally given in "cps" — characters per second. At the accepted figure of 5 letters (or characters) per average word, a printer speed of 10 cps, or 2 words per second, becomes 120 words per minute. The advertised speed of printers for small computer use ranges from about 10 cps (120 words per minute) to over 100 cps (1200 words per minute).[5]

Advertised speed is to actual speed as advertised miles per gallon estimates are to actual mileage. When you are typing on an old fashioned typewriter, your speed when you type the word "the" can be 150 words a minute, while your speed in typing "42,917 zebras (Grebe) #802 @ $17.82 ea. = $764,780.94" may be 12 words a minute. Your average speed might be 50 words a minute — but your *rated* (maximum) speed is 150.

So it is with printers. Actual speed can be anywhere from one-third to two-thirds of the advertised speed. That's still pretty good, especially considering that you never have to retype because you've done all your editing on the screen.

66.

Advertised printer speeds are about as reliable as advertised miles per gallon.

---

5. Printer technology is at the point where huge "ink jet" printers that squirt letters on the paper can print "personal" letters at speeds approaching 100,000 words per minute. That's a complete "personal" magazine subscription letter at the rate of 10 per second! And you worried that America was falling behind in the technology race.

What printer speed do you want or need? No simple answer. I have talked to people who were happy with a 10 to 15 cps printer. And I've talked to others who were quite annoyed at sitting around waiting for their printer to print out a long report, mailing list, etc.

An interesting compromise is the technology that lets a printer be printing one thing while you can be using the computer for something else. This "printer spooling," as it is called, is done automatically by some computers, while you can add either hardware or software to make other computers do it.

Making your printer decision

For many people, the choice is simple, at least as to whether to choose dot matrix or typewriter quality. For others it is confusing and complex. Most are in between.

Here are three compromise solutions:

— Rent. Computer printers are rentable from some computer stores and from equipment rental companies, sometimes for as short a period as a week. Actual intensive use with your own computer and your own workload is the best test of a printer.

— Share. If two people who can't decide between dot matrix and typewriter quality printers get together, they can share the usage. That's my situation. I have a typewriter quality printer, and a nearby friend has a dot matrix printer. Each of our computers will operate each printer. When he needs better quality work, he borrows mine. When I need higher speed or graphics capability, I borrow his. A happy solution.

— Wait. Low-cost ink jet printers that combine the best features of both are said to be just around the corner. Maybe several corners.

67.

Rent a printer for a week or a month before you buy one.

68.

If you can't decide between a dot and a typewriter printer, find someone else in the same predicament, and jointly buy one of each.

Financial Matters

"I'll Pay Your Outrageous Price if You'll Give Me Terrific Service."

Here is a sensible strategy to consider for buying a computer, especially your *first* computer. It doesn't always work, but the risks are small, and the benefits if it succeeds are considerable.

The assumptions made are these:

☐ The prices at retail computer stores are likely to be 15% to 25% higher than mail order discount prices.

☐ The higher local price presumably goes, at least in part, for a support staff who can install your system, and give you assistance after the sale.

☐ But retail stores *are* in business to make a profit, and the less after-the-sale time they have to spend, the more profitable they will become.

☐ Mail order computer sellers rarely have much interest in you once the sale is made.

☐ Retail stores have some interest in repeat business, and like to be able to refer potential customers to satisfied local users.

With all this in mind, the following strategy presents itself. Here, as I remember it, is what I said at the time I bought my Apple system from a local computer store:

Bear: "I have now decided that I want to buy this Apple II+ computer with 48K of memory, two disk drives, and a Video black and white monitor. Your price on this package is $2,310. Here is the current price list of a large mail order discount house. You can see that my price from them, including shipping, and excluding sales tax, would be $1,906.

"Now, I am willing to pay you that extra $404, because I fully expect that you will give me extraordinary service, expert advice, help me out with loaner machines in times of need, and generally be available for aid, assistance, and consultations at all reasonable

69.
Offer to buy locally at retail prices only if you can negotiate extra or special services.

hours, and perhaps a few unreasonable ones. On that basis, will you accept my check for $2,310."

To no one's amazement, they did. Nothing in our arrangement was protected (or, probably, protectable) in writing. It was a good faith agreement. The fact that the store's only helpful employee left soon after, to be replaced by a series of less and less helpful folks, until finally the enterprise went out of business, is probably immaterial. It was a good gamble on my part—and I am aware of many instances with other people where it *has* turned out to be successful.

Some people feel comfortable using an entirely different approach. In a similar circumstance, they would have said to the local store, "You're asking $2,310 for the system. I can buy it for $404 less by mail. I can't see paying you all that extra money for at best a few hours of your time after the sale. But I am willing to pay you an extra $100. So if you'll give it to me for $2,000, you've got a sale. Otherwise, it's off to the telephone I go."

I have talked to people who feel comfortable with this approach, and who say it works quite often, although not all the time. If one dealer turns it down, there are always others willing to accept a smaller profit.

Machines won't take over the world entirely so long as we have the little thrill that comes when we add a column of figures and get the same total we did the first time.

—Kodiak, Alaska Mirror

It's OK to Haggle

Almost no one pays the sticker price on a car. Even people who hate bargaining will "make an offer" when buying a home. But very few people feel comfortable dickering over the price of a refrigerator, a television set, or a computer. Perhaps the word "haggle" is inappropriate, with its connotations of the Turkish marketplace. But it is, nonetheless, entirely reasonable and proper to negotiate the terms of your purchase of small computers and other related equipment.

Most people don't do this. But those who do tell me that it almost always works—and when it doesn't, they go to another supplier who *is* willing to talk price.

These are the areas that can be negotiable:

The total price. Most dealers pay anywhere from 30% to 50% less than their "sticker" prices. There is room for negotiation. Some dealers would rather make $100 on a $3000 sale than lose the sale entirely—knowing that satisfied customers are likely to return for other supplies and goods from time to time.

The terms. Some dealers carry their own contracts; others have working arrangements with local banks or leasing companies. And some are open to "creative" financing. One man told me he wanted a $6,000 system. "Look," he told the dealer, "I won't haggle on the total price. I'll give you $2,000 now, $2,000 in six months, and $2,000 in a year, but I want the equipment now." He got it.

Try-out period. A purchase can be made subject to your satisfaction, with the option to return everything for a full (or 90% or other negotiated percentage) refund within, say, 30 days.

Delivery and installation. You can but ask. I once bought a system from a dealer 150 miles away, with the stipulation that no payment would be made until the equipment was "up and running" in my office. If you have any doubts or reservations about your abilities in this regard, then ask.

Warranty length. If the dealer has his or her own repair facility, or access to one, then it is entirely reasonable to say, "I'll buy this if you'll personally extend the warranty from 90 days to a year" (or two or three, for that matter).

Training. Some dealers and distributors have regular classes in the use of their equipment, lasting from a few hours to a few days. If this is not available, or if you feel the need for more personal instruction, you may wish to ask for 5 or 10 or 20 hours of teaching as part of the deal—your place or theirs.

The thing to remember is that it is very much a buyer's market, and likely will remain so indefinitely. A sensible salesperson or manager knows perfectly well that if you are dissatisfied with the deal you are offered, you can go to the place in the next shopping mall over, or, indeed, deal with any of the hundreds of mail order discounters who advertise regularly in computer publications and daily newspapers.

What It Really Costs to Buy a Computer

Let's start by considering what it really costs to buy a razor. About two bucks for my Gillette Atra. Oh, and then a new blade (at about 30 cents each) every two or three days. Plus shaving cream and after shave lotion. Not counting the Band-Aids, over the anticipated five-year life of this particular $2 razor, my total cost will be about $300.

Of course, if drugstores sold only "total shaving systems" (all

70.
It is OK to haggle with dealers over price, terms, a try-out period, warranty terms, training classes, and delivery and installation costs.

the supplies needed for five years of shaving) for a mere $279.95, I suspect that beards would suddenly become more popular.

This approach to selling is actually *known* in textbooks as the "razor and blade" school of marketing. You can virtually give away the razor, and your fortune will be made on the blades — because people buy 'em one at a time, and never think about the total real cost.

Razors = hardware. Blades = software. And if the general populace ever contemplated the actual total cost, most people would be inclined to return to counting on their fingers and doing word processing with a ball point pen. Atari, Intellivision and the like would be in big trouble, because while millions of people seem willing to buy a $100 game unit and *then* buy $400 worth of game cartridges over the next year or two, almost *no* one is going to spend $500 all at once for the complete game system.

The only reason small computers manufacturers don't give away their computers and then make zillions on the software is that there are thousands of software sellers, but only a small handful of game cartridge makers, so they can't count on the follow-up business themselves. *Some*one will get it, but it's likely to be someone else.

A computer store owner told me that an average first-time computer buyer will spend an amount equal to the initial purchase each year for the first three years on software, additional hardware, repairs, lessons, and the like. Of course this will vary considerably from person to person and computer to computer, but it seems safe to say that the typical customer who thinks he or she is making a $1,000 purchase is, in reality, making the initial payment on a $4,000 purchase.

How is all this extra money spent? Leaving out psychiatric care, there are four categories ("opportunities" as one trade magazine called them) in which additional bucks can be spent:

One-time-only start-up costs

There is the cost of delivery and installation, if available, and if you wish it done (you probably do).

There is the cost of instruction and training, either from the vendor or from outside sources.

There is the cost of converting what you are doing now to electronic form. This can range from setting aside (but not throw-

You keep adding components until you exceed your yearly income.

—James Warren, computer consultant

71.

In the long run, most people will spend three or four times as much money on software, repairs, lessons and additional hardware as on the original computer purchase.

ing out, please!) your ten-cent pencil, to spending thousands of dollars to have someone type all your financial records, customer lists, and other data into the computer.

And, most significantly, there is the sometimes sizeable (but well worth it) cost of operating your *old* non-computer system simultaneously with the new for a few months at least. (See page 115, where I explain why this is the single most important piece of advice in this book.)

Additional hardware: essential

Just as one car manufacturer used to list the rear seat as an "optional extra" in order to keep the base price of the car down, there are likely to be additional bits and pieces of hardware not figured into the original price, but which you will come to realize, often within a few days of purchase, are essential to your work or pleasure.

For example, when I bought my Apple, I thought I was getting all that I would require to be off and running: the computer, two disk drives, a printer, and the necessary cables. Before too long, it was clear that there were *ten* additional things that I would like to have had. I am going to identify these ten things, not because they will all be relevant to every small computer buyer, but as an indication of the *kinds* of things most people face:

1. *More memory.* The subject of memory size is discussed in detail on page 78. The basic Apple came with 16,000 bytes of memory. I felt the need to buy 32,000 more (in the form of plug-in modules that fit inside the computer), and I still could probably use 16,000 more of the little devils.

2. *Printer "interface" card.* In order to run my particular printer off that particular computer, a $200 interconnection gadget had to be plugged into the Apple. As with so many extras, I don't understand (or *need* to understand) what it does; I only need to know that without it, the printer doesn't work.

3. *"Integer" card.* As I understand it, my model computer is slightly different from the previous model, so that programs written for the previous model don't work on mine. By installing an electronic bit of wizardry, this year's model will behave like last year's model and run last year's programs. About $100.

4. *Television connection box.* While a computer monitor plugs directly into the computer, a home television does not. In order to play games in color (this is important; who wants a

black-and-white Pac-Man?), this device must first be installed in the computer. About $25.

5. *Z80 Softcard*. As with the integer card, there are thousands of desirable programs that only run in a system called CP/M. This $400 item plugs into the Apple and makes it run like a CP/M machine.

6. *Lower case unit*. The first few hundred thousand Apples sold did not produce lower case letters on the screen. For a mere $100 or so, invested in yet another plug-in device, the lower case alphabet appears.

7. *Shift key*. Without lower case letters, there was no need for a normally-functioning shift key. So the shifting function was put into a different key, elsewhere on the keyboard. One has the choice of learning to send the pinkies *up* instead of *down* to find the shift, or buying a gizmo that makes the key labelled "shift" shift. Anywhere from $20 to $50.

8. *Fan*. Gadgets 1 through 7 all give off a little heat. When most or all of them are installed, it may grow uncomfortably warm inside the computer. Hot parts wear out faster, as Xaviera Hollander may have pointed out in another context. A small cooling fan is strongly recommended. About $100.

Man is the lowest cost 150-pound non-linear all-purpose computer system that can be mass-produced by unskilled labor.

—Apochryphal NASA report on why we send humans to the moon instead of robots

9. *Carrying case.* One of the joys of the Osborne and similar one-piece computers is that they can be carried from place to place with relative ease. Separate-component computers are no easier to move around than six-unit home stereo systems. But independent manufacturers do make some satisfactory suitcase-type carriers specifically designed to carry the needed parts of a multi-part computer.

10. *Constant voltage transformer or electrical surge preventer.* Either of these devices, described on page 175, provide much peace of mind, and may actually work.

The total cost of all of the above, around $1,500, is just about equal to the original cost of the Apple.

Additional hardware: non-essential

All popular computers have a wide array of additional hardware available, provided either by the manufacturer or by independent companies vying for a share of the market. One can easily spend double or triple the cost of the computer itself in buying non-essential hardware. (I realize that one person's "non-essential" may be another's "utterly necessary." For instance, if you are buying a computer to compose music on, then a music synthesizer unit is essential.) Here, then, are the ten most common non-essential (for most people) but awfully nice hardware items:

1. *Printer buffer or spooler.* With most computers, you can only do one thing at a time. While the printer is printing, you cannot do other things with the computer. This plug-in device controls the printer independently, so you can be typing in, editing, playing games, or whatever, while the printer is grinding away. Generally $100 to $300.

2. *Number pad.* Some computers have a separate array of number keys, as on a calculator, off to the right of the main keyboard. For many of those that don't, a plug-in number-pad module can be added on for $100 or less.

3. *Voice synthesizer.* A unit that produces intelligible albeit mechanical-sounding human voices can be added on to many computers. The main uses appear to be in applications for blind people, and in various games. The novelty and wow-your-friends value is high: you can type in any words or sentences and the computer speaks them back to you. Cost: $200 to $500.

4. *Game controllers.* Some computers come with built-in "joy sticks" or levers and knobs needed to play many games. Some do not, and even for those that do, serious game players prefer more sophisticated "professional" controllers, at $50 to $100.

5. *Music synthesizers.* The computer is capable of creating a wide range of musical sounds, including faithful imitations of many instruments, but additional hardware (and software) is required actually to produce the sounds. The cost can be from $100 to $1,000 or more, depending on complexity.

6. *Speeder-uppers.* Some people grow bored or irritated waiting for old-fashioned computers to do in seconds what newer models can do in fractions of a second. Some very sophisticated hardware is available to make computers do various functions at higher speed: loading programs, sorting records, etc. Often they are gadgets that plug into the computer itself.[1] Cost: $100 and up.

7. *Modems.* The modem is the device that enables a computer to send and receive information over ordinary telephone lines. They are discussed on page 82. They are essential if you wish to have your computer "talk" to another computer, whether to get current stock information, send electronic "mail," or dip into the library of the *New York Times*. They range in price from $100 to about $400.

8. *Clock/calendar.* An electronic clock/calendar can be installed, so that your computer will always know the day and time (and, if you have a voice synthesizer, it will even tell you out loud). Some people find it useful to keep permanent track of the day and time that a certain program was written or run. About $75.

9. *Graphics equipment.* There is quite a range of gadgetry to assist people who wish to use computers in a visual way. You can draw directly on a graphics tablet, and your drawing will be stored electronically, and can be reproduced with a special kind of printer called a graphics plotter, or displayed and manipulated on the screen ("Let's see how the floor plan would look if the kitchen were over here instead . . ."). Prices start around $300 and climb rapidly.

10. *Hard disk.* A hard disk, or a Winchester hard disk is a

'Graphics tablets' transfer drawings directly into a computer.

---

1. There is a wonderful story told by Tracy Kidder in his splendid book *The Soul of a New Machine*. A man whose job involved trying to figure out how to make a certain computer do operations in fewer and fewer billionths of a second went off one day and left this note on his computer: "I'm going to a commune in Vermont and will deal with no unit of time shorter than a season."

means of storing a great deal more information than on a soft, or floppy disk. Hard disks are sealed units that plug directly into computers, and can hold from 1 million to 10 million bytes (characters) of information. (Ten million bytes is about 2 million words, which, at an average reading speed, would take a human 14 8-hour days to absorb.) The price range is from $2,000 to $5,000 depending on capacity.

Anything you can't spell won't work.

— Will Rogers

What software will you need?

Elsewhere I suggest that it makes more sense to choose the software before the hardware. Since software accounts for anywhere from 5% to 50% of the cost of a complete computer package (20% is typical), it is a significant cost item. In anticipating costs over three to five years, the major variable is game playing.

While dedicated users might want or need one word processing program, one number processing or "spreadsheet" program, and whatever specific applications are relevant to their business or hobbies (accounting programs, engineering programs, stamp collecting programs, etc.), it is likely that, once acquired and put into operation, these programs will last for many years. New ones in other areas may be added, but it is such a bother to upgrade or change old ones.

Games, however, are always changing, and not cheap. Most sophisticated computer games are in the $25 to $50 range, and there are plenty of people who buy 5, 10, 20 or more a year. Thus if games are to be played, their cost must be taken into consideration when calculating expenses.

73.
Repairs will average about 10% of the cost of hardware per year — less when it's newer, more when it's older.

This is a blank disk worth $3.00

This is a sophisticated accounting program worth $300.00

What repairs will be required?

No one knows but the statisticians, and all *they* know is that it is reasonable to budget about 10% of the cost of the hardware for repairs each year. Maybe a little less when it's newer, and a little more as it ages.

In summary

It is possible to buy a complete computer system (computer, memory unit, and printer) for under $1,000, when the memory unit is a cassette recorder rather than a disk drive. Complete systems involving one or two disk drives and a printer generally range between $2,000 and $5,000, with the average about $3,500. Software can add from 10% to 30% to these amounts.

Financing a Computer Purchase

We can quickly dispose of the four traditional methods of financing the purchase: banks and finance companies, sellers who carry contracts, credit cards, and lease/purchase arrangements. Just a few words on each.

Banks and finance companies

Depending on the daily state of the economy, many traditional lenders are willing to make computer-buying loans payable over a period of three to five years, at anywhere from prime rate to five points over prime. A last resort method.

Computers can solve all kinds of problems except the unemployment problems they create.

—Laurence J. Peter

Seller carries contract

All larger and many smaller companies are capable of doing this. Often a 20% or 25% down payment is required, but the interest rates are generally better than what banks offer.

Credit card

Even if the total purchase price exceeds the limit on your bank credit card, there are ways around that. One is the fact that limits are negotiable, especially for a one-time-only special purchase. Another is an agreement with the seller, who is authorized in writing to charge your credit card account regularly, up to its limit. If you have a $1,000 limit, for instance, and want to make a $4,000 purchase, the seller may agree to give you the equipment for the first $1,000 he or she can charge, with the understanding that the account can be charged at least $200 a month until the

$4,000 is paid. The dealer retains legal ownership until the full amount has been charged.

Lease/purchase plan

Independent leasing companies buy the equipment from the dealer, then lease it to you for a monthly payment equal to anywhere from 3% to 10% of the purchase price. After three to five years of making payments, you own the equipment (or have the right to buy it for 10% of its initial cost). The main advantage over direct purchase is that there is little or no down payment. There may also be tax advantages in leasing instead of buying.

Become a dealer

While some companies screen potential dealers carefully, and require substantial intitial purchases, others seem pitifully grateful to have more dealers, and make minimal or negligible demands. One man, for instance, was in the market for a good daisy wheel printer. Instead of paying $2,500 to $3,000 for a Qume or a Diablo, he became a dealer for a smaller but good-quality company. He bought a "demonstrator" model at a large discount and on good terms offered by the manufacturer. And he ended up paying for the entire purchase by selling printers to friends and neighbors at 10% over wholesale. In applying for a dealership, it is appropriate to have a letterhead of some sort, identifying you as a computer sales or service organization, at the very least with an undefined name, such as ABC Industries.

Become a commissioned salesperson

Even if you are not the sort of person who is comfortable in the role of a door-to-door high pressure salesperson, you can work with a computer store in a low key way. One man who wanted a Kay-Pro computer made such an arrangement with a computer store. They loaned him one as a demonstrator (which he regularly used in his own business) and deducted $200 from his own purchase price for every one he sold. After seven sales, all to business associates and friends, he owned his "demonstrator" free and clear.

Become a demonstration site or center

Some enlightened companies or dealers acknowledge that it is virtually impossible to get an adequate demonstration in a computer store or dealership. They are willing to make equip-

74.

The cost of new equipment can be reduced by becoming a dealer, salesperson, or demonstration site for some of the equipment.

ment available under favorable terms (lower prices and/or a payment plan) to users who will permit potential buyers to come in and see the equipment in operation. The county I live in made such a deal with the Burroughs Corporation. Burroughs is making all kinds of financial concessions, in return for the right to have people from other government agencies nationwide come here and see their hardware and software in action. This approach has been used for equipment worth a few thousand as well as for stuff in the millions. A small mail order company in Chicago, for instance, secured its mailing list programs for half price in return for allowing four visitation inspections a year. A software publisher offered its array of financial programs on extremely generous terms to early buyers, in return for evaluations and testimonials about the programs.

Get someone else to buy it for you

A surprising number of people told me stories about how they acquired their computer equipment for little or no out-of-pocket expenditure, by getting someone else to buy it for them. Three brief examples should suffice.

1. A small company specializing in data entry (typing other people's information into a computer) was charging 15 cents to type in a customer's name and address. They approached their largest client with this proposal: We want to buy a new IBM Personal Computer for about $4,000. You buy it for us, and we'll type in your next 40,000 names at no cost to you. The client agreed. They got $6,000 worth of service for their $4,000 investment, and the data entry firm got a "free" computer.

2. A small computerized typesetting company wanted a second Radio Shack computer. They suggested to their largest client that if the client bought them the machine (for about $2,000), they would get all their typesetting at half price for a year. Another deal that made everyone happy.

3. A bookkeeper wanted to computerize her business. She suggested that each of her 30 clients put up $100 in advance, to finance her purchase of an IBM PC. In return, she agreed to deduct $10 from their monthly statements each month for a year. The clients all agreed, and the purchase was made, financed 1/30 by each client, who hardly noticed the amount (and got back a 20% return on their investment to boot).

75.

Ingenious users regularly find ways of getting other people to buy their computer equipment for them.

The toughest decision a purchasing agent faces is when he is about to buy the machine that will replace him.

—Laurence J. Peter

Warranties

Computer Warranties Are Absolutely Shameful and There's Not Much You Can Do About It

Consider this scenario: You buy a cigarette lighter for 79 cents at the drugstore. Because of a manufacturing defect—one that is well-known to the manufacturer, who has decided not to correct it or to recall the product—the lighter explodes, causing your $100,000 house to burn to the ground. The manufacturer thereupon informs you, "Not only are we not going to pay for your house, we're not even going to refund the 79 cents you paid for the lighter."

Could anyone really try to get away with that behavior in this day and age? And would the buying public just sit there and accept this? The surprising answer is that this is precisely what is done throughout the computer industry: a munificent warranty extending all of 12 weeks and 6 days, followed by *no responsibility for anything,* even if equipment they *knew* was defective destroys your business.

The standard of the computer industry, for both hardware and software, is a 90-day warranty!

It is almost inconceivable to me that manufacturers have so little confidence in their products that they only stand behind them for what is, in effect, 65 business days. Furthermore, the manufacturers very specifically and elaborately decline to take any responsibility for damages that the system might cause to you or your business, *even if they were well aware of the defects in what they sold you*!

Very few people I've talked to have ever read or thought about the small type that appears in the literature with almost all computer stuff—hardware and software—that you buy.

76.

Most computer hardware and software is warranted for a shamefully short 90 days.

To counteract all those years of their putting these words in small, discreet type, here is a typical warranty in large, hard-to-miss form:

> **Manufacturer makes no warranties, either expressed or implied, with respect to this product, its quality, performance, merchantability, or fitness for any particular purpose, nor with respect to the manual describing the product. The product is sold "as is." The entire risk as to its quality and performance is with the buyer. Should the product prove defective, the buyer (and not the manufacturer, distributor or retailer) assumes the entire cost of all necessary servicing, repair, or correction, and any incidental or consequential damages. In no event will the manufacturer be liable for direct, indirect, incidental, or consequential damages resulting from any defect in the product, even if the manufacturer has been advised of the possibility of such damages.**

77.

If defective merchandise damages other equipment of yours, most warranties let the manufacturer off the hook even if they knew about the defects in what they sold you.

78.

Extended warranties or service contracts are rarely a good financial investment, but may be worth it for peace of mind.

I'm not a lawyer, but I've read enough to know that this kind of warranty is very rare in the consumer world. Product liability extends well beyond the cost of the product itself. If a headache pill kills someone because it had the wrong stuff in it, the manufacturer's liability goes well beyond refunding the ten cent cost of the pill. If a $6 bolt causes the collapse of a hotel lobby bridge, killing scores, the liability goes well beyond $6.

Inevitably, I would imagine, consumerists and consumer law will be devoting more time to the multi-billion dollar small computer world. But for now, there are really only four alternatives to consider with regard to warranties:

1. *Take whatever they choose to dish out.* (Most people *are* wimps in this regard. Through a combination of eagerness to get started and a child-like innocence saying that surely nothing will go wrong, we are indeed victims of the manufacturers and their

clever lawyers who write warranty statements like the one above.)

    2. *Buy an extended warranty or a service contract.* (These can help in some distressing situations, but not in many others, as I will explain momentarily.)

3. *Negotiate your own warranty.* This is a real possibility, either when you buy a complete small system from a single source, or a large system from the manufacturer, but not, of course, when you buy a $300 computer at the supermarket.

4. *Fight back.* A few lessons in Computer Consumer Karate are given on page 225.

Extended Warranties and Service Contracts Will Solve Some Problems, but Not Others

Following the end of the generous 12-6/7-week warranty that is the industry standard, it may be possible to pay extra for a warranty covering an additional time period, ranging from nine months to two years, depending on the manufacturer.

Some extended warranties simply extend, without alterations, the same warranty that was in effect for the first 90 days. Others toss in additional conditions, rarely (remarkably enough) to the consumer's benefit. These might include, for instance, adding a $50 or $100 deductible clause, or narrowing the conditions covered by the warranty so as to exclude certain parts or certain kinds of problems.

As with buying *any* insurance policy (for that is what an extended warranty or a service contract really is), two elements to consider are the financial aspects and your own peace of mind.

There are discoverable limits to the amount of change that the human organism can absorb.

—Alvin Toffler, Future Shock

To take a typical example, let us say you have paid $5,000 for your computer, disk drives, printer, etc. A service contract will cost you in the vicinity of $500 a year. (Ten percent is a rough rule of thumb in these matters). Now, let us say that you knew, with absolute certainty, that out of every ten people in your position, (each paying $500 a year), in any given year, one would have a $2,000 repair, two would have a $1,000 repair each, and seven would have no repairs at all.

How much of a gambler are you? Is the peace of mind worth $500 a year to you? Obviously it is for many people. But others will opt for "self-insurance," meaning they put $500 each year (literally or figuratively) into an insurance fund. If they go for years without major repairs, they've made good money. If they need that $2,000 repair on their 91st day of ownership, they shed tears. That's what insurance gambling is all about.

But there is one more important factor to bear in mind: when things *do* go wrong, they may not be covered by your warranty or service contract for one of two common reasons:

1. The problem was with the software, and software is almost never covered by a *computer* warranty. (It is also the most common source of recurring problems.) Software may have a short, non-extendable warranty of its own.

2. Even if it is a hardware problem, it may not be at all clear which element of the hardware needs help. If they come from different manufacturers, and are covered by different warranties or service contracts, there could be a situation in which *no one* will assume responsibility. (In fact, carrying this one step further, it may be unclear or even hopelessly confusing as to whether the problem was *caused* by hardware or by software. This all-too-common dilemma is discussed on page 216.

It Is Possible to Negotiate an Extended Warranty or an Independent Repair Contract

Although the vast majority of small computer buyers accept without question the warranty offered and the repair situation available, there can be alternatives.

Negotiated warranty with dealer

Large buyers of systems from large manufacturers regularly negotiate warranty conditions, especially when they are dealing with other than the industry giants. They say, in effect, "Nuts to your crummy 90-day warranty. I'll give you my business if you give me a three-year warranty." This sets the suppliers' cost accountants to work to figure out if the deal makes sense (manufacturers keep careful, if secret, records of expected time between failures of their equipment), and, more often than not, a deal is struck.

The small computer buyer has no leverage with the huge companies, but *may* have some with the dealer or packager. Since the prices are negotiable anyway (see page 92), the dealer simply figures additional repair costs into the negotiating position. (Many dealers have arrangements with high school whiz-kids who come in after school and fix computers for minimum wage or less. Don't feel sorry for the dealers.)

If, for example, you say, "I'll buy this system, but I want you to

79.
Many large and some small buyers are able to negotiate extended warranties as part of a purchase.

IF OTHER PRODUCTS WERE SOLD

INTRODUCING THE NEW

Chevrolet

- ★ Full 90-Day Limited Warranty
- ★ Six Convenient Repair Depots Nationwide
- ★ Learn To Drive It In Only 6 Months
- ★ Ltd. Service Contract Available – Only $1500/Year

THIS WEEK'S SPECIALS AT
SAM'S RECORD STORE

LENA HORNE:
GREATEST HITS

33⅓ RPM Record

DEVO
BURNT CIRCUITS

42½ RPM Record

PAVAROTTI
sings
GERSHWIN

A 33⅓ RPM disk that plays only counter clockwise

SPECIAL ADAPTER

Lets your 47¾ horizontal turntable play 33⅓ records vertically at 35½ RPM

(Almost as good as the original.)

THE **BEE GEES**
AT **EPCOT CENTER**

PLAYS ON
29¼ RPM VERTICAL
TURNTABLE ONLY!

LIKE COMPUTER PRODUCTS . . .

THE NEW SHREDDING BLADE

for your **CUISINART**

Comes complete with 578-page technical & instructional manual

SHARPEN PENCILS
WITH YOUR TOASTER

The Cosmotron
Mark III
bolts onto
any standard
household
toaster . . . !

**PERFORMANCE YOU NEVER
DREAMED OF from your TOASTER**

Installs in hours . . . a lifetime of pleasure.

CAUTION: installation may void your toaster
warranty and/or cause hives to break out on your
neck.

ARCHYTRONIC INDUSTRIES

we make

SHIFT KEYS

for your
typewriter

Although IBM
typewriters are
capable of typing
capital letters,
IBM does not
supply a shift key

ARCHYTRONICS

manufactures an
IBM compatible*
shift key. Install
one and enjoy
the experience of

UPPER CASE
LETTERS

* in most cases

include full service (parts and labor) for two years," the worst they can do is snicker and say, "No," at which point your friendly Yellow Pages will guide you to another dealer who may be more eager to make a $3,000 to $10,000 sale.

Independent repair contract

In many computer repairs, the ratio of labor costs to parts costs is anywhere from 10 to 1 on up to 100 to 1. So, if you can locate a repairperson who works for modest hourly rates, you can very likely get inexpensive repairs.

Happily, such people can often be found in and around high schools or community colleges that have active computer class offerings. I've talked to several people who had made repair contract deals with the schools, or with individual students, at wages ranging from $10 to $20 an hour.

The only real problem several of these people reported is that of getting used to carrying on a serious negotiation or business discussion with someone who is not old enough to drive a car.

The Delayed Warranty Scam

A man who works in a retail computer store once told me something that at the time seemed very peculiar and extremely baffling: if he could induce a computer-buying customer to fill out the warranty registration card before leaving the store with his or her purchase, the salesman would get a $150 bonus, direct from the manufacturer. This seemed an amazingly high bonus for an $1,800 sale. But, as it turned out, there is method in the madness.

As lamented elsewhere, most computers come with a 90-day warranty. Obviously it costs the manufacturers money to make in-warranty repairs, and equally obviously, they do not lose money when they charge for out-of-warranty repairs.

Apparently, a great many buyers, justifiably distressed with the puny warranty, are simply not sending in their warranty registration until something actually goes wrong with their equipment, whether that is 3 or 300 days after they have bought it.

There would seem to be no law that *makes* you send in a warranty card promptly. Indeed, if you buy a Christmas present

80.

High schools with computer departments may offer repairs by teenage whiz-kids at bargain prices.

81.

Some customers wait to send in their warranty cards until *after* something goes wrong, whether it is 3 days or 300 days after purchase.

computer on sale in September and send in the card, the warranty would have expired before the gift is opened.

So one manufacturer, at least, has done its cost accounting, and figured out that they will save *more* than $150 if they can start the warranty clock ticking before you leave the store.

Is the manufacturer's behavior ethical? Is the customer's delayed-registration behavior ethical? This is not a book on moral philosophy. But I did think you should know what some people are doing—and why you may be asked to leave your signed warranty registration behind in the store.[1]

---

1. Say, how about offering to split the bonus with the salesperson who encourages you to do this?

82.
Some manufacturers offer a big bonus to the saleperson if he or she fills out and sends in your warranty card for you.

PART THREE

USING COMPUTERS

The one single most important thing of all. How do you learn more? How computers are used and misused. About programming. Games. Miscellaneous matters.

The One Single Most Important Thing of All

This is a rather complex section, but believe me, it's worth the price of admission. If I were permitted one and only one thing to say to people who are contemplating a relationship with a computer, I would say the things in this section. These are the ideas that I desperately wish someone had not only *told* me when I got my first computer, but beat me over the head with, watched me closely to see that I heeded them, and put itching powder in my socks every day that I didn't.

The problem is that it is so easy to *say* — but so hard to convey the importance of it — especially since it won't *really* be important for perhaps half of the people reading this. Which half? Well, as John Wanamaker said about his marketing budget, "I know half my advertising dollars are wasted. The trouble is, I don't know *which* half."

Let's work into this with yet another automotive analogy. What if seat belts were even more uncomfortable than they are now, and so expensive that they added $1,000 to the cost of a new car. But they also would save upwards of 100,000 lives a year, world-wide, if everybody wore one.

So if the King of the World decreed that everyone must install and wear seat belts, you could imagine the outrage. Opponents would point out, to begin with, that if there *were* no seat belts, 97% of us still would never die in an auto accident. Why penalize the vast majority for that unlucky 3%?

Of course if seat belts *weren't* mandatory, the relatives and loved ones of the deceased 3% (and the deceased themselves, through spirit transmission) would probably be saying, with great vigor, "Why didn't you *tell* me? Why didn't you *make* me?"

Well there it is. It's that sort of thing. I'm going to tell you with

83.

There is a strong tendency to "junk" the old system as soon as a new computer works correctly the first time. Doing so is the worst mistake a new computer user can make.

as much conviction as I can. And you've got to promise that you will never, ever come up to me on the street and say, "Boy, have I had a miserable computer experience. Why didn't you warn me about that stuff you were discussing on page 116 of your book? I mean *really* warn me."

For half of you, then, here goes. And the other half better read it too.

Many individuals and businesses acquire a computer to take over some aspect of their lives or their activities. They "computerize" something. And as soon as the computer is up and running, they abandon — often irrevocably abandon — the old technology, the old method.

Don't.

I believe that it is absolutely essential not only to keep the technology of the old method as long as possible — but actually to continue *using* the old method, alongside the new — for a minimum of three months.

As soon as the computer does its first little thing correctly, there is an overwhelming, almost irresistible tendency to embrace it totally, to switch everything over onto the computer as quickly as possible.

Untold grief has been experienced by individuals and businesses that have fallen into this trap. The new computer works wonderfully for a few hours, a few days, even a few weeks. So out with the old horse-and-buggy methods and machinery. Throw out the kerosene lamps when the electric power arrives (and break your neck stumbling in the dark with the first power failure). Dispose of your wind-up watch when you get your digital model (and find yourself trying to meet a tight schedule in a distant city when your battery dies and you can't find a store that sells your size). Put all your addresses and phone numbers into a home record-keeping program, and toss out your dog-eared address book. (And then here comes Christmas, and you can't find your main disk, and your back-up disk was sitting on the refrigerator and got erased by magnetism).

Keeping the old and the new going side by side can be trivial in some cases — storing the kerosene lamps, keeping a wind-up watch in your luggage, hanging onto the old address book — or it can be extremely complicated and expensive. Even when it is the latter, it is still well worth doing.

To paraphrase Pascal talking about belief in God, if you *do* keep the back-up system going and never need it, you've spent a little extra time and money, but haven't really suffered. But if you *don't* keep the old system going, and you *do* need it, you're in big, big trouble.

Few people disagree with all this advice. Even fewer follow it. I know. I'm one of those who has suffered more than once. When the new computer (or new program) works well the first time, there is a giddy feeling of joy and well-being. Life is worth living. There is a real feeling of infallibility. Invulnerability. The notion of taking out *any* time, much less a great *deal* of time to write all the numbers by hand into the old ledger book even once more is anathema. Senseless. Antiquated. And then . . .

. . . and then. Consider these case histories: one from my own experience, and the rest selected from many conveyed to me by sadder and possibly wiser computer users.

Lost: $28,000 worth of names

Every morning, 50 to 100 letters came in asking for product information. The names and addresses were typewritten onto "Master Addresser" cards — an old-fashioned spirit duplicator-based system. Filing away the cards among tens of thousands in shoeboxes was slow and inaccurate. Selective mailings to certain customers were virtually impossible.

When the computer arrived, not only were all new names and addresses typed directly in, but teams of typists were engaged to work three shifts a day typing in all the old names as well.

The system had a few bugs, but on the whole seemed to be working well. Typing Master Addresser cards was discontinued, and when all 80,000 names were in the computer, with copies of all disks made and stored in another location, the 80,000 Master Addresser cards were donated to the Catholic Church.

And then . . . No one knows how it happened. Some flaw in the program or in the computer. But about six weeks after the system was up and running, somehow, one day, 4,000 names disappeared. They weren't on the original disk, and they weren't on the copy. In retrospect, it may have been the copying program that was flawed, and in the process of adding a few names to the end of a disk, 4,000 names disappeared from the front.

84.

No matter how expensive, inconvenient, or annoying it is, keep the old system running parallel to the computer system for at least three months.

In old movies of Africa, the natives either welcome the stranger as their savior and make him king, or they blame him for all their troubles and set him on the coals. So it is with the computer, which is crowned by some and cooked by others.

—Martin Greenburger

The experts came in and solved the problem, and it never occurred again. But those 4,000 names—valued at about $7 each—were gone forever. A $28,000 loss. The cost of continuing to use the old system along with the new for three months might have been about $800.

Out to pasture too soon

It was one of the most modern stud farms in America. Thoroughbred horses worth millions of dollars were treated like visiting royalty.

Elaborate and extensive breeding and hereditary records were kept on every stallion and every customer. Data on tens of thousands of horses, going back eight and ten generations. All the record-keeping was in the charge of the same Kentucky gentlewoman who had been keeper of the files for close to half a century. And then came the computer.

Extensive and elaborate programs were written to take care of all the duties previously handled by "Old Gillian." After a few weeks of rigorously testing the systems, "backwards and forwards, up and down, and twice sideways from Sunday," the computer was put in charge, and Old Gillian was turned out to pasture.

"Data entry"—typing in the names and numbers—was considered a low-level task, and was given to two lightly-trained secretaries. The programs worked fine—but the *instruction manual* written for the low-level users contained several unclear points. They weren't unclear to the man who wrote the manual; *he* knew how the program worked. And they didn't *seem* unclear to the typists, because they never asked questions. They just blithely typed things in wrong.

The errors were not discovered for more than four months, at which time it was far too late to reconstruct the facts. Through lost business and loss of reputation, the owner of the farm reckons his out-of-pocket loss at nearly $50,000—and it would have cost a tenth of that to keep Old Gillian for another three months, duplicating the computer's work in her old-fashioned reliable way.

The lost novel

John V. had fair success as a novelist, banging out a new one every couple of years on his old Smith Corona portable. A slow typist, and a meticulous editor, John was a perfect candidate for a word processing system, which he dutifully acquired and taught himself to use with aplomb.

Like many users of word processing, John felt no need to commit anything to paper. All his words were stored electronically on disks. All disks were copied every day, with one set kept at the computer, the other stored in a fireproof safe in the garage. Good computer "housekeeping," as far as it went. And then disaster struck.

After a long and creative day at the keyboard, John had entered several crucial chapters onto his "original" disk. Then, in the process of making a back-up copy, he somehow put the original and the back-up disks into each other's slot. He copied the *old* disk on top of the *new* one, thereby erasing ten hours of hard work—an act so demoralizing, so depressing, that John literally gave up work on that particular novel. He had not looked at it for three months at the time he communicated with me (a letter typed on a Smith Corona typewriter!).

Returns from downstate have been delayed

With much fanfare and publicity, the county went over to computerized vote counting. "No more 2 a.m. reports," they proclaimed. "With this high-speed system, the total count should be available within an hour of the closing of the polls."

Some places that computerize voting keep the old system in place for at least one election. The punched ballots are counted by hand at slow speed after they are counted by computer at high speed. But this county did not feel the need. Budgets were tight, and if they could spare the pay for the "usual" 15 ballot counters, so much the better. And besides, the earnest young man from the computer company was *so* reassuring.

The polls closed at 8 p.m., at which time the absentee ballots on hand were run through the machine. The results almost immediately appeared on the screen: 999,999,999 votes for one candidate, 0 votes for the other. A real Albanian result—and a bit surprising, with only 120,000 registered voters in the county.

The young man worked quite frantically over his machine, as ballots came flooding in from all over the county. Three hours after the polls closed, the urgent call went out for the human beings who had counted ballots in the past—but it was nearly midnight, and most of them were unwilling to get out of bed to lend a hand.

At 4 a.m., they gave up, and called the Registrar of the nearest county that had similar equipment—a mere four-hour drive away. The ballots were loaded into two Sheriff's cars, and by nine in the morning, they were ready to be run quickly through the high speed voting computer. The results were flashed back home a mere 14 hours after the polls closed.

The $250 saving in not keeping the old system going in parallel was greatly surpassed by the overtime salaries, gasoline, and other expenses accrued, not to mention depriving the electorate of the results of several crucial races for more than half a day.

The unkindest cut

When the big printshop got its brand new paper-cutting computer, the only way to make room for it was by getting rid of the old "guillotine" paper cutting machine, operated by a brute force and the power of leverage.

The new machine was, in fact, a computer-controlled power blade. All the coordinates of a series of cuts were typed in and stored in the disk drive built into the machine. With the push, then, of a single button, the machine would go through its paces, moving great slabs of paper hither and yon, making precision cut after precision cut.

At least that's what it said in the advertisement. In practice, when the machine worked at all, it behaved more like Sweeney Todd, the mad barber, making random cuts wherever it seemed to feel the need. By now, the old hand-powered machine was several hundred miles away. A printshop without a paper cutter is like, well, a chef without a knife. Not too many customers want 3-foot by 4-foot letterheads. So the printer went, hat in hand, to his chief competitor to beg (and, ultimately, pay handsomely for) use of the other man's old-fashioned cutter. It was three months before the computerized machine was back in service.

My files are full of tales like these: devastating problems involving inventory control systems, accounts receivable files, check-writing activities, typesetting, maintaining a huge stamp collection, income tax records, general ledger woes, and on and on.

In every case, precisely the same series of events occurred:
(1) Computer arrives.
(2) Old system abandoned too soon.
(3) Computer fails.
(4) Big problems.

> The general rule is that the more dependent you are on anything, the more apt you are to become infuriated . . . when it does not work to perfection. . . . We have deluded ourselves into believing that a machine can function perfectly, and when that delusion is exposed by failure, we become utterly enraged at the machinery. Of course, we are really angry at ourselves.
>
> —Dr. Mel Mandel
> (Psychiatrist)

In every case, the cost and bother of keeping the old system going in parallel with the new was far surpassed by the cost and bother of the computer failure.

As with most new machines and systems, many of the problems that ultimately will occur happen during the first few months. This is especially true of programming errors, a major bugaboo of new systems.

Many people will read this and decide that:

(1) This is a trivial matter, or

(2) It can't happen to *me,* or

(3) This is a risk I am willing to take, and therefore I will do nothing.

Some of those who do nothing will have computers that run beautifully forever, and they may write me "I told you so" letters. And some of those who *do* pay heed and run the old and the new together for a few months will *also* have perfect computers and wonder why they bothered.

But if only one person—well, I'd actually prefer several dozen, or perhaps twenty-two thousand—follow this advice *and* are spared agony and expense when the computer fails, I shall rest easy in Writer Heaven.

85.

"Computer literacy" has many meanings— none of them essential for most people in most situations.

How Do You Learn More?

Computer Books and Magazines

"Computer literacy" has become a major catch phrase for the decade. "Achieving computer literacy" is perceived as a worthy goal for all. "Computer illiteracy" is a sorry fate, to be avoided at all cost. And so on.

"Computer literacy" can have many meanings, just as plain old ordinary literacy does: Can you do nothing more than sign your name (check-signing or financial literacy)? Can you talk to people well enough to buy a hat or locate the bathroom (conversational literacy)? Can you write a letter? an essay? a sonnet? a novel? Many different levels and kinds of literacy—every one of them either important or unimportant, depending on the circumstances. It is meaningless to say simply *"Literacy is essential."* [1]

Most people on earth will live their lives and die without ever having laid fingers on a small computer. (Some people have already achieved great success in the computer world without having any technical or programming skills. They *do,* of course, have business skills or game-conceiving skills or other creative skills.) And most of us lie somewhere in between. It may be nice, or even desirable, to achieve some level of "computer literacy"— but the world will somehow go on if we don't.

Books and magazines are a place to start. Goodness knows, there are enough of them. In fact, the sheer number of computer-related publications is quite mind-boggling. And their numbers

If automation keeps up, man will atrophy all his limbs but the push-button finger.

—Frank Lloyd Wright

---

1. My favorite tale in this regard is the short story by Somerset Maugham about a church janitor, or sexton, who is fired when the minister learns he is illiterate. On the way home, he craves a cigarette, but cannot find a smoke shop in the neighborhood. He opens a shop there, prospers, and after a few years he is the millionaire head of a national chain of smoke shops. He manages to hide his illiteracy for years, until one day a business associate finds out. "Good Lord, man," the associate says, "As an illiterate, you have become one of the richest men in the country. What would you have been if you *could* read and write?" "Sexton of St. Anthony's Church," the man replies!

are increasing at a rate unprecedented in the history of the book and magazine industries.

Books

I have spent over a hundred hours in bookstores and libraries staring at computer books, and a good deal more time, later, with those few I chose to take home with me. Some specific titles you may wish to consider are provided on page 268.

But on the whole, I was neither encouraged nor impressed. For example, I actually looked at every single one of the 1,808 computer books on sale at the largest computer book store in California. I established the following rules:

1. If I could understand the title, then I picked the book up (1,522 were picked up).

2. If I could understand the jacket notes, then I looked at the table of contents (1,192 passed this test).

3. If I had meaning for all the words in the table of contents, I turned (this was arbitrary) to page 49. (Got this far with 622 of them.)

4. If I genuinely understood every word on page 49, I did the same with page 98, and then with page 137. (Down to 29 books.)

5. Then I applied the criteria I used to use in grading term papers: Is it true? Is it relevant? Is it enlightening? That enabled me to set aside books of computer cartoons, jokes, anecdotes and trivia.

Four books remained, so I bought them: Kidder's *The Soul of a New Machine,* McWilliams' *The Personal Computer Book* and *The Word Processing Book,* and Joseph Deken's *The Electronic Cottage.*

Of course the same situation prevails with books as with new technology, as discussed on page 33. If you don't see a computer book you like now, wait a few days. During 1983, computer books were published in America at the astonishing rate of 5 new titles a day — nearly 2,000 over the course of the year!

It seems clear, both from my informal interviews with customers in bookstores and especially from the data on best-selling computer books, that the prime customers are people who already *have* a certain computer, are somehow dissatisfied, and are hoping to get more pleasure or usage from it.

In fact, in one recent week, 17 of the 20 best-selling computer books were "How to" books for specific models: "How to get

86.

The vast majority of computer books fail to meet these four criteria: a good computer book must be comprehensible, true, relevant, and enlightening.

87.

Most computer books are for people who already have a computer and want to get more out of it. Many people who buy books for this reason are disappointed.

more out of your Apple II+" . . . "Programming for the IBM Personal Computer," etc. The overlap in content is extensive: for instance, the more than 30 books on using the Timex-Sinclair are virtually indistinguishable from one another.

Magazines

Over 100 computer magazines, newspapers, and newsletters are available, with new ones emerging every month. Both readers and advertisers seem insatiable in their desire to spend their money in a never-ending flow of magazines on the subject of small computers.

Most computer users to whom I have spoken subscribe to one or two, and "check out" half a dozen others at the store, buying those with articles or advertisements that interest them. It seems not uncommon to spend from $10 to $20 a month on these publications.

Many people seem to have strong feelings about which magazines are good and which are not. There are strong advocates of *Byte* or *InfoWorld* or *SofTalk* or *Personal Computing* or whatever. I have no specific advice or recommendations. I do try to spend a few hours a month browsing through computer magazines in the public library, but I have yet to subscribe to one.

Computer Courses

People who want to learn more about computers through formal coursework have many options available, as purveyors of academic materials have *also* discovered the extremely high level of interest (and willingness to spend money) in this field. Courses range from the very general and occasionally superficial ("What this electronic revolution is all about") to extremely technical ("Applications of FORTRAN in bridge design"), and at prices ranging from free to thousands of dollars.

In all large cities, and many smaller towns, live courses are available through five different kinds of agencies: users' groups, computer shows, colleges and universities, alternative learning centers, and proprietary schools. And courses are offered by mail to people living anywhere in the world.

Colleges

Nearly all colleges and universities now offer computer classes — often available to the non-degree-seeking public. This is especially true of the more-than-1000 community or junior colleges. These are commonly offered at little or no fee, and the teachers are likely to be working computer professionals doing this in their spare time.

Alternative learning centers

There are hundreds of them around the country, sometimes independently run, sometimes affiliated with churches or social agencies. Teachers can list any course they wish in the catalogue, ranging from divorce workshops to pickle making. Many com-

88.

None of the more-than-100 computer magazines is an absolute "must read." Overlap is enormous. Browsing regularly in a library is more economical and probably more efficient.

puter offerings are to be found at costs of just a few dollars up to perhaps $100. The courses are likely to be less academic and less formal than those offered by the more traditional schools.

Proprietary schools

Proprietary (i.e., money-making) schools of all kinds offer computer courses to the public. Some of them are business colleges that have added computer divisions; some have been established by major computer corporations (such as Control Data) to train people in their own (and sometimes other) equipment. And some are newly started by entrepreneurs riding the boom. (Last year: real estate license school. This year: computer school. Next year: paramedical assistant school.)

There is certainly nothing wrong with the notion of proprietary schools. Some do outstanding jobs, albeit often at a higher cost than public schools. (The higher price may buy access to newer or better equipment—or it may buy the school owner a new yacht. It is always wise to check schools out with the Better Business Bureau and the local Chamber of Commerce.)

89.
Some major universities offer low-cost correspondence courses in computers and programming skills for people living anywhere in the world.

Courses by mail

Here, too, there are both private profit-making companies and public universities offering computer courses by mail. The private companies (N.R.I., Cleveland Institute of Electronics, etc.) generally offer a complete, organized program of study (programming, computer repair, etc.), covering a period of a few months to several years. These organizations advertise regularly in *Popular Science, Popular Mechanics,* and similar magazines, and a list of accredited home study schools may be obtained without charge from the National Home Study Council, 1601 18th St. N.W., Washington, D.C. 20009.

90.
College credit and degrees can be earned for computer skills learned outside of school.

While a dozen or so universities offer correspondence courses to people living anywhere in the world, none has a cohesive *series* of courses designed to provide a unified program of study. Still, the costs are often much less than the proprietary schools. It is possible to put together your own program by selecting a course or two from here and a course or two from there.

See page 270 for information on two useful books. One lists all correspondence courses at all schools, the other (by yours truly) tells how to get college credit (and degrees) based on knowledge of computers, programming, and other life experience learning.

Support groups

Local computer clubs and societies often have both formal and informal classes on computer use. Support groups are discussed further on page 205.

Computer Shows

There are many different kinds of computer shows. For people thinking about buying a computer, and for those who already have them, certain shows can be interesting, useful, enlightening, and lots of fun. Others can be tedious, dreary, and a waste of money.

Most shows are put on by independent entrepreneurs, who rent a big exhibit hall, and then rent booth space to manufacturers, dealers, distributors, computer stores, users groups, publishers, and others who have something to offer to the computer-buying public. A hefty admission price (anywhere from $5 to $25) is charged to the public for the privilege of going in and looking at or buying things.

There are three kinds of audiences for such shows: OEM's, ISO's, and EU's.

OEM stands for "Original Equipment Manufacturer," although in practice an OEM is someone who assembles already-made equipment from one or more manufacturers, perhaps adding some software of his or her own, and offers a complete package for sale to the public. Exhibitors at OEM shows do *not* sell to the general public, and the shows are of much less interest to people like me. It is nice to know that the people who make the springs that push keyboard keys back up when you push them down have a place to exhibit their wares, but the audience is rather specialized.

ISO's are Independent Service Organizations, which is computer industry talk for retailers. ISO shows are especially interesting, since manufacturers large and small pull out all the stops to try to interest retail stores and computer consultants in their products, both present and future. The main ISO shows are called COMDEX (COMputer Dealers EXposition), and are held in Las Vegas each December and Atlanta each spring. (My first COMDEX

91.
It is possible, and often enlightening, for "civilians" to attend dealer or trade computer shows.

experience is described on page 200.) Although such shows are not meant for the general public, it isn't hard to get in; I shall describe how later in this section.

EU's are End Users — the general public — you and me, and without us, there would *be* no computer business. At least half a dozen different firms are in the business of putting on end user computer shows, ranging from one day in a shopping center mall in a small town to a week in a major exposition hall in Chicago or New York.

End user shows

Most end user shows are totally eclectic. All manufacturers are invited, along with distributors, local stores, consultants, and so forth. There might be a 40-foot booth from IBM with flashing lights and smiling ladies across from a tiny booth rented by a teenager to try to sell his space game program.

Some shows, however, are devoted to a single computer (for instance the AppleFest shows held around the country each year); others are devoted to all the ramifications of a certain computer language or program (a CP/M language products show; a VisiCalc program show).

There are seven kinds of reasons that people go to end user, or consumer computer shows. Most people to whom I have talked are generally satisfied in six of these goals, and almost always frustrated in the seventh:

1. *What's new*. In all but the most puny shows, there is an opportunity to see more hardware and software in one place than any computer store or dealer is likely to have. Sometimes the goods are genuinely new (the Osborne was first shown at a consumer show in San Francisco in 1981); sometimes it's just stuff that is new to you. Either way, there is ample opportunity to fill your shopping bags (there are always some booths that give away shopping bags), with material for later perusal.

2. *Hands on experience*. Some booths, both hardware and software, offer the opportunity to try things out. Sometimes there are prepared demonstrations (for instance, the purveyors of a quite sophisticated aptitude testing program that would require four or five hours to go through entirely, offered, at one show, a 5-minute and a 15-minute abbreviated version to give a flavor of the entire program).

Any sufficiently advanced technology is indistinguishable from magic.

—Arthur C. Clarke

SHOE TICKLER

Some of the new game demonstrations may have long lines waiting, while some of the more esoteric booths may be quite grateful if you sit there for an hour trying out (as I did at one show) a crossword puzzle making system.

92.

Retail, or end user computer shows often offer tremendous bargains on hardware and software purchases made at the show.

93.

Price wars often develop, resulting in even lower prices toward the end of a computer show. Disks and printers are most often heavily discounted.

3. *Buying stuff.* Many consumer-oriented shows permit exhibitors to sell things right at their booths. This can range from disks at $2 each up to multi-thousand-dollar systems. Quite often, there are remarkable bargains offered, especially toward the end of the last day of the show, because the exhibitors would much rather sell things at little or no profit than have to lug them away.

Prices will, in fact, change regularly through the course of a show, as price wars develop among various booths offering similar or identical goods. At the last four or five shows I've been to, the most volatile items have been disks and small printers. I went to one show with the thought of buying an Epson printer. The first day of a three day show, the prices at the various booths selling Epsons ranged from $550 to $600. New, hand-lettered signs kept going up, and by the end of the third day, I bought my Epson for $450. Same thing with disks. I have seen generic (no brand name) disks going for as little as a dollar each, and name-brand boxes of ten dropping, during the course of a show, from $40 to under $20 per box.

4. *Educational events.* Many shows offer a series of lectures or seminars on subjects as diverse as how to use WordStar, how to start a computer consulting business, and how to use Fortran in mechanical engineering applications. Sometimes the lectures are a part of the admission price; more often, they are paid for separately by those who wish to attend. Many shows sell either tapes or transcripts of the lectures at a price lower than one pays to hear them in person.

5. *Networking.* Computer shows are excellent places to meet people. Informal users groups are spontaneously formed by two or three people who, standing around the Gizmotronix booth, discover that they have all had similar problems, and have various ideas about how to solve them. Similar interactions occur at the seminars, the snack bars (one has to do *something* there besides eat the dreary food served at most events), and the "hospitality lounges" (booths or nearby rooms rented by larger manufacturers to offer a place to sit down, relax, perhaps even have a drink).

6. *Entertainment and souvenirs.* Many computer shows really *are* shows. In order to attract attention to their booths, various exhibitors use magicians, acrobats, mimes, comedians, tightrope walkers, people in various elaborate costumes, and that all-time attention getter, scantily-clad damsels. (Perhaps 80% to 85% of attendees at most shows are males.)

Furthermore, they pass out balloons, toys, pens, pennants, badges, buttons, rulers, flags, keychains, noisemakers, hats, and, in the case of the second-cleverest convention booth I've yet seen, cushioned shoe insert pads, imprinted with the company name.[1] Finally, there are always contests of all kinds. Most of them, sadly, are just lotteries and other non-creative raffles, but often there are a few that reward creativity or tax the intellect.

7. *Talking to manufacturers and suppliers.* This is the one that sounds entirely reasonable, but rarely works. I have spoken to a great many people who have shared my experience of going to a show with the expressed intent of talking to the manufacturers of certain equipment — either as an owner, to get further information or satisfaction in some complaint; or as a potential owner who needs more information than a neighborhood dealer could supply.

One sees badges on people in booths indicating that they are the president or vice president of their company. I am quite convinced that these badges have been pinned on dummies acquired from some local Rent-a-Booby service to impress the public with the importance of the booth. These *cannot* be the real officers, or the company would be down the tubes in a month. Two examples will suffice.

• In the fall of 1982, *Rolling Stone* magazine selected the Brother $200 electronic typewriter as one of the outstanding products of the year. On noting that there would be a Brother booth at a nearby computer show, I went with the intention of trying out this wonder. There were five people running the Brother booth. Three were Japanese gentlemen whose badges indicated they were company officers, and who spoke remarkably little English ("Roaring Stone? What is Roaring Stone?"), but, when they understood what I wanted, assured me there was *no* such product, nor was there *likely* to be. The other two folks in the booth were decorative females handing out brochures on other Brother products, but that was the limit of their communicational abilities. The first ads for the Brother $200 electronic typewriter began appearing within a few weeks, and the product itself reached the stores soon after.

94.

Shows are great for looking at stuff but generally unsatisfactory for talking to exhibitors or getting questions answered.

---

1. The cleverest by far was the Australian pavilion at the Montreal World's Fair in 1967. The entire exhibit consisted of a large room full of huge and comfortable easy chairs. When you sank exhaustedly into one, a mellow voice through a speaker built into the chair started extolling the virtues of Australia.

• I had been having a lot of trouble with my EasyWriter word processing program. My letters to the company went unanswered, and my long distance phone calls produced little useful advice. At one show, my intent was to buttonhole someone from the manufacturer, to see if I could get some satisfaction. The top officers of the company were there, but they left their buttonholes home. I couldn't get anyone even to listen to my lament, much less to offer any advice. I was prepared to spend the $150 needed to upgrade my program to a more sophisticated version — *if* I had my questions answered satisfactorily. After this show, I junked my EasyWriter and spent the money on a competitor's program instead. Small potatoes, sure, but those $150s do add up.

These are most clearly *not* wimpish situations that I somehow got into. Nearly everyone to whom I have spoken has had similar experiences. Peculiar, but there it is.

Getting the Most out of Computer Shows

Checking out shows in advance

I've been to well-advertised heavily-promoted shows that were an utter waste of time. A couple of dozen not well-equipped booths, mostly local stores, and a lot of totally irrelevant items. (Britannica I can understand, I guess, but why were there three different manufacturers of shrink-wrap plastic packaging machines at one miserable little show? Maybe they had arrived a week early for the Delicatessen Show?).

95.

Some heavily-promoted shows are real duds. The main variable is the number of exhibitors. Under 50, forget it. Over 250, worth a trip. Over 500, don't miss.

The best assurance of a good show is past experience. All northern California enthusiasts know, for instance, that the San Francisco Computer Faire, held each spring, is a grand show, growing grander every year. There are similar events in many other large cities, well worth the hefty admission price.

When in doubt, it is not a bad idea to talk to people as they are leaving a show, or to eavesdrop on conversations. When I came out of one quite unsatisfactory show, for which I had paid ten bucks, I almost got up the nerve to approach the poor suckers waiting in line to buy tickets. (Would I have failed to go in if someone had warned *me* while I was waiting in line? Probably not, until I had experienced at least one very poor show.)

Another good indicator is the number and nature of exhibitors. Sometimes ads or programs will identify the participants. If there are fewer than 50, it may not be worth your effort, especially if most are just local dealers or stores. Over 100: fair. Over 500: can't fail; there are bound to be things of interest.[1]

Strategy for getting in to trade shows

Shows specifically for dealers can be among the most interesting. But the general public is not admitted. However, *potential* dealers are most welcome, since they are excellent prospects for buying lots of equipment to stock their new businesses. All it usually takes to get a ticket to a trade show is a business card (and a modest admission fee). So if you've ever thought about going into business, however remotely, you might want to invest a few dollars in a business card for Intergalactic Amazotronix Industries, or whatever, and head on in.

Strategy at the show itself

Computer shows can be truly mind-boggling. There were, for instance, about 1,200 booths at the COMDEX show, and I had about 16 hours to spend there. Deducting time for walking, eating, bathrooms, and watching the acrobats and clown shows, I realized I had about 30 seconds per booth, or, perhaps, 3 seconds per product. Clearly impossible.

There are two common strategies followed: that of the blitzers and the planners. Blitzers race madly up and down the aisles, filling shopping bag after shopping bag with anything that looks vaguely interesting. Then, after a couple of hours of this, they repair to the dining area, their motel room, car, or other less frantic spot, and pore over the literature, identifying the 10 or 50 or 500 products or booths deserving of closer attention, which are thereupon visited in the time remaining.

Planners get the show directory early in the first day, and with that and the obligatory map of the hall, identify (based on the descriptions in the directory) the "musts," "wants," and "maybes" with various codes on the map. They then plan the shortest route that will take them to these places, and if time remains at the end, *then* they may allow a little serendipity to enter their lives.

I don't go as far as Kingsley Amis's Lucky Jim, who decided at an early age that there was no point in acquiring new information because it pushed out an equivalent amount of information he already had, leaving him just where he started. As the new electronic marvels buzz away furiously, some of what they do will have value. But, as an inevitable accompaniment, they will preserve what ought to be torn up, discarded, cast aside, or should never have been born.

—Edwin Newman

---

1. Actually, I tend to rate shows by the number of shopping bags I fill. There are 1/2-bag shows, 3-bag shows, etc.

96.

Most people are *capable* of learning as much as they desire about computers, but many are intimidated by an unsatisfactory early experience, or by what they've heard. Avoid the "I never tried it because I can't do it" fallacy.

You're Smarter than You May Have Thought (A Short Pep Talk)

I have talked to hundreds and hundreds of people who were eager to report their computer experiences. The stories range from devastating to glorious. When people tell me mournfully that they don't think they are ever likely to get involved in computers—they just can't imagine how to begin—it has seemed appropriate to report this actual case history, as conveyed to me by the lady in Boston to whom it all happened.

There was a lady who sort of thought she might like to find out what computers were all about. But she kept putting it off, because she felt intimidated before she even began her quest. Some of what she had read and heard had led her to believe that she lacked the manual dexterity to interact successfully with a computer.

(On the day she had that thought, she successfully and single-handedly took command of a 4,000-pound machine whose proper operation required her to coordinate and synchronize independent activities of her left hand, her right hand, her left foot and her right foot, and to monitor, with eye and ear, various gauges and sounds, while looking over her left shoulder. She backed her car out of the garage.)

She had read just enough computer ads to be able to fret about the apparently incomprehensible vocabulary of bits and bytes and modems not to mention peripherals and programming and other concepts that made "learning computers" sound like an academic enterprise well beyond her mental abilities.

(On *that* day, she utilized the concepts of accounts payable and receivable, cash flow management, double entry bookkeeping, information storage and retrieval, mathematics, and inference. She balanced her checkbook. Then she performed an act which, amazingly enough, according to a Gallup survey, more than half the people in America have never done: she voluntarily read a book other than the Bible.)

She tentatively set foot in her neighborhood computer store. She felt uncomfortable and out of place in the sleek high-tech environment. She *did* find it impossible to communicate with the young man who was on duty at the store, who looked at her with a mixture of pity and disdain when she apparently failed his initial vocabulary test.

She left the computer store in confusion and mounting despair. While shopping at the supermarket that very afternoon, she impulsively bought a Commodore VIC-20 computer off the shelf, between the paper towels and the photographic film, took it home, read the manual, hooked it up, plugged it in, turned it on, started enjoying herself, bought a couple of other books to supplement the not-always-great manual, played games, started in on a home bookkeeping system, made a few tentative stabs at learning programming, found she enjoyed it, bought a book on programming, took a class in programming, wrote programs, bought a larger and more sophisticated computer, helped automate her

Shopping at home with your television and home computer is just as much fun as shopping at a Russian department store. The available merchandise is limited, and you can neither touch it nor examine it until after you have bought and paid for it.

—Arthur Elmont

husband's business, gave lectures on overcoming computer fear, taught classes in computerization, and finally opened her own computer service bureau in the storefront vacated by the bankruptcy of the computer store she had first visited.

Not everyone will take it nearly this far, of course. But anyone who has enough smarts to read this book, and enough interest in computers to read this book is, beyond doubt, capable of succeeding with computers if he or she but wishes.

Computers certainly aren't for everyone. But the only way to find out is to dip your toe in the waters. If the waters are cold and uncomfortable, then at least you'll have found out first hand, and not by hearsay, intimidation, or being warned off by inept lifeguards. It is better far to try now and discover you'd rather not, thank you, than to wait and wait, and then find out that way back in the 1980s, you had a chance to plunge into computers but, in the words of the slogan Guinness Stout once used, you "never tried it because you didn't like it."

How Computers Are Used and Misused

Cataloguing Your Necktie Collection: Trivial or Unnecessary Uses of Computers

In response to my standard question, "How are you using your small computer," a Chicago businessman proudly told me that he was using his IBM PC to keep track of his neckties. He could tell at a glance how many striped, patterned, and solid color ties he had, what they had cost, when they were last cleaned, and how often he had worn each one.

I dared to hope that he had found a few other uses for his $5,000 worth of machinery, but that was the one he wanted to talk to me about.

This kind of situation is extremely common. No, I don't mean cataloguing other items of clothing. I mean the equivalent of using your 1938 Hispano-Suiza 12-cylinder touring car solely to go buy your morning paper. As *Time* points out, "for many household operations . . . microcomputers are clearly inferior to simpler and less expensive devices. Like fingers."

Consider a few examples, chosen from hundreds that I found in the literature, or heard about from computer users.

Educational trivia

There are at least three geography programs on the market that do little more than flash a map on the screen and ask the student to identify the state or country, and name its capital city. Others offer endless arrays of arithmetic problems, spelling problems, multiple choice questions in history, and so on.

There *are* many exciting uses for what is called "CAI" (computer-assisted instruction). But the mere fact of using a computer

The lasting benefits of the computer age on our society may ultimately prove as great as those of the CB radio.

—Charles Haas

97.

Many people use computers to do things far better done with a few 3×5 cards or a pencil. The "I've got it so I'd better use it" notion often leads to trivial or inefficient uses.

137

doesn't automatically make a lesson wonderful. The same tedious, uncreative people who gave us tedious, uncreative textbooks are now giving us tedious, uncreative computer programs.

David Grady puts it nicely in his article, "A Hard Look at the World of Educational Computing": "With a world full of good books to read, songs to sing, and pictures to paint, computer-based exercises should have to earn their way into the school day by delivering at least as much value as whatever they replace . . . Sad to say . . . the replacement of existing tedium with the latest, most up-to-date tedium is an activity as old as the schools themselves."

Personal finance

There is a good deal of computer literature touting the merits of using the computer to keep track of personal finance: accounting, bookkeeping, bills to pay, income tax data, and so forth. And indeed many people *talk* about this aspect as one of the justifications of buying a computer. But I have the feeling from talking to many people that very, very few of them are actually *doing* this sort of thing.

Perhaps they agree with *Money* magazine that "family finance programs generally either are unnecessarily complex or simply duplicate what you can do with a $30 calculator and a little patience . . . Probably in less time than it takes to set up the budget program and tally monthly totals for income and expenses, you could do the same job with a calculator and a ledger."

James Fallows, writing in *Atlantic* in 1982, did the appropriate calculations: "At the end of the year, I load the income-tax program into the computer, push the button marked 'Run' and watch as my tax return is prepared. Since it took me only about six months to learn . . . I figure this approach will save me time by 1993."

Home information

A lady in Canada told me that her family's main use of their Commodore computer was storing vital family information: an inventory of their possessions, recipes, and their 35-name Christmas card list.

Again, there's nothing whatever *wrong* with this. It just seems an extravagant use of sophisticated equipment for a trivial end.

98.

The mere fact of using a computer doesn't make school lessons or business programs *better*, just *different*.

99.

The time it takes to learn a new program may be greater than the amount of time it saves you over the next ten years.

And it may not even be the most efficient way to handle things. Robert Cowen, writing in the *Christian Science Monitor* points out that "it would be tedious to type recipes into a computer when they are more easily stored and retrieved from cookbooks, card files, and envelopes of clippings . . . Why glorify the trivial?"

Not all inappropriate uses are trivial. There are many, many cases where a computer was successfully used for something, until someone figured out a better way of doing it with*out* the computer.

For example, Alan Cadan runs a million-dollar necktie business from his home. From the *Wall Street Journal,* we learn that "a $10,000 computer system was acquired last year, but he prefers to use clipboards to keep track of things . . . . The computer could track the inventory, but it is simpler and quicker to subtract each day's shipments from what's on hand to keep a continuous inventory count, Mr. Cadan says."

Another example: a large school system thought they required a computer to assist teachers in preparing lesson plans. They learned of several commercially-available systems with which, for instance, a teacher considering a lesson on the Spanish Armada, could push the necessary buttons and on the screen or printer would appear a one- or two-page summary of the relevant information.

Before they spent nearly $50,000 on such a system, they hired a sensible consultant. The consultant determined that there were about 10,000 separate printouts available in the system. He hired unemployed teachers to write out the factual material for 50 cents a page. Then he built, from cardboard and cheap wood, a rack along the hallways of the school building, 25 bins high and 400 bins long, thus containing 10,000 compartments. The rows and columns were labelled with colors and symbols. The actual energy for this information storage and retrieval system was provided by the children, who were sent to the hallway to retrieve a sheet from "Red Kangaroo 7"—which the teacher's index indicated was the sheet on the Spanish Armada. Total cost: about a quarter of the electronic system; no breakdowns, more involving, and more fun.

A final example, reported by the *Wall Street Journal*: American automobile manufacturers have developed very expensive

If we were to stop promoting computers for inputting or generating data that are insignificant, trivial, irrelevant, inconsistent, contradictory, incorrect, redundant, obsolete, unworkable, worthless, misleading, confusing, and incomprehensible, then will there be enough data left to build the much touted Third Wave "information society" that everybody seems to be talking about?

—Jack Hokikian

and sophisticated computer systems for keeping track of inventories of expensive parts in warehouses all over the map. Japanese auto manufacturers, on the other hand, build their parts factories right next door to their car factories, thereby eliminating not only the need to keep track of inventories, but even the need for inventories themselves.

100.

Don't buy a $10,000 solid gold sledgehammer to drive in a two-cent thumb tack.

What's the lesson in all of this?

Don't buy a $10,000 solid gold sledgehammer to drive in a two-cent thumb tack.

What People Really Do with Their Computers

In the course of talking to hundreds of people about their small computer experiences, I determined that there appear to be ten kinds of things they do with their machines. Most of the things are easy enough to predict, but three of them (5, 9, 10) came as a surprise to me.

I list the uses in what I would guess to be the order of time spent with each, the most popular first.

1. *Games.* Still, and perhaps forever, the most common use of microprocessor technology.

2. *Electronic filing cabinet.* Recipes, household inventories, Christmas card lists, neckties, whatever. Storing "non-volatile" (unchanging, or seldom-changing) data is a computer use that a stack of 3×5 cards can generally do just as well.

3. *Personal finance.* Keeping track of the checking account, income tax data, net worth, depreciation schedules, mortgage payments, portfolio management, etc.

4. *New skills.* Learning to type, foreign languages, cooking lessons, academic subjects, appliance repair, whatever.

5. *Trivial uses.* Cataloguing the necktie collection, and the like, as previously described.

6. *Word processing.* Writing personal letters, reports, short stories, novels, note-taking, etc.

7. *Business use.* Small businesses that are not the main source of income, or activities related to an office somewhere else. Accounting, mailing lists, general ledger, bookkeeping, etc.

Almost certainly within 10 years [by 1976], we will have on the market a small appliance that can be plugged in like the radio or the TV set . . . which will enable any student from first grade through college to get all the information he needs . . . from a centrally-located computer.

—Peter Drucker

Some people take their small computers wherever they go.

8. *Research.* Tying in with other computers and data bases to get library information, stock prices, newspaper articles, etc.

9. *Practicing for the office.* Businesspeople who already have, or are expecting to have computers come into their business lives and who, concerned or terrified by the prospect, are working with small computers at home to be better able to deal with the office computer.

10. *Cuddling.* There is a whole subset of people who have a small computer for the same reason they subscribe to *Mother Earth News.* They may never do anything about it, but it really makes them feel good to know that they are somehow tuned into What's Really Happening. As Sherry Turkle writes in *Computer as Rorschach,* " . . . the relationship with (their) home computer carries longings for a better and simpler life in a more transparent society. *CoEvolution Quarterly, . . . Runner's World,* and *Byte* magazine lie together on (the) coffee tables. Small computers become the focus of hopes of building cottage industries that will allow the hobbyist to work out of his home, have more personal autonomy, not have to punch a time card, and be able to spend more time with his family and out of doors."

The Abagail XZ-2700

101.

A significant subset of people buy a small computer not because they want one or need one, but because they feel ownership is an essential part of "what's happening" and they want to be "with it."

About Programming

What Programming Is

A program is the set of instructions that tells a computer what to do. I understand the basic philosophy of programming, although I have never actually written a program, and I probably never will. (See page 144 on your right *not* to be a programmer).

It is easy enough to talk about programs in ordinary English. Here, for example, is a program:

1. Enter an amount of money in dollars and cents.
2. Multiply the amount of money entered in Step 1 by .04.
3. Add the number obtained in Step 2 to the number entered in Step 1.
4. Display the number obtained in Step 3 on the screen after the words, "The total amount of your purchase, including Nevada sales tax, is:"

This clever little program might be entitled, "Program for Calculating Nevada Sales Tax."

At this time, it is unnecessary and unimportant to know what actual keys are punched to tell the computer this. In fact the specific words, numbers, and symbols will differ from one programming "language" to another. The simple fact is that it is possible to type in a series of logical steps that make the machine go through its paces.

Within reason, everything that can be expressed in words can be rendered into programming instructions.

Expanding on the above example, let us say you have a Las Vegas gift shop. With every purchase, you type in the buyer's name and address, the item(s) purchased, and the price of each. The computer stores this information and calculates the sales tax and the total price.

For your monthly sales tax reports, it is possible to add to the program:

The problem with the home market is that the computer has been a solution looking for a problem.

—Kathleen K. Wiegner

5. Take the amount calculated in Step 2, and store it away in a file called "Sales Tax."

6. On the first day of each month, take all the numbers stored in the file called "Sales Tax," add them together, and print them following the words, "Total sales tax for the month just ended is:".

Once again, these are the sort of things one says to a programmer, whose job it is to figure out how to communicate the instructions electronically to the computer.

For a final extension of this example, let us say that you get in a special shipment of bullfight paintings on black velvet. You wish to notify your best customers of this event. Let us say that the code number for black velvet bullfight paintings is 117.

Now you wish to have the computer search through its memory to find all customers who have the following specifications:

a. Their product code number is 117.

b. The amount of money entered in Step 1 above is over $100 (you only want to write to the big spenders).

c. Their Zip code is a number no lower than 90001 and no higher than 92999 (you want to write only to people living in Southern California, the black velvet capital of the world).

The programmer, then, is the person who takes the available data, the capabilities of the machine, and the desired result, and figures out how to get from here to there. (The five *kinds* of programming are discussed on page 147.)

Notice that I did not say that the programmer figures out the *best* way to get from here to there. There is rarely if ever a single solution to a given programming need. If my need is to have one number added to another number, the program *could* say:

1. Multiply the first number by 8.
2. Multiply the second number by 6.
3. Divide the result of Step 1 by 4.
4. Divide the result of Step 2 by 3.
5. Add the results of Steps 3 and 4 together.
6. Divide the result of Step 5 by 2.
7. Print the result following the words, "The sum of the first number and the second number is."

This inelegant program *will* do the job of adding two numbers together, and will take a computer only a few millionths of a second longer to perform than the more elegant "Add the first number to the second number" would take.

The time difference hardly matters in many situations, but

Technological progress has merely provided us with more efficient means for going backwards.

— Aldous Huxley

when a program requires thousands or even millions of separate calculations, the saving of a tiny fraction of a second thousands of times can be quite significant.

Another example of programming elegance: The story is told that when Enrico Fermi was a lad, his mathematics teacher gave the third-grade class some busy work, so he could attend to some personal business: "Add up all the numbers between 1 and 100. A prize to the student who finishes first with the correct answer." While the rest of the class was dutifully writing down $1 + 2 + 3 + 4$, Fermi, in about ten seconds, raised his hand with the correct answer. He calculated thus: $1 + 100 = 101$; $2 + 99 = 101$; $3 + 98 = 101$. So there will be 50 pairs totalling 101. $50 \times 101 = 5050$. At least as elegant as whatever he won the Nobel Prize for some decades later!

Programmers find it a challenge to seek elegant solutions. There is, in fact, a large and intriguing book called *The Psychology of Computer Programming,* which discusses this matter in detail. Programming is truly as much an art as a science.

102.

Computer programming is as much an art as a science. Good programmers seek "elegant" solutions, which may not be faster or better, just somehow nicer.

Stand Up for Your Right Not to be a Programmer

Many programmers think that programming is so wonderful, so elegant, such fun, that anyone who does not want to become a programmer must be a few bricks shy of a load. This is roughly analogous to a happy stable cleaner failing to comprehend why *every*one doesn't enjoy shoveling manure as much as he does.

Programming *can* be a challenging, creative, entertaining, rewarding, personally satisfying thing to do. Goodness knows, it is still a growth industry, and there are probably going to be more job openings for competent programmers than almost any other white collar job over the next 10 or 20 years.[1]

But you do not *need* to understand programming to use computers successfully any more than you need to understand enzyme action in order to enjoy a good meal.

This is a fact that many people seem not to have grasped. Over and over again, I hear the lament, "I want to get into computers — but I don't see how I'll *ever* learn programming." The registrars

103.

You don't need to understand programming to use computers any more than you need to understand electronics to use your stereo.

---

1. Of course that's what they said about teachers in the '60s and space scientists in the '70s, and they were wrong on both counts then.

offices at half a dozen colleges and universities I surveyed told me the same thing: programming classes have high initial enrollment — *and* the highest dropout rate of any classes by far.

Some people drop out because they just can't understand what's going on. But the majority, I am convinced, drop out (as I did, from the only programming class I ever tried to take) because it becomes clear to them that what they are learning is unnecessary for their goals. As long as *some* clever programmers are able to make computers operable by non-programmers like me, there is no *need* for me to learn anything whatsoever about it.

There is a real problem in that many people who really enjoy something cannot comprehend that some otherwise reasonable people have no interest whatsoever in their thing. ("You don't want to go cross-country skiing even a *little* bit?" No. "You don't want to eat even a *little* of this squid soufflé?" No. "You don't want to learn a few of the *simplest* programming instructions?" No.)

And yet, here I am, bopping through my new word processing program, for which programming knowledge is not supposed to be needed, when I have the need to delete one of my files. I am all done with it, and I want it to go away forever. The manual starts talking about issuing a "DOS command," and informs me that "You are not allowed to BSAVE anything to the output disk."

Now, just as I can recognize that a written message *is* Japanese, even though I cannot *read* one word of Japanese, so, too, do I recognize that "BSAVE" is a programming instruction, along with "words" like GOTO, HIMEM, BLOAD, MID$, PARAMS, PEEK, and POKE.

There is no *need* for this. At the very least, the manual could have told me exactly what keys to hit to delete a file. Better still, they could have cleverly put a little routine into the program that causes the necessary steps to happen "automatically" when I type in something like "Delete File #3."

(One of the things that makes new generation computers like the Apple Lisa and the Epson QX-10 so appealing is that they *have* taken those steps in elegantly simple ways. With the Lisa, you simply use your electronic "mouse" to point at a picture of a wastebasket on the screen and the file in question goes away. Less cute, but just as simple, with the Epson, you press a button on the keyboard labelled "Delete File." Either of those actions initiates a long and intricate series of electronic steps, resulting in the deletion of the file — but the user doesn't need to know about that any

They tell me computers are growing more "user friendly" — but you still have to wear goggles and get out in the mud and crank them.

—Marina Bear

104.

Many computer systems that claim no programming knowledge is needed lie. It *shouldn't* be needed, but programmers tend to forget how little non-programmers know (or want to know) about programming.

more than he or she needs to know that one must pump a little gasoline through a carburetor into a cylinder, compress it, and set fire to it 10 times a second in order to make a car go. You just "step on the gas" and it all happens, just like magic.)

My word processing program is by no means an isolated event. I have learned to look carefully through the instruction manuals of programs in which I have possible interest. Even in some relatively simple game programs, one is told that to modify one aspect or another, "Simply enter the program, and on line 2470, change GOTO 640 to GOTO 780."

I am aware that there are people in the world who know how to "enter" a program, but why must I be one of them? I regularly follow instructions correctly when I neither know nor care why I am doing it, as long as I achieve the desired result (use unleaded gas; close cover before striking; align left side with line A unless tray 2 is in use).

It only requires a few square inches of paper to tell us non-programmers *how* to do things, instead of *what* to do. So let's stand up for our right *not* to learn programming if we'd rather not.[2]

---

2. I will be getting angry letters, one-third of them anonymous, from programmers, saying, in effect, "You poor shnook. Don't you realize that . . . " Well, I'll bet that my backhand is better than yours, my calligraphy more elegant, and my vegetable soup tastier. Everybody doesn't have to do everything well. Or at all. Thank you.

The Five Levels of Programming, and Who Will Use Them

Having just established that it is totally unnecessary to learn programming, I shall now describe the five levels of programming that it is not necessary to learn.

These are, it seems to me, important distinctions to make. People use the word "programming" in many ways, but can be referring to quite different levels each time: "By 1990, all college graduates will need to know programming." "Programming skill required for this job." "There is no need ever to learn programming."

Level 1: Machine language programming

Elsewhere, I have brieflly described how, at its most elemental level, computers are, in effect, a series of off-on switches. The number "21," for example, is represented by six consecutive switches in the off-on-off-on-off-on configuration. The number "9" consists of switches in the off-off-on-off-off-on order. How does one add "21" to "9"? There is an elaborate internal logic that "tells" the machine what to do with these two arrays of switches, when separated by yet another array of switches that corresponds to a "+." *Somehow* (and I neither know nor care how), the computer ends up with switches in an off-on-on-on-on-off pattern, which stands for a "30."

The machine language programmer is one who actually understands what goes on inside the machine itself. Only a tiny percentage of programmers can do this. Some people regard them as the elite of the field. Others regard it as a peculiar and largely unnecessary (if hard to acquire) skill, not unlike being able to recite Shakespeare while balancing a jug of water on your head.

Level 2: Programming with programming languages

The reason it is not necessary for most people in most situations to know anything about machine language is that the clever folks who have devised the various programming languages have done all the work needed to master the machine.

For example, when you hit a "+" key on your $6.95 pocket calculator, the very act of hitting the "+" key puts into action all

By 1976, 75% of college graduates will be expert programmers, and will go into jobs in the computer industry.

— Popular Science, May, 1965

those elaborate off-off-on-off switch manipulations needed to combine one set of switches (i.e., one number) with another. Because someone figured out how to do this wonderful shortcut once, and packed it all into the "+" key, no one ever has to do it again.

The people who developed the various programming languages have taken a lot of incredibly complicated sets of machine behaviors, and combined all the dozens or hundreds or thousands of steps required to execute them into a single shorthand character or collection of a few letters. The programmer must understand what all these shorthand designations do, but has no need to understand *how* they do it.

105.

The philosophy of programming remains constant, no matter which programming "language" is being used. It is therefore much easier to learn a second programming language than a first.

FOR MONTHS, I HAD BEEN HEARING COMPUTER PROFESSIONALS EXCITEDLY DISCUSSING COMPUTER SYSTEMS THAT OPERATED WITH EUNUCHS.

I WAS AFRAID TO ASK.

TURNED OUT THEY WERE REFERRING TO A "HOT" NEW OPERATING SYSTEM, DEVELOPED BY THE BELL SYSTEM, CALLED "UNIX."

OH.

There are dozens of programming languages in use. They all have the effect of making the computer do many internal maneuvers from a single keystroke (or two). The most popular programming languages have names like Basic, Pascal, Fortran, and Cobol. I believe they are mostly acronyms for various things, but I am incapable of remembering what.

People talk about one programming language being more *powerful* than another, which means that it can do more complex things with fewer keystrokes.

Some languages are designed to be most useful for certain categories of users: scientists, or businesspeople, or beginners, or children. But the *philosophy* of programming remains constant, so that a person who has become "fluent" in one programming language will find it much easier to learn a second language than a person starting from scratch. ("Fluency," incidentally, is an apt term. Some universities that have foreign language requirements for its graduates will now accept fluency in Fortran or Cobol or other popular programming languages to meet that requirement.)

Level 3: Program changing

Some people can edit someone else's manuscript or correct someone else's golf swing to make them better when they are incapable of writing or swinging on their own. Similarly, there are people who may not be able to create an elaborate program from scratch, but who have the skill to make creative changes in other people's programs.

To do this requires a knowledge of programming languages, and also a good sense of the real world needs of users of various programs. For example, one writer had a word processing program that was capable of putting footnotes at the bottom of a page. But the original programmer had not taken into account *really* long footnotes, which would have to lap over onto the next page. The writer found a program modifier who was able to delve into the program itself line by line, find among the thousands of lines the few dealing with footnote instructions, and make certain minor adjustments to accommodate long footnotes.

The modifier told me she could *never* have written such a complex program from scratch, but she was able to do a bit of fine tuning on someone else's work.

Another example: most mailing list programs print out name and address labels with the "standard" five-digit Zip code. But

106.
It is much easier to learn to change, modify or adjust other people's programs than it is to learn how to write your own programs.

Programs can be altered manually (using pencil and paper) or electronically (directly on the computer).

when the Postal Service announced a nine-digit Zip code, these programs were unable to cope with it. I spoke to several mail order companies who went out and hired program modifiers to go through their programs and make the necessary changes so that there would be room for nine characters in that particular location.[3]

Program modifying is a very tricky business. John Muir said that every time he moved a rock, he found that it was tied to everything else in the universe. So it is with programming. Many people have found, to their utter dismay, that making a very minor change in Line 2740 can make a tiny change in 6 other lines which in turn are tied into 18 other lines. Several people used the Rubik's Cube analogy in trying to describe how they got further and further in over their heads.

(Correct practice would dictate making a copy of a program before tampering with the original. But there are programs which are electronically uncopyable which can *still* be tampered with.)

Level 4: Program adjusters

Some programs are designed to be changed by the customers. The method of making the changes is explained — sometimes clearly, sometimes cryptically — in the instructions to the program.

As a simple example, my label printing program, designed to print name and address labels, was written for rolls of "one-across" labels (one label per row). The original programmer has made it possible for me, the know-nothing, to change the program. The screen asks me, "Do you want to change the program?" I type, "Yes." It gives me a "menu" of possible changes: number of labels per row, horizontal size of label, vertical size of label, number of lines of printing per label, etc.

By following relatively simple instructions (either on the screen or in my manual), I have made basic changes in the program, which are then permanently stored on the disk. I have no idea what I did, but I have achieved the desired result, thanks to the clever person who wrote the program.

One more example. My word processing program is designed for 8-1/2 by 11″ paper, which contains 66 lines per page. I recently

There is no danger of machines running amok, unless, of course, they have been programmed to run amok.

—John Hargreaves

3. It now appears, however, that it was not a computer-knowledgeable person at the Post Office who announced the "nine-digit Zip" for it turns out that we are supposed to put a hyphen between numbers five and six, hence *ten* spaces required. This sort of thing will keep the program modifiers in business.

had occasion to write a lengthy paper on forms provided by an Australian publisher — in "A4" metric size, which is slightly different in both dimensions.

By invoking some built-in "change the dimensions" rules of the program, again with no knowledge whatever of the technology or programming changes I was making, I was, in a matter of seconds, able to change the program to a 70-lines-per-page metric model. I was given the option of storing this *new* size permanently on the disk, or using it temporarily and returning to American sizes later.

The more skilled the original programmer, the easier it is for non-programmers to adjust programs to suit their needs.

Level 5: Program users

When you put a quarter in the Pac-Man game, you are using a very clever and quite complex computer program — without giving any thought whatsoever to that fact.

Someday, if all goes well, the great majority of programs for small computers will fit in the same category. Just as you give no thought now to the gears and pulleys that spring into action when you turn on your electric typewriter, so, one day, will you give no thought to the elaborate, sophisticated program that makes your word processor process words.

It is *that* kind of computer usage that will enlist legions of new participants in whatever kind of computer revolution we've got going today.

What*ever* the total number of humans interacting with computers, my prediction is that participation in the five categories I have described is likely to be roughly logarithmic in nature. By that, I mean that for every one machine language programmer there will be something like 10 programmers, 100 program modifiers, 1,000 program adjusters, and 10,000 program users.

I don't want to process words, I said. You will learn, she assured me. . . . We have the HardWriter Program, the ImpossiCalc Program, (and) the Try-And-Index-It Program. . . .

—James Kilpatrick

107.

Most computer users will *never* be programmers. Some will learn to modify other people's programs. A small percentage will become programmers.

Games

What Are You Doing in There, Harry— or It's Really All Right to Play Games

Without exception, games are the things that computers do best, and yet some manufacturers and dealers foster the attitude that it is somehow undignified, unbusinesslike, and/or *wrong* to play them.

When my friend Harry bought himself an IBM Personal Computer a few months ago, he announced in somber tones that it was *For His Business*. Day after day, he sat in his study with the door closed, familiarizing himself with the equipment, and setting up his business records. Or so he told his wife and children.

But from time to time, decidedly unbusinesslike beep-beep-beeps came wafting under the door. They would stop quite suddenly when Pat would knock on the door and ask Harry what he was doing in there.

Harry, and many, many other people have somehow been intimidated into believing some of those *Wall Street Journal* ads: "This Computer Means Business." "The No-Nonsense Computer." "You Won't Be Using Your QX-44 To Play Games." "Business, Not Monkey Business." And so forth.

What nonsense. That's like selling a pencil and saying it's great for doing accounting, but you better not use it for writing poetry and love letters or drawing pictures of flowers.

Here's why I say that games are what computers do best: an ideal computer program, whether for bookkeeping or zapping invaders from Arcturus III, should have these characteristics:

- comprehensible instructions
- possible to learn in a reasonable time
- runs without flaws
- a positive experience for the user (not necessarily *fun* but at least satisfying).

108.
Many people feel guilty about playing computer games on computers they bought for business purposes. But games are still one of the things computers do best.

PAC-MAN
SNAC-MAN
BLAC-MAN
FLAK-MAN
TRAC-MAN
✳ ASTERO ✳
YAK-MAN

ATARI

Some games have elaborate
sound effects.

With few exceptions, most computer games meet all four
characteristics — and many non-game programs do not.

For those of us who love virtually *all* games, and will contentedly play "Button, button, who's got the button" for an hour
with a three-year-old, it is difficult to remember that there are
actually some people who do not enjoy games. My only message
to them is, don't reject computer games until you've given them a
try. There's an awful lot more to them than the shoot-em-up space
games and the ultimately tedious Pac-Man.

(I am a little bleary-eyed as I write these words, having been
up until one in the morning last night playing *Adventure* with a
friend. The feeling is very much the same as having spent the
evening in the company of *two* intelligent, creative, and fun-to-be-

with people. And so it was. John Fremont was one, and the other was programmer Gordon Letwin who made the game available for small computers.)

I've got two more reasons (justifications? rationalizations?) for playing games openly, instead of hiding behind locked doors like Harry to indulge:

One is that I somehow signed on with a remarkably non-competitive family. They don't even like keeping score in tennis. Many computer games are one-person games — or at least one live person (me), matching wits with one or more clever programmers. The electronic equivalent of chess by mail. Maybe not as good as face to face, but better than none at all.

The other reason is the relaxation and reward aspect. After a long spell of *working* at the computer (even writing a book like this is work for me), I promise myself the reward of at least a short game before going back to the real world.[1]

Games Are Cheap Entertainment

I have heard many complaints about how expensive computer games are. Well, yes and no. I have paid anywhere from 50 cents (a $10 disk with 20 games on it) to $40 for a single game, and with rare exceptions, I've felt that I was getting good value for money spent.

109.

Computer games may seem expensive to buy, but when you calculate cost per hour of enjoyment, they are cheaper than most forms of entertainment.

It depends on how you look at it. I look at it on a per hour basis. If a $10 game bores me after 15 minutes, then that game is costing me $40 an hour. If it remains challenging for four hours, then it is costing me $2.50 an hour.

Consider the following significant chart:

Event	Cost Per Hour
Visit to psychiatrist	$60+
Broadway musical	$20
Meal at good restaurant	$15

1. I can hear the clucking already. It's unhealthy. Should be out getting exercise. Playing with electronic friends is weird. Well, as I told a clucking relative (who plays games with Thomas Middleton all day long — by doing Double Crostics), *anything* done to excess is liable to be unhealthy and/or weird. When the Grand Inquisitor of Betelgeuse VII frightens me more than Reaganomics or the nuclear arms race, then I'll admit I'm in trouble.

Week at fancy resort	$ 6
First run movie	$ 3
Hard-cover book*	$ 2
Magazine*	$ 1
Paperback book*	$ .50
Good computer game*	$ .25
Sunsets, parlor games, etc. etc.*	$ .00

Games Are Fun, but Do Not Necessarily Develop Computer Literacy

Some of the more pious apologists for the right of teenagers to spend their lunch, job, or mugging money on 25-cent video arcade games suggest that there are significant learning experiences involved, and that valuable skills are being developed leading to familiarity with computers (or, as it is often called, computer literacy). The philosopher Dr. Bruce Colman has pointed out, in this regard, that in the 1950s, these same folks would have been defending our youth hanging out in pool halls on the grounds that three-cushion shots were helping them learn Newtonian physics.

There are (however) three generally-accepted redeeming social values of computer games (in addition to the fact that when more people are having fun, the average mental health level of the world improves.

• They are valuable tools for learning about things other than computers. Learning that comes about as the result of playing a game is not only painless, but often faster and more lasting. The better the game, often, the better the learning.

Educators have come up with some pretty good learning games. Some are as simple as playing Hangman in French or Spanish to help learn those languages. Some are as complex as elaborate simulation games where the student is running a store or business, buying stocks and bonds, or trying to get his 747 from Vladivostok to Rio de Janeiro as fuel-efficiently as possible.

Some are skillful blends of already-popular computer games and teaching skills. My favorite (and the favorite of many others, clearly, since it was among the top three selling programs for a

110.

Don't expect to learn computers by playing games. Most computer games contribute to computer literacy about as much as playing billiards contributes to learning Newtonian physics.

---

* These items, of course, can be shared, passed along, or re-used, thereby reducing the cost per hour.

long time)[2], is called MasterType. Unlike various other Learn-to-Type computer programs, which merely adapt standard classroom techniques to the screen, in which the computer takes the role of the teacher ("Type the following sentence . . ."), MasterType has the student manning a space station. "Evil" letters and words slowly descend from space toward the station. The only way to stop them is to type the word correctly on the keyboard. If you do so, the word disappears (to be replaced, perhaps, by a longer or more complicated word heading your way).

After each round, your speed and accuracy figures appear on the screen. You can move through dozens of different levels and skills, practice just numbers and the stuff *no* one can type fast (like #$%&!?)[3], and teachers can add their own words or phrases to the lessons.

● They are valuable tools for learning about computers. There are said to be games and other pleasurable learning experiences involving actually "getting into" and altering the very programs that run the games. In doing so, one learns about programming while playing the game. (Many programmers to whom I have talked say this sort of thing is unnecessary, since they think programming itself *is* like a huge and wonderful logic game.)

● They sharpen the mind and exercise the brain. There are learning theorists who believe that, just as jogging and lifting weights prepares one for *any* form of athletic competition, be it volleyball or horse racing, so does brain exercise prepare you for *any* kind of mental endeavor, from taking tests to robbing banks. (Willie "The Actor" Sutton, famous and pretty successful bank robber, used to solve crossword puzzles and acrostics intensively for weeks before a job, to get his head in shape for the split-second endeavor. Mr. Sutton's take presumably would have been even higher had he had the opportunity to hone his intellect on sophisticated computer games.)

---

2. Program or software sales are "charted" into the Top Ten or Top Forty each week, just like hit tunes.

3. Say, do you suppose that's why comic characters swear by saying "Oh, #$%&!?" Perhaps they are all bad typists[4] and they express their anger this way?

4. Of course most of them have only three fingers on each hand.[5]

5. Did you notice, this is a footnote to a footnote. Literary history may be made here on this page today!

Let us assume that the computer is a faster working, more compact library. But just as today's students don't know how to use the library, tomorrow's will be helpless when confronting their tiny, inexpensive, speedy computers with their tiny, unexercised, hopelessly sluggish minds.

—John Simon

111.

Some computer games appear to have the effect of sharpening the mind and exercising the brain.

Satori Games
presents

THAT'S WHERE THE MONEY IS

The Bank Robbery Game
for Home Video Systems

First choose the weapons you think you'll need — guns, gas masks, ropes, etc. Be careful you don't carry too much, or you'll move too slowly and get caught by Edgar the Guard. But if the randomized Tear Gas Spray hits you without a gas mask, its off to The Hoosegow! Watch out for rival gangs led by Big John D., Jesse and the Boys, and Patty and the Girls who want to rob the same bank! If you can Blow Up the Vault (you didn't forget the dynamite, did you?), if Edgar the Guard doesn't get you, and if you've positioned your Getaway Car in just the right place, you'll Escape with the Loot, and Meet Your Moll in Miami Beach.

HOURS OF FUN FOR CHILDREN OF ALL AGES

Miscellaneous Matters

What Word Processing Is All About

Dozens of lengthy books have been written solely on the subject of word processing. There is no way I can explain it thoroughly in a tiny space. The reason for mentioning it at all is simply this: if I had known more about what word processing could do for me, I would have started using it several years sooner than I did.

112.
Word processing is one of the things computers do best. Once many people get started, they rarely return to pencils, pens, or typewriters again.

The basic idea of word processing is simplicity itself. Like the man who was thrilled to discover that he had been speaking in prose all his life, my first response to word processing was, "Oh. But that's what I *already do* with my typewriter, pencil, whiting-out fluid, scissors, rubber cement, and stapler."

All of the above are indeed word processing tools, since word processing can be considered the process of getting words from the brain of one person to the brain of another person in the best possible way (easiest, most efficient, cheapest, prettiest, and/or fastest).

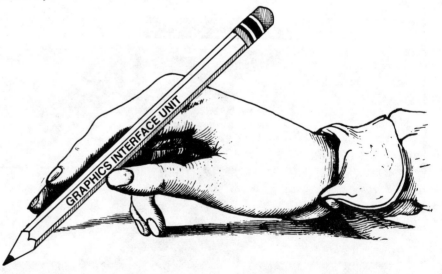

A pencil (that is to say, a User Controllable Graphics Interface Input Module) is one of the simplest word processors. I can make certain marks on a sheet of paper, which will have meaning for certain other people. If I make a mistake, I can use the Character Delete Unit cleverly affixed to the other end of my pencil, and make the word go away. If I want to put additional words into an already-written sentence, I can write them in the margin and draw little arrows. And if I want to move an entire sentence or paragraph to another location in my text, I can physically remove it with scissors and glue it into its new location. Finally, if I notice that I have spelled "pterodactyl" wrong throughout my essay, I can read through it carefully, changing every appearance of the incorrectly spelled word.

What I am doing is processing my words. Causing them to exist, changing them, and moving them around. Given those basic functions, the *only* differences between a ten-cent Ticonderoga No. 2 word processing pencil and a $10,000 word processing computer system are those of ease and efficiency of use, price, prettiness of output, and speed.

Using a word processing program

When I wish to send some words out into the world, whether a one-page letter to my Aunt Helene in New York or a 200-page book, I start by loading my word processing program into the computer (by inserting a disk and typing a four-character instruction or command).

Now I am ready to start typing in my words. I do so on the keyboard which is almost identical to that of my old-fashioned typewriter. Instead of seeing the words on paper, I see them on the television screen of my monitor. If I make a mistake, I can backspace and make the correction, insert new words, or delete words right on the screen. If I want to move a sentence or a paragraph or a page from one part of my text to another, I can electronically lift a word, a sentence, or a paragraph out of one place and insert it in another.

If I discover that I have typed in "George Washington" throughout my essay on tennis racquet restringing, when I should have typed "Thomas Jefferson," I can simply instruct the computer to go through my text and automatically change every occurrence of "George Washington" to "Thomas Jefferson."

If I worry about my spelling in general, I can call up a "Dic-

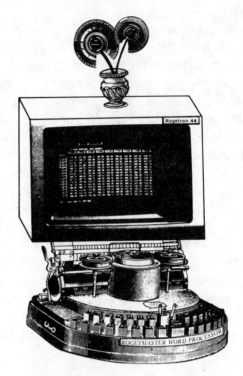

113.

Unless you spend 1000 or more hours a year at a typewriter, word processing may not be cost effective (if you buy a computer solely for that purpose), but it certainly improves the quality of life.

tionary" program which will match every word in my text with a large electronic dictionary, and show on the screen any that don't match, and *may* be wrong.

If I am writing something that will require an index, I can insert a certain invisible symbol next to each word or phrase in the text that I will also want in my index, and when I am done, I can push a few buttons and out comes a completed index.

Finally, and for me most importantly, everything I write is stored electronically on a disk. I can write and print out a rough draft of something, read it over, make corrections with a pencil, insert the changes onto the disk, and print out a final copy, whether a day or a year (if I haven't lost the disk) later.

So much for ease, efficiency, and speed. My computer beats a pencil or a typewriter hands down on all these counts. Now a few words about price and prettiness.

Price

Is all this ease, efficiency and speed worth the $5,000 or so that the equipment cost? Or even the $2,500 it would have cost to get minimally acceptable machinery? For me, the answer is an emphatic "Yes," because I have estimated that processing my words electronically saves me more than 200 hours a year. If the equipment lasts three years, if my time is worth more than $8.33 an hour (I fancy myself that it is), then I'm ahead of the game.

But for many other people, the answer is an equally emphatic "Maybe," or "No," at least when considered in purely financial terms. If word processing just saves a few minutes a day, one's time would have to be worth hundreds of dollars an hour to make it pay. For many, ease and efficiency more than make up for the lack of cash savings. But there are also many who would be much better off with a good $400 correcting typewriter and $4,600 in the bank. (See page 137 on "Cataloguing Your Necktie Collection.")

The other important consideration is what else you may be doing with the computer. If, for a hundred dollars more you can add word processing to the computer you are considering for accounting or mailing lists or playing games with, all well and good. Most buyers will pay $500 extra to add air conditioning to their Buick. But if all they want to do is sit still and keep cool, there are better ways than buying a $12,000 air conditioner that happens to have a Buick attached.

"Did you hear about the lady who confused her food processor with her word processor?"
"No, what did she get?"
"Minced words."

Prettiness

The way processed words get to the other party is either by being sent over telephone lines to the other person's computer ("electronic mail"), or, more commonly (nowadays, at least), by being put on paper, and getting the paper to the other person. Most people seem to agree that *any* mechanically reproduced character is going to be more legible (if not necessarily prettier) than most handwritten ones. However for almost all public documents (i.e., things that will be seen by another person), typewriter-quality printing is unquestionably prettier, and thus preferred by most people.

The various considerations (including prettiness) in choosing a printer are discussed on page 86, and the notion of going directly from computer-entered words to typesetting is covered on page 165.

"Did you hear about the lady who confused her word processor with her food processor?"
"No. What did she get?"
"Minced words."

Dealing with the Noise

While computers themselves are virtually silent in their operation, computer-driven printers are not only noisy but relentless. If this affects the harmony of your household as it did mine, there are steps that can be taken other than trial separation.

In older times, when I often used to spend my evenings pounding the keys of an IBM typewriter, the regular clack-clack-clack, compounded by the fact that my office was in the next room down from the bedroom, caused my wife to wonder why I couldn't be a writer like John O'Hara, who wrote from nine to five every day, with an hour off for lunch (or, perhaps, like Will Shakespeare, whose quill was presumably a few decibels quieter than an IBM).

In one way, the computer helped preserve family harmony, because I was able to type into it and store my words on disks—and then, at reasonable hours, run the words out all at once through the printer.

But it is the relentless aspect of computer printers that causes other problems not only in my life, but, I deduce, in those of many others (because of the proliferation of equipment designed to do something about the noise). Most background noises, in both home and office, are variable and random. Typewriters clack for a while, pause, and clack on. Phones ring occasionally. Pencils are sharpened. Doors slam. Psychologists have noted that continuous (i.e., relentless) stimuli are much more likely to drive people bonkers—hence the success, for example, of the Chinese water torture.

Once you start printing out your files, records, text, or mailing labels on a computer printer, it may go on, without interruption or hesitation (if you are lucky) for hours and hours. And *this* is the kind of noise that seems to drive some people crazy.

One solution is to turn the printing on just before leaving the office or the home. I used to do this. After the third time that the paper or labels jammed in the printer shortly after I left, causing the printing of 6,000 lines on top of one another, shredding the paper and perhaps damaging the printer rollers, I abandoned this practice.

A second solution is ear plugs. A popular brand called Flents seems to do wonders blocking out clacking, but still letting essential sounds like ringing phones and crying babies come through.

114.

While computers are themselves silent, the relentless noise of most printers is annoying to many others in the environment. Soundproofed boxes that fit over printers are a good solution.

Printer Enclosure

SO QUIET, YOU CAN NEST A CHICKEN ON IT!

A third solution is a special sound-absorbing foam pad for the printer to sit on. These are available from computer stores and computer supply catalogues for under $20.

The ultimate solution is a soundproofing enclosure for the printer itself. The printer is surrounded by a box made from soundproofing material. A hinged door permits access for inserting and removing paper, changing ribbons, etc. Depending on the size of the printer to be enclosed, these boxes range from $300 to $500, and are available from computer stores and computer supply catalogues.

Finally, if no other solution is feasible, but noise continues as a problem, there *are* totally silent computer printers that produce words on paper by sending electrical impulses through specially-treated paper. They are inexpensive and fast, but because of the silvery tone of the special paper, their use is limited to producing rough drafts, or other uses in which black on silver is appropriate (none of which leap to my mind at this moment).

It Really Pays to Shop Around for Supplies

There may be some good arguments for buying your computer and some programs at or near retail price from your local dealer or store (see page 91 for these reasons). But can there be any reason, anytime, to pay $5 for a disk that can be bought elsewhere for $2?

There is a huge price difference between supplies bought at retail and supplies bought from discount houses or at computer shows. By "supplies" I mean, in general, anything that either gets used up (paper, ribbons, labels), or things that are so standard and so uncomplicated, no instruction or advice is needed in their use (disks, typing elements, cables).

Many people probably buy goods at "retail" for the same reason they buy 17 cents worth of postage stamps for 25 cents from a vending machine: convenience and immediate need. But if you can plan ahead, and are willing to tie up a little money in inventory, the savings are immense.

Disks are a typical example. Major brands, at this writing, have a retail price of around $5 for a 5-1/4″ floppy disk. In quantity, the price can come down to $3.50 to $4 each. But it is not uncommon to find these disks at $2 to $2.50 at discount houses, and often

115.
It is risky to start a long printing operation and leave the room. If the paper jams on line 3, you're in trouble.

116.
For extreme noise-sensitive situations, there are totally silent thermal printers.

117.
It really pays to shop around for supplies: paper, disks, ribbons, etc. The variation in prices can be 100% or more.

under $2 at computer shows, when the inevitable price wars that
start at these affairs between various booths get into full swing. (At
one show, the price of brand-name disks was dropping about five
cents an hour. I waited until near closing time and bought a large
supply at $1.80 each.)

If you aren't likely to be going to a show, where do you find the discount sellers? Primarily from advertisements in the many computer magazines. (Some magazines don't accept discounting ads, to protect dealers, or to increase the likelihood of the magazine being sold in retail stores, but many do.)

Often the lack of sales tax (if you buy from out of state) more than offsets any shipping charges that may be added.

Of course what you *don't* get from a discounter, usually, is service or advice. This is why it may not be wise to buy hardware or software this way, unless you know exactly what you want, and are willing to sacrifice the personal service, attention, and emergency help that a local dealer *may* be able to provide.

Typesetting by Computer

This subject will be of interest to about 7% of the people and zero interest to the rest. But, darn it, it took me four years to find out all this stuff, so permit me to share it with the 7% and the rest of you can skip along.

Typesetting is the production of words that look like the ones you are reading now. For most professional purposes (books, reports, magazines, pamphlets, advertisements, etc.), it is much classier and more impressive-looking than `typewriting, which is what you are reading now.`

Traditionally, the way you get material typeset is to write or type out the words you want typeset, and bring them to a typesetting service, which uses large and expensive photographic equipment to produce the words. Depending on the number of words set, you will pay anywhere from two cents to ten cents a word to have this done. And if you want to make a few minor changes after the job has been done, you usually have to have the entire text reset.

There are now some typesetting services that let *you* do the difficult and expensive and time-consuming work of actually typing in the words. Then you send them your disk, and they run it through their machines to produce the typesetting.

There are three main advantages to this system:

1. You have full control over quality. You can see all the words of the finished job on your own screen or printer (even though they will not look as classy as the finished job), and make any needed corrections or additions yourself.

118.
When a high-quality print-out is essential, it is possible to get book-quality typesetting from small computers by sending a disk or tape to certain typesetting services.

2. *Because* you have done all "keyboarding" yourself, the cost of typesetting is much less — often less than one cent per word.

3. All the work is saved and stored on a disk, so that if you want to make some revisions for a later printing of the same material, *all* you have to do is make the corrections; you don't have to retype the whole thing.

The main disadvantage of this process is that you have to type in a whole bunch of additional commands, so the typesetting machine will "know" just what you want: when to put a word in boldface or italics; when to change to a different typeface; when to indent a paragraph; and so forth.

I have my poor to feed.

— Emperor Vespasian, rejecting a mechanical appliance that could do the work of three

The second disadvantage is that you have full control over the quality. If something goes wrong, you have no one to blame but yourself.

One of the customers of the small typesetting business of which I am 25% owner forgot to type in the command which told the computer to go out of italic type. And so, instead of one word in italics, she ended up with about 31,776 words in italics. The machine is dumb. It can only follow the instructions it is given. The owners of the machine are smart. They charge for the number of words set, regardless of whether they are what the customer had in mind (if it was indeed the customer's error).

A typical line that our customers produce might look like this:

```
<4MM>This is a  <3>good <4> example
of computer typesetting.  <F>How do
you like it?
```

"<4MM>" means use typeface number 4 (a boldface type) and indent two spaces. "<3>" means switch to typeface 3 (an italic) until further notice. "<4>" is the further notice, meaning go back to typeface number 4. <F> means go to a larger size type.

It's really quite easy to learn, and the finished line would come out looking like this:

This is a *good* example of computer typesetting. How do you like it?

Different services have different codes that must be entered. There is no consistency here whatsoever. Some services can accept words typed on a wide variety of computers and with many different word processing programs. Others, like ours, are *only* for people with a Radio Shack Model 1, which, thankfully, is a lot of people.

Locating these services

You can generally locate these typesetting services in the Yellow Pages under, remarkably enough, "Typesetting." Often the ads will say if the company accepts computer input. Some will only accept words shipped to them over the phone lines through a modem. Some will only accept a disk that you mail to them. Some will accept either.

And if you happen to have an Apple, TRS-80 Model 1, or certain other small computers (or would like the keyboarding done for you), you can reach the service I own part of, Baskerville and Company, at 100 N. Franklin St., Fort Bragg, California 95437. End of advertisement.

Faith in machinery is our besetting danger . . . as if it had a value in and for itself.

—Matthew Arnold

"Typesetting" with your printer

There are typing elements (daisy wheels or thimbles) available for some printers that look a lot better than most typewriting, although not quite as good as most typesetting. Still, for many purposes, proportionally-spaced typing with justified (even) right margins looks pretty good, as per this sample:

Learning the Commands

Probably the best way to learn the Cursor Commands is by remembering that the command character represents in most cases the action that the command is supposed to produce: i.e. "F" for forward, "B" for backward, etc. This is called a

Printed with a Silver Reed printer with proportional print wheel

The simulated boldface words are produced by an instruction in the program that tells the printer to move the paper a tiny fraction of an inch and hit the same letter again.

Of course it is not possible to change from one typeface to another on a home printer, without the big nuisance of stopping and changing print wheels.

PART FOUR

PROBLEMS WITH COMPUTERS

Sources of problems. The nature of
problems. Psychological problems.
Dealing with repairs. Two ultimate
solutions.

Sources of Problems

Computers Are Much More Fragile than the Manufacturers Want You to Think

In older times (back in the '70s), most computers were installed in special computer rooms. Philosophical and religious reasons aside, the main reason for doing this was because computers were very delicate machines, highly susceptible to moisture, heat, dust, static electricity, and assorted other factors.

They still are.

However, the manufacturers are well aware that no one is going to buy a $69 Timex-Sinclair, much less a $10,000 Apple Lisa, if they are told they must install it in a dust-free, temperature- and humidity-controlled room with anti-static flooring, a special electrical transformer, and possibly a lead roof.

To be sure, small computers *do* work fairly reliably on kitchen tables, laps, and in smoke-filled offices. But I am convinced that many of the problems that occur, and repairs that are required, could have been avoided if users had more appreciation for the delicate nature of their beast.

There are four general kinds of problems to worry about: environmental, mysterious forces, mechanical, and human beings.

The environment can cause problems

As indicated, computers tend to be more fragile than manufacturers often imply. There are certain steps that can be taken to diminish the likelihood of problems caused by factors in the environment — dust, smoke, heat, moisture, dandruff, hair, etc.

Notice, however, that this section is not called "How to avoid . . ." or "How to solve . . ." The reason is that it just isn't worth it, either in cost or effort, to eliminate the problems entirely. If a $20 dust cover can reduce the number of dirt-related

119.
Computers are really much more delicate than most manufacturers would like users to believe.

Computers are sensitive to temperature extremes.

breakdowns from one every 50 days to one every 300 days, then it is well worth it.[1]

While dust and dirt are unwelcome in all elements of a computer system, they can do the most harm on disks and in disk drives. Consider the illustration below.

120.

Particles as small as those in cigarette smoke or dust can cause big problems in small computers.

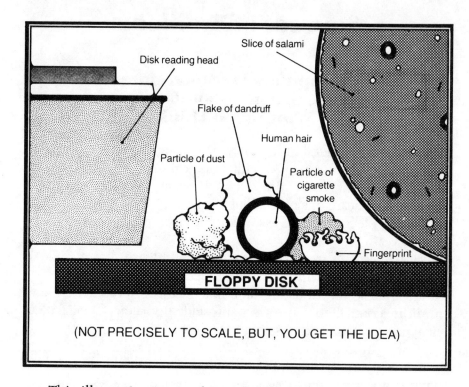

Disk reading head

Slice of salami

Flake of dandruff

Human hair

Particle of dust

Particle of cigarette smoke

Fingerprint

FLOPPY DISK

(NOT PRECISELY TO SCALE, BUT, YOU GET THE IDEA)

This illustration more than anything else, reminds me of just how fragile my system really is. Of course every grain of dust, particle of smoke, or flake of dandruff won't destroy your work. And, thankfully, many of the times when an error message is flashed, trying again will cause the operation to work, often because the offending particle has been pushed to the side the second time through.

The best way to minimize dust and dirt problems is by careful housekeeping, and by following certain simple (but oh, so easy *not* to do) rituals:

Inanimate objects are classified scientifically into three major categories: those that don't work, those that break down, and those that get lost.

—Russell Baker

• always put disks back in their paper or plastic sleeves when they are not in the disk drive.

---

1. The value of a dust cover is greatly enhanced when it is used. Many are bought, but few are used regularly. Nailing it to the wall as a talisman against grime has little effect.

- get (or knit) a cover for the computer, the printer, the disk drives, whatever machinery you have, and use it all the time.
- never smoke around the computer.
- never touch the shiny parts of either disks or tape.
- vacuum the area around the computer regularly (and carefully, so as not to stir up dust).

Other environmental factors pale in comparison, but may be worth mentioning briefly:

Moisture: Many manufacturers give humidity recommendations for their machinery, but unless you are inclined to carry your computer into the Turkish bath with you, there should be no

121.

Good "housekeeping" in the area of the computer is essential: regular vacuuming, using a dust cover on the computer and other machinery, always putting disks and tapes away, etc.

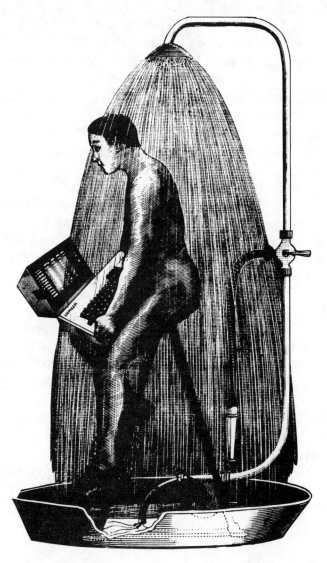

Not recommended

Actual path of a gamma ray through typical home.

major problem. Minor ones, or long-term ones, perhaps. I live near the ocean, and I can already see tiny spots of rust on some of the mechanical parts of my printer. Printout on the wall, as it were.

Temperature: Again, there are unlikely to be heat or cold-related problems within the range of what is found in normal (or even abnormal) homes and offices.

Gamma rays: There is probably some top secret manual for computer repair people, in which they are told that when all else fails, they can always blame the problem on gamma rays. *Omni* magazine confirms, however, that if one of these rays, which regularly come wafting down from outer space, should pass through a computer, it is liable to wreak havoc in the most subtle ways (for instance, erasing just a tiny part of the information on a disk or tape, such as a minus sign in an important calculation). Some big computer users shield their computer rooms with lead to ward off gamma rays and other particles that may be invented from time to time.

Unless you have run clean out of important stuff to worry about, it is not necessary to worry about gamma rays.

Mysterious forces can cause problems

Many of the things that go wrong with computers and in computing can be traced to problems with electricity, magnetism, and other mysterious forces. It really isn't necessary to understand the nature of the forces as long as you are aware of what they can do, and, to the extent feasible, what can be done to guard against them.

"Guard against" is indeed a matter of feasibility, always: a trade-off between cost, effort, and the number and nature of problems. If all is going generally well, why buy even a $100 gadget to prevent voltage surges. But if massive problems are occurring every few hours, a $500 "constant voltage" system might seem like a bargain.

Here are the five kinds of problems that are most likely. I've had four of them. None has been totally debilitating, but none has been a whole lot of fun, either.

1. *Too much power.* Normal household electricity in the United States and Canada is somewhere between 115 and 120 volts. The power companies try to keep the amount of electric

current in this narrow range, but often they do not succeed.

As with the engine of your car, if the available horsepower rises or falls a little, there is probably going to be no problem. But a giant voltage surge is like strapping a jet engine on your rear bumper: at the least, the power surge will cause loss of control, and it might well destroy the machinery.

I have been trying for three years to learn whether huge power surges are something that occur every three days or every three decades. I telephoned five electric companies and they all assured me that there is *no such thing* as a giant power surge. I telephone three manufacturers of power surge preventing equipment, and they left me with the impression that unprotected computers (and quite possibly computer users) are being fried to a crisp with astonishing regularity.

It is possible to buy, rent, or even borrow from your power company, devices that record the highest voltage coming through a circuit during a certain time period. If you worry about fried fingertips, or if you are having otherwise-inexplicable problems, it might be worth a try.

But I should think much greater peace of mind will come from investing the $50 to $100 necessary to buy a surge preventer: a gadget you plug into the wall, and then plug your equipment into. It works something like the overflow drain in your sink. If a huge wave of power comes gushing through, it only permits 120 volts to reach your computer.

Think of it as the computer equivalent of a St. Christopher statue on your dashboard. It'll probably never be needed, and when it is, it may not work, but oh, the peace of mind in the meantime.

2. *Too little power.* This is a much more common, and much harder to solve problem. You know the phenomenon of house lights dimming for a moment when a refrigerator or freezer motor comes on. That is because it takes more electricity to start up a motor than it does to run it, and so for that fraction of a second, power is diverted to the motor from lights—and from your computer.

Computers are regularly dealing with information in temporary memory banks. Temporary means that if the power fails, even for a fraction of a second, the memory goes blank, or gets garbled in some manner. If the power drops 5 or 10 volts, there

122.

Voltage surges may be rare, but they can destroy a computer. A $50 surge preventer is probably worth the peace of mind it brings.

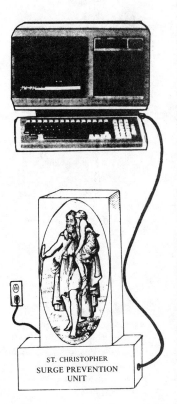

ST. CHRISTOPHER
SURGE PREVENTION
UNIT

123.

Voltage drops won't hurt the computer, but may cause baffling problems, even if they only last a fraction of a second. The solution is a constant voltage transformer.

Laddermation Industries Inc.

User-powered alternative energy sources are available.

124.

If power failures are a recurring problem, battery back-up systems are available, but bulky and expensive.

will probably be no problem. If it drops 15 or 20 volts, or more, there may be a problem, depending on what the computer was doing at the instant of the drop.

Power drops can never cause damage to the machinery itself, any more than too little vermouth destroys a martini. But power drops *can* interfere with the programs being run.[2]

There are two solutions to this problem, both of them rather expensive. One is something called a *constant voltage transformer,* which takes any line voltage between about 50 and 150 volts and transforms it to a nice steady 117 volts. This device is fine as long as the power stays on—and indeed the printshop mentioned in the last footnote ended up getting one. But the $300+ expense is rarely warranted unless the problem is acute.

When the problem is that the power goes off entirely, whether for a few seconds or, as regularly happens in our neck of the woods, for many hours at a time, the solution is a battery backup system for the computer. When the power from the wall plug stops, the batteries take over so fast that nothing in the temporary memory is lost.

It is very unlikely that small computer users would want or need such a system, since it is usually possible (and good practice) to transfer stuff from the temporary memory to the permanent memory every five or ten minutes, so the worst that can happen is losing a few minutes' work. (The batteries in question, by the way, are not small flashlight type, but a series of large automobile-type batteries.)

3. *Static electricity.* Static electricity is the stuff that sometimes gives you a small shock when you touch a metal doorknob, and which enables you to slide across a shag carpet in leather shoes and "stick" balloons or playing cards on the wall. (Look, if you want a book on physics, then buy a book on physics; that's all the explanation you are going to get from me.)

Static electricity can have an effect on the innards of your computer, and it's never a good effect. It can happen even if you don't slide across the floor and stick a balloon on your disk drive.

Large computer installations generally have special anti-static flooring or carpets. (One can buy anti-static spray for existing

2. Sometimes more than "once in a while." I once brought a small computer into a printshop to do some work. Every time one of the big presses started up—which was about six times an hour—the computer fouled up.

carpets, too.) While this is not a major problem with small computers, most manufacturers recommend keeping the machinery in a rugless room.

4. *Magnetism.* Magnetic waves kill computers. Let us say that you have taken 10 million little iron balls and arranged them on the table to spell out the third act of King Lear. What happens if a strong magnet is passed over your creation? Well, exactly the same thing happens to all the little particles on the surface of the tape or disk in your computer in a magnetic field, and, just as with the iron balls, the information is gone forever.

This can be a major problem, not because of fiends who sneak into people's houses armed with giant electro-magnets, but rather because there are hidden magnets at work all around you. Virtually all electric motors are magnetic to some extent—even the ones in your computer, disk drives, tape recorder, and printer. It is wise housekeeping practice, indeed, never to leave disks out and about, especially near typewriters and other office machinery, telephones, television sets, air conditioners, stereos (especially the loud speakers), or any other electrical stuff.

5. *X-rays.* The only place one needs to worry about X-rays is when carrying computers or computer tapes or disks through an airline check-in device. Most of the people to whom I have talked have had no problem when they asked to have their portable computer or box of disks *not* X-rayed. One woman, however, told me that she was not even allowed to bring her Osborne onto a plane; it had to travel as checked baggage. One wonders why. ("Take this plane to Havana or I'll compute the value of pi to 400 places!")

125.
Magnetism is the worst enemy of computers. It erases or distorts electronic information. And there are magnets all over the place, especially in stereo speakers and many electric motors.

Mechanical problems

Even though many computers are advertised as having "only seven moving parts," or something equally impressive, the fact is that they also have thousands of *non-moving* parts. Many of these non-moving parts are either soldered or otherwise fastened to other non-moving parts.

Anything that has been fastened to something else has the potential for becoming unfastened. And, of course, anything that can potentially happen, probably will.

Other terrible things can happen when a computer is jostled, jarred, banged, or shaken. But the most common thing is to have soldered connections come undone. When this happens, there is the potential for a major problem, because while the re-soldering itself might take 30 seconds and a nickel's worth of material, it can take a $50-an-hour technician two hours to find the broken connection.

The watchword, then, is to treat your machinery as gently as possible. When big computers have to be moved, they are carried in elaborate and expensive vans that are virtually giant self-propelled boxes full of foam rubber. The same care should be taken with small machinery—even (or perhaps especially) that which is supposed to be portable.

Another concern: there are so many little parts in a big computer, some of them can fail, and the machine will still work in certain ways. It may be quite a while after a jostle that a problem appears. I once had a computer moved about 150 miles. The allegedly-experienced movers used an unpadded van. Disaster. For literally years afterwards, problems were attributed to the effects of that fateful move.

Once, I found myself in a most amusing (as well as distressing) "Catch 22" situation. I lived about 150 miles from the nearest repair depot for a certain computer. A service call, including the repairman's driving time at $60 an hour, would have cost at least $400. So I opted for their "walk-in" service ("stagger-in" would be more appropriate, inasmuch as I had to climb a long flight of stairs carrying a 90-pound machine). The first time I brought it in for repairs, they diagnosed the problem as loose connections, and fixed same. By the time I got it home, it was not working. When I brought it back, they said, "The connections must have come loose from jostling on your way home." After this scenario had

126.

Computers have very few moving parts, but they have thousands of stationary parts. It may only take a minute to repair a loose connection, but it may take an expensive technician a long time to find it. Move computers as little as possible, and gently when you do.

If it works, it's out of date.

—Stafford Beer

repeated itself twice more, it was clear that I was in a hopeless situation. The very act of taking the computer home from the repair facility was precipitating the next breakdown. Faced either with moving my office to a corner of the repair depot or getting rid of the machine, I sold it—to a business just a few miles from the repair place.

Human beings can cause problems

Many computer books or manuals for beginners contain a reassuring statement like this: "No matter what you do, it is impossible to damage the computer itself because of programming or other minor errors on your part."

I don't want to alarm you unduly, but that isn't totally accurate. In the course of talking to hundreds of people who had computer problems, I learned of two kinds of problems that were achieved by beginners or near-beginners who were quite astonished by the havoc they were able to wreak.

The more commonly occurring problem arose from putting a disk into a disk drive incorrectly. Disks are square, and have two sides, so there are eight ways they can go into the necessary slot. Only one is correct (or two, in the case of some disks). Inserting a disk incorrectly is akin to rubbing a cat's hair the wrong way. The disk may get all scrunched up, and manage to throw the pick-up head out of alignment—an annoying and often expensive problem. (A few brands of disks actually indicate on the label how they are to be inserted, but most do not. Pity.)

There are eight ways to put a disk into a disk drive—only one of them correct.

Although it is said to be impossible to write a program that will destroy a computer, three novices told me that they nearly did just that. Apparently what they did was, in effect, write a program that told the disk-reading head to "Go to point A" and, when it got there, "Go to point B" and when it got there, "Go to point A," and so on, literally *ad infinitum,* except the mechanical parts will wear out or fall off long before infinity arrives. In fact, probably by next Wednesday.

Another common error wrought by humans is that of inserting or removing a disk from a disk drive while the drive is still turning. This has roughly the same effect as removing a phonograph record from the turntable without lifting the tone arm. Never insert or remove a disk while the red "drive in use" light is on.

127.
Although some people dispute this, it seems actually to be possible to write a program that will physically damage a computer.

This is an unsolicited testimonial for 'Elephant' brand computer disks. The disks themselves seem quite nice—but then so do everyone else's. But the Elephant people do two things no other disk-maker does, for which they are to be commended: Every disk has a special label with big red arrows, to diminish the chance of putting it into the disk drive the wrong way. And every disk holder, or envelope, has these valuable and well-written instructions.

Aside from dropping it to the floor or pouring yogurt into the works, the only other common problems that can be wrought by humans involve turning a computer off at inappropriate times. If a computer is turned off while it is doing something, it may not only fail to complete its task (adding, sorting, printing, etc.), but may also destroy or foul up the data it was working with. The effect is equivalent to turning off the lights when the juggler has six plates in the air at once. Absence of whirring or clicking noise is not good evidence; many computers do important things silently. Normally the screen will tell you when a certain task has been completed.

NEVER FORGET.

Even though we guarantee your Elephant Flexible Disks to meet or beat all industry standards, we can't promise they'll forever retain their memory—unless you promise you'll forever do (or don't do) the following things:

1. DON'T TOUCH THE SHINY PARTS. (The exposed "plastic" slits or dots that show through the black paper liner.) And don't touch them with anything. They're vulnerable to fingerprints, dust, coffee spills, cigarette ashes, sneezes, and maybe even dirty looks. The best way to keep things from touching them is to keep the disks inside their protective sleeves whenever you're not actually using them.

2. DON'T JAM THEM INTO THEIR SLOTS. Ease them gently into their drives, so they don't bend, scratch, or otherwise become offended.

3. BEWARE OF MAG-NETISM. The disk's "memory" comes from a critical arrangement of the tiny magnetic particles on the disk's surface. Therefore, exposing the disk to close contact with any kind of magnetic field (which you'll find in and around television sets, electric motors that run fans, typewriters, air conditioners, etc., as well as the coils in most loudspeakers) can muck up the arrangement of particles—and your disk will end up either with amnesia or madness.

4. HANDLE LIKE GLASS. Which means don't bend them, sit on them, drop things on them, use them to prop up table legs, etc. If you do so, they will spite you.

5. KEEP THEM COM-FORTABLE. Meaning between 50°F to 125° Fahrenheit (10° to 52° Celsius). Intense heat or cold can cause lost memory or weakened sensitivity. As an egregious generality, though, if the room's comfortable enough for you, it's more than comfortable enough for your disks.

6. IF IT'S IMPORTANT, COPY IT. Let's face it: the information on the disk is usually worth a whole lot more than the price of the disk. (Just in man-hours alone to re-create the stored information, let alone in what it could cost you if something like your entire accounts receivable file should all of a sudden "forget.") So by all means, if the data is valuable, make a copy of the disk and store it someplace safe—like a deposit box or fireproof vault.

Made in U.S.A.
© 1981 Leading Edge® Products, Inc., Canton, MA 02021

Poor Disk Management
Can Cause Problems

Admittedly, that advice does not precisely fit in the category, as promised on the cover, of "things I wish someone had told me . . ." The precise category of this one is, "Things a lot of people and books told me, which I agree with, and know as well as I know my own name, and have vowed to do, but don't."

Here is the situation.

Let us say you have just finished a long session at the computer, typing in names and addresses, or writing a story, or entering medical data, or doing your income taxes. When it's time to stop, all your work is now stored on plastic—either a disk or a cassette tape. What happens if that disk or tape is lost, stolen, or destroyed by fire? Clearly, it represents *at least* the loss of a vast amount of time and energy.

It can be far, far worse than that. For example, businesses that have lost their customer lists or accounts receivable records have gone bankrupt. Doctors who lost their patient records have prescribed medicine to which there was a fatal allergy.

The solution is so obvious, it is almost trivial: copy your tapes or disks and store the copies elsewhere.

It is, one might say, as obvious as the fact that wearing seatbelts saves lives, and that smoking cigarettes causes lung cancer.

We humans are really peculiar creatures—90% of us don't wear our seat belts; tens of millions of us suck on tubes of burning vegetation; and vast legions of us don't take that extra minute at the end of a session with the computer to perform the simple acts that will prevent disaster.

The reason, of course, is that no one expects the disaster to be their own. (I was once hired to write a slogan for a big safety organization. My unwieldy but accurate creation was, "If they had been asked one minute before the fatal crash, none of the 250,000 people who died without seatbelts on in cars last year would ever have expected to die in a car crash. But they all did.")

Oddly, the thing that most people, including yours truly, regularly do is diligently make a copy of their data—and then store it on the shelf alongside the original.[3] Admittedly, this fits in the

128.

Always copy all disks and tapes and always store the copies somewhere else. If you only do this 99% of the time, then the 100th time will be the time that amazing events happen and you will lose all your data.

---

3. This isn't *quite* as crazy as it sounds. At least if one set of data is destroyed by the computer, there will be a back-up set—*which should immediately itself be copied!*

same behavioral bin as wearing your raincoat under your clothes, or storing the key to your safe in your safe for safekeeping. But faced with the alternative of making a copy of the data, and transporting it all the way to my garage, where I have a fireproof file box . . . well, there are always good reasons at the time. I'll try to do better, I really will. And so should you.

One of the most tragic of the many "lost data" stories is that of the big hospital in Canada that installed a sophisticated computer in its X-ray department. More than 50,000 crucial patient records were entered. There was a rigorously-enforced procedure to make and verify a copy of the Master Tape every day, and then to store the copy in another building on the hospital grounds. When the X-ray wing of the hospital burned to the ground one night, in the debris was found the charred remains of the Master Tape . . . and alongside it, the charred remains of the back-up tape.

The stone age may return on the gleaming wings of science.

—Winston Churchill

Handle disks only by the edge.

The Nature of Problems

The Dreaded 99% Factor

Is something that works 99% of the time satisfactory? "It all depends," said the statistician (who later drowned in a river with an average depth of nine inches). If your car worked 99% of the time, that means you'd have it for all but 3.667 days of the year, which isn't bad. If a baseball player got on base 99% of the time, even George Steinbrenner wouldn't fire him.

But suppose you had a pair of shoes that were comfortable 99% of the time—meaning that every hundredth step you took caused agonizing pains to shoot up your leg? And how about a game of Russian roulette in which you win 99% of the time. Is that good enough? Suppose, for instance, there were 100 guns on a table, and only one was loaded. What would it take to get you to pick one up at random and fire it at yourself?

Yup. There are times and places when a 1% "error" rate isn't *nearly* good enough. And the world of computers is one of those places.

I have been involved in many situations in which a computer expert assured me something or other could be done. "Piece of cake" is a phrase much favored by such people. And then what happened was a 99% success rate, which turned out to be exactly the same as total failure. Let me explain.

One example: I had purchased WordStar, a quite complex and very popular word processing program, on an 8″ disk. When I converted to a system using 5-1/4″ disks, it was necessary to convert the programs and files onto the smaller disks. Could this be done? "Piece of cake," they said. Just like copying a 90-minute tape cassette onto two 45-minute cassettes. No problem.

Well, for reasons that I have never understood, the copy was 99% accurate. With our name and address records, that was barely tolerable. One wrong letter out of 100. No big deal if "Washington" comes out "Sashington." (Of course if it puts an "S" instead

129.

In the performance of a computer, 99% accuracy isn't nearly good enough. The difference between 99% and 100% is huge.

It figures that if you can go out and buy a Julia Child cookbook, follow the directions and get a respectable souffle, there's no reason why you should settle for less from millions of dollars worth of machine.

—Suzanne Garment

of a "W" in Mr. Whitman's name and you may have lost a customer or gained a law suit.)

But where the 99% factor really did us in was with regard to special commands in the program. All characters are not created equal. Say you came to a fork in the road, and there you saw a sign like this:

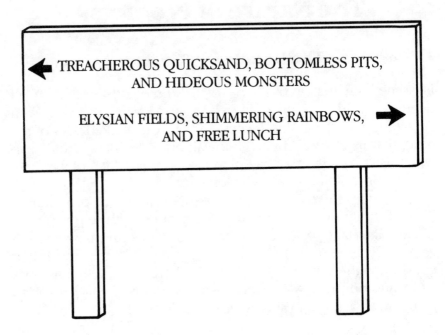

This sign has about 100 characters. They are *not* equal in importance. If the third "O" fell off, the message "BOTTMLESS PITS" is still pretty clear. But if both the arrows were missing, your afternoon hike would have a 50-50 chance of turning quite unpleasant.

It is the same in a program when the 1% turns out to be a key command character, not just an ordinary letter.

For example, when my WordStar was converted, one of the things that was lost was the command that told it to *stop* under-lining. To underline a word in the text, there is a symbol you put in front of the word or words, telling the computer to underline everything until a certain symbol is encountered again a little later on. My converted WordStar never stopped once it started. I wanted to underline *one* word, and ended up with a manuscript with *4,216* consecutive underlined words.

That's one of the more explainable errors. Most of them were too complex or esoteric for me to understand. But the simple fact was that the converted WordStar did not work satisfactorily, and I abandoned it.

I have subsequently had, read about, and been told about dozens of examples of distressing situations involving the 99% factor. Of course sometimes it is 97% or 99.5% or even 99.9%, but the principle is always the same.

There is no heavier burden than a great potential.

—Linus (Peanuts)

As a professional musician who was attempting to use his home computer to compose music put it to me, there are at least 50,000 separate pieces of information in the orchestral score to Tschaikovsky's 1812 Overture. If the second oboe misses one command (note), no one will ever notice. But if the guy who fires the cannon misses one command, the whole piece is ruined.

Dealing with the 99% factor

It can't be avoided; it can only be acknowledged and understood. It is the reason one should never buy brand new programs or equipment (see page 25, Never Be the First Kid on Your Block . . .). And it should be taken into consideration whenever data are being manipulated in any fashion: transferred from one place to another, copied, printed out, revised, whatever. The difference between 99% and 100% is huge. Much, much bigger than the difference between 98% and 99%. You have every right to demand and expect 100%, just as the pilot of a single-engine plane has the right to demand and expect 100% of his or her engines to work. Anything less is unsatisfactory. Sadly, many people are so pitifully grateful to have the 99%, they don't insist on the 100%.

The Incompatibility Problem

There was a kid in our high school whose main claim to fame was that he had a small collection of 11″ 27-1/2-RPM phonograph records. In the late 1940s, when "long playing" recording technology was just becoming available, there were no industry standards. Different manufacturers and inventors were experimenting with various sizes and speeds. Pat's father had reasoned that Americans were used to the 11″ size (the height of ordinary typing paper), and to put precisely one hour of sound on an 11″ disk (which *also* seemed logical) required a speed of 27-1/2 RPM.

Thankfully for us, if not for Pat's father, all the record and phonograph manufacturers got together and agreed on a size and a speed, and that is why your 12" 33-1/3 RPM records can be played on virtually any record player now being manufactured.

Unfortunately, there never were any agreements among computer makers and program makers. In fact, if anything, they went in the opposite direction. For many years, for instance, IBM had its own unique systems that were compatible with nothing else, except other IBM machines — the theory being that once you got all your data entered, you were an IBM captive for life.

So we have reached a point where there are, amazingly enough, more than *10,000* different variations possible in the way that information can be stored on a small computer disk or tape.

130.

There are major compatibility problems among the various brands of computers analogous to having long-playing records of many different sizes and speeds.

Please understand, I am not referring to the *content* of the disk, but just the way it is structured. It is as if long playing phonograph records were made in 100 different sizes and 100 different speeds (= 10,000 variations). A 42-5/8 RPM 9-3/4" disk *might* play on a 43-1/4 RPM 9-1/4" turntable, or it might not, and even if it did, it might sound funny.

If this were the case, undoubtedly entrepreneurs would spring forth, offering devices to slow down or speed up turntables, and services to "reformulate" beloved records onto disks of different sizes.

Well, that sorry state of affairs is just where we are in small computers. *Some* of those 10,000+ variations will work on systems set up to handle *other* variations — sometimes quite well, and sometimes with minor or major problems. Sometimes information can be moved from a disk with one of the 10,000 variations to a disk with another set — and sometimes this works well, sometimes slightly, and often not at all.

In my experience, computer experts are far more confident than they have any right to be about compatibility. I have either experienced, or been told of dozens of situations in which a promised compatibility was, in fact, quite incompatible, or, perhaps worse, tantalizingly almost-compatible (the 99% factor).

Here are seven of the factors which can vary from system to system, and which may contribute to incompatibility:

1. *Size of disk.* Most small computers use either 5-1/4" or 8" diameter disks, which are not interchangeable. There are a few systems that work on 2" "microdisks" and, recently, a few with

Altering disk size is
impractical.

3-1/2″ "hard disks," all incompatible with each other. Data theoretically *can* be moved from one size to another, but not always reliably.

2. *Density of disk.* Ordinary disks are single-density. A given amount of information can be stored on them. Double-density disks are the same size, and look the same, but it is possible to store twice as much information in the same space on them. Single-density disks may work on a double-density machine, but not vice versa.

3. *Sides to disk.* Some disks have a recording surface on one side only. Others can record on both sides. A double-sided disk drive can handle single-sided disks as well, but not the reverse.

4. *Sectors on disk.* Information is stored in little electronic "corrals" on the disks. The way in which they are arranged can affect whether or not the information can be found and retrieved. A 16-sector system won't be able to find things on a 13-sector disk. There are special programs (my favorite is called Muffin) that quite reliably deal with this problem.

5. *Hard or soft sector.* This refers to the number of "index" holes drilled in the disk, to help guide the computer mechanism to find any given part of the disk. Hard sector disks have lots of holes; soft have only one. I have no idea which is better, or why; I only know that they are not compatible with each other.

6. *Memory size.* This is discussed in detail on page 78. A disk produced on a computer with a larger memory may not work properly on a machine with a smaller memory.

7. *Different disk operating systems.* The Disk Operating System (or DOS, pronounced to rhyme with "loss") is a set of instructions that tells the computer how to interact with the disks. DOS's are complex things. DOS manuals run into hundreds of pages. The same computer *can* run on various DOS's, but problems can arise when data entered under one DOS are dealt with using another DOS.

131.

There is a lot of hardware and software one can buy to overcome incompatibility problems, but don't expect 100% accuracy.

What to do about incompatibility

There are several things that can be *tried* — but with no assurance of success. This is the area where the dreaded "99% factor" is most apparent. There are possible solutions with both hardware and software.

1. *Hardware solutions.* Various manufacturers have devised electronic devices that can be installed in computers to make

them do things the original designers didn't have in mind. For instance, there are many desirable programs that will only run in an operating system called CP/M. For a mere $400 or so, it is possible to buy a little unit that plugs into slots inside certain small computers that enable them to run CP/M programs. Comparable units exist for other "emulations" (means of allowing one computer to emulate another).

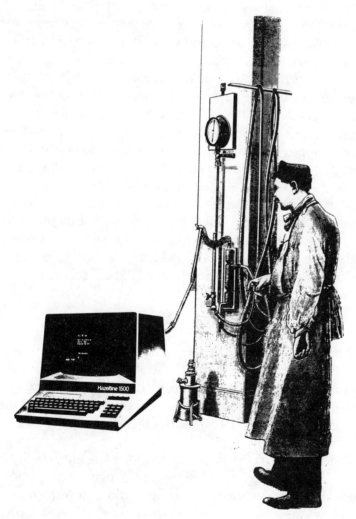

2. *Software solutions.* Apple, for instance, offers a special "Basics" disk which, when run, temporarily turns a newer model Apple (which requires 16-sector disks) into an older model Apple (which required 13-sector disks). That sort of thing. There is a

whole series of fairly expensive programs, called "Move-It" which are designed to permit one model of computer to "talk" to another. One can buy, for instance, an "Osborne to TRS-80" Move-It; an "IBM to Kay-Pro" Move-It, and so on. Not everything can be moved thus, and not everything moved arrives in precisely the same condition in which it left (the old 99% thing again), but I've heard from quite a few happy Move-It users.

3. *Modem solutions.* Modems, which allow computers to interact by telephone, are described elsewhere (on page 82). An interesting side effect of modems is that when data has been "translated" into the special electronic form necessary to pass over telephone lines, it may be possible to "fool" the data into moving into a new home when it arrives at the other end. For instance, even though there is no way to use Apple disks on an IBM Personal Computer, people have told me that when they send their Apple data through a modem, if the computer at the other end of the phone is an IBM, not an Apple, much of the data will, in fact, settle in on the IBM. But not all.

Clearly, there are some situations in which problems of incompatibility have been solved, or resolved. But there are an awful lot more that continue to cause confusion and distress.

Will there *ever* be industry-wide standards? Don't hold your breath. It's on the list right after 27-1/2-RPM 11" records.

Software Failure

In my earlier years in the computer wars, I used to be surprised at how often there were errors in the software I was using. The errors ranged from relatively minor (but annoying) occasions in which directions were incorrect, or columns of numbers did not line up evenly, to total disasters in which huge quantities of data were lost forever.

132.
Software is often sold with major errors because it is difficult and expensive to pre-test it in all the ways people will use it.

As one more accustomed to books than electronic data, I knew that a publisher would never knowingly issue a book with chapters missing, an incorrect index, and a few pages upside down. How, then, could a software "publisher" sell a program with obvious errors in it?

The answer, I have learned, is that it is virtually impossible to test a software program in all the different ways that a customer is likely to use it. It's like some of the product recalls you read about. The doll company may have tested and "childproofed" its new Winking Wendy 17 ways from Sunday. Then some three-year-old discovers that Soldier Sam's combat boot is precisely the right size and shape to pry off Wendy's head, does so, swallows it, and subsequently expires.

Once, for example, I bought a well-reviewed mailing list program, to store names and addresses, print labels, etc. It worked just fine for the first few weeks. Then one day, it utterly failed, in the most alarming way. More than 1,000 names and addresses had been typed in, and suddenly, none of them was there any more. Furthermore, the copy we had faithfully made was ruined, too.

What had happened was this: the company that developed this program had tested it thoroughly on lists of a few dozen names. It worked splendidly. But what they did *not* know was that when the very key was struck that filled the disk to capacity, a series of events was triggered that erased the disk — and failed to notify the user. Midway through our 1,117th name, then, the disk erased itself, but we didn't know this, so we went blithely on, typing in dozens more names, and then made a perfect copy of our now-blank disk.

The supplier was appropriately chagrined. They had not felt the need to test the "disk full" situation. Too bad, they said, and promised to send us a corrected disk when they had solved the problem. What about the $100 in labor costs to re-enter all those records? Too bad, they said again.

As it turned out, the new disk they eventually sent was labelled "Version 2.6" which meant it was probably the 17th revised version (1.0 to 1.9, then 2.0 to 2.6). Clearly we were not the only people finding errors.

Not all software failures are quite so devastating. Many are minor annoyances, and quite a few simply require making notes in the instructions to the effect that at a certain point, for instance, one must hit the 'return' button twice instead of just once, as printed. (See page 194, "Don't Ask Why . . ." for more on this.)

The important point here is that when something dreadful happens, many beginners immediately assume that *they* must somehow be at fault. Not neccessarily so. And it isn't just the low-priced small-company software that is less than perfect. IBM, for instance, sold many thousands of its Personal Computers with a word processing program that turned out to have numerous defects, and was finally recalled and replaced.

What, then, do you do if you believe you have defective soft-

133.
The newer the software, the more errors it will have. Early buyers are usually the guinea pigs.

ware? Despite the miserable warranties generally offered, I've found most software houses quite reasonable about making adjustments—at least to the extent of replacing something defective with something less defective (or, in not a few cases, with something just as defective, but in different ways).

Since all it takes to develop software is a small home computer and a good brain, some software "companies" turn out to be one person, sometimes a precocious teenager, working out of his or her kitchen. When you telephone the company and the phone is answered, "Hello," this is probably the reason. One-person companies are likely to be very kind and often helpful, but they are much more limited in the help they can provide if the problem turns out to be an extremely complex one, involving the logic of the program itself.

And if all else fails, there is always the Computer Consumer Karate (see page 225).

A Tiny Error Can Be Incredibly Disastrous

134.

Tiny, almost invisible little programming errors can destroy a large business.

The annals of communication are full of horror stories in which a tiny little error had a devastating effect. A probable error in translating a Japanese statement may have led to the atom bombing of Nagasaki. A typing error, "He is no*t* in London," instead of "He is no*w* in London," caused an international incident. Jimmy Carter's translator had him saying, in Polish, "I want to make love to the Polish people," instead of "I love the Polish people." And so on. For want of a noun the sentence was lost; for want of a sentence the meaning was lost, etc.

The mushrooming effect of tiny errors is nowhere better seen than in computer programming. A "+" where a "−" is wanted can, if not caught, give a company incorrect financial information that might result in its ruin.

Are such things always found? Not on your life. In many perfect crimes, not only will the culprit never be caught, the very nature of the crime may never be known. Similarly, some of the worst computer disasters are still hidden in the electronic circuits of a machine.

I can think of no better example than the wee little mistake that cost me $40,000. Before *and* after the tragic events, I would have said that it was impossible that such things could happen. Surely two intelligent men (my partner at that time was a bank president) could never let such a thing go so far, unnoticed. Not so. Here is what happened:

Our business was selling books by mail. We ran advertisements. People would write in with orders, and we would send them books. As our business grew, we installed a computer, in part to help us keep track of which advertisements were producing the most orders.

We decided to find out whether offering an "800" free telephone ordering service would increase our business. We ran a few test advertisements with an 800 phone number in it. It was, of course, essential that we carefully keep track of the number of telephone orders, to compare them with the number of orders by mail.

Our programmer fixed things so we could enter a "T" on the computer to indicate a telephone order, and the weekly report the computer prepared would keep a separate tally of the T's.

Within a month, it appeared that we had a winner. We were getting hundreds of "T" orders. So we began putting the 800 number in all our ads. The $1.25 per call we were paying the 800 service company was clearly a good investment.

When the time came to do our income taxes, nearly a year later, it was very clear that something was terribly wrong. All the extra money that *should* have come in from the telephone orders wasn't there.

Finally, we learned that due to a bizarre programming error, *all* orders received on even numbered days of the month were tallied as telephone orders, while *all* orders received on odd days were tallied as mail orders. The 800 service had not increased the number of orders one iota. People simply ordered by phone instead of by mail. But the computer was telling us otherwise.

By the time we learned this, we had paid for an astonishing 32,000 telephone calls, at $1.25 each, for a totally unnecessary expenditure of $40,000.

We later heard that the programming company had fired the programmer who made the blunder. But there was no question of trying to get our lost money back, because we had signed the "standard" contract, saying, in effect, that no matter *what* the programmers did, up to and perhaps including selling our daugh-

Like sex drives, card tricks, and the weather, computers tend to be discussed in terms of results rather than processes, which makes them rather scary.

—Martin Mayer

ters into white slavery, we could not take legal action.

Could this disaster have been prevented? It would be nice to think that a militant, vigilant manager would have caught the problem early on, but I am not optimistic about that. The error was so subtle, the programming company so sure of itself, and the results so plausible, we had no reason to be suspicious.

Recently, some larger computers were recalled because, after several years, someone discovered they were deleting every 40,000th "9." Can you imagine some of the subtle problems *that* caused!

The main lesson learned is the crucial one stated forcefully on page 115: Whenever you start something new with a computer, keep a parallel, non-computerized system going, regardless of the bother and expense, until you are 100% certain that the computer is working correctly.

Don't Ask Why, Just Keep on Going

I have had literally hundreds of experiences in which the following sequence of events happened:

1. Something undesirable happens. The printer doesn't print. The disk drive doesn't stop whirling when it should. The moon-landing rocket crashes when it should have landed smoothly. The alphabetizing program produces Z through A instead of A through Z. Any one of scores of unwanted events.

2. I do many things. I read the instructions. I check that everything is plugged in right. I repeat the procedure (and it still fails). I ask questions of friends or the ceiling, whichever is closer. I fret. I think evil thoughts. I try again and again, and it still doesn't do what it should. Then suddenly, unexpectedly . . .

3. It all works perfectly. I haven't the remotest idea why. Was it something I did? Was it passage of time, allowing something to cool down (or warm up?) Had I made the same mistake over and over again until now? Were my prayers answered?

135.

Many problems somehow correct themselves. It is usually a poor use of time to try to figure out what happened and why; plow onward gratefully.

At this point, there is an overwhelming temptation to stop what you were originally doing, and to try to find out what went wrong and why or how it was corrected. I strongly advise against this. To attempt to do so is almost always extremely time consuming and, worse, totally unproductive.

My father, who was an accountant in his early years, once worked for a boss who insisted that the books balance each month down to the last penny. If, after totalling thousands of complex transactions (without a computer!) the two sides of the ledger were off by three cents, dozens of hours of work were put in to find the discrepancy. Hundreds and hundreds of dollars to find a few pennies.

For some people, this kind of perfection is a necessity — or at least a worthy goal. For most, it simply doesn't make sense.

So it is with trying to find out what went wrong with the computer *after* it is no longer wrong. (The exception, of course, is when the same wrong thing happens over and over again, in which case it *is* important to know why.) But the great majority of computer mysteries are one-time-only events, so even if you *could* figure out why the disk drive didn't turn on or the paper jammed or you typed a "w" and got an "m" or why you lost the car keys or what happened to Amelia Earhart, it might be momentarily gratifying, but in the long run, as well as in the medium and short run, it won't do you any good.

Psychological Problems

The Causes of Anguish

Some people *want* to be told if they have terminal cancer. Others never want to know. Some people *want* to know if they're going to be surrounded by child beggars on their trip to the Taj Mahal; some people even open the brown envelope from the IRS before the rest of the mail.

In other words, there are people who want to plan for the worst, well in advance, because it helps them deal with the problems if and when they come.

Elsewhere, I discuss the matter of how to *deal* with anguish and despair. Some people will want to know the kinds of things that *cause* the anguish, because it may help them prepare, if only psychologically, for the hazards that lie along the road.

For those people, I have some things to say about the four kinds of situations that have caused me the most distress, and how I dealt with them. Those who wish to fly blind may proceed at once to the section on sugarplum fairies, puppies, word games, paper folding tricks, and chocolate chip cookies.[1]

Working with accurate but poor instructions

When I was very young, my grandfather bought me a book on how to play chess. It started out telling me that the king was the tallest figure, and the bishop had a slot in it, and there were 32 black squares alternating with 32 white squares. By about page three, it was discussing the merits of the *en passant* strategy that Capablanca used in Havana, 1927, as contrasted with Keres' use of mid-game center-board strategy.

---

1. That section is not in this book. Watch for it in the forthcoming sequel, "166 Wholesome Activities to Occupy Your Time at the State Home for Former Computer Enthusiasts."

The same author—or someone that he has trained—is now busily engaged in writing computer instructions. I am no longer surprised, but am regularly annoyed and often depressed by the very poor quality of the written materials that accompany computer-related products.

Consider just one example out of the dozens that I have done battle with in recent years.

The 187-page manual for my word processing program starts out like this:

> "People write words and sentences on pieces of paper to store them for future use. The computer uses magnetic diskettes for the same purpose . . . We don't have to worry about how the computer physically uses the Test Files, any more than we need to worry about how the computer can turn our thoughts into bits and bytes . . ."

I was encouraged. Perhaps an English-speaking human was writing to me. But by page 35, I was faced with prose like this:

> "Memory End/256 . . . where HIMEM is. When the parameter is 150, HIMEM is in its normal location at $9600. This number is reduced when special printer drivers or the spooling module are loaded above HIMEM."

Working with inaccurate instructions

This is sort of like working for days on a mammoth jigsaw puzzle, and then discovering that the last three pieces are missing. The frustration of doing an immense amount of work, in attempting to learn a complex new procedure, and then coming upon a missing instruction, or a clearly incorrect instruction, is highly distressing. To *not* come upon it, and learn sometime later that the reason for continued failure had nothing to do with one's own inadequacies, but rather with the inadequacy of the instruction writer, is devastating, and probably ulcer-producing.

Obvious equipment failure

The only thing more distressing to me than obvious equipment failure is this:

136.
It isn't that you're dumb; it's that most instruction manuals are badly written, incomplete, and/or inaccurate.

137.
Computers are capable of subtle, extremely difficult to detect errors, such as changing every 19th "7" into a "3".

Non-obvious equipment failure

This is the computer equivalent of walking around all day with your slip showing, or a huge crumb in your mustache[2] or a "kick me" sign that someone has stuck on your back.

Although there are supposed to be "error messages" that flash to tell you when something is going wrong, this does not always happen—sometimes because the kind of error is one that does not have detectors, and sometimes because the error detection system is, itself, malfunctioning. Elsewhere, I recount the disaster when the "disk full" message didn't come on, and I blithely typed in thousands of words that were lost forever—the computer equivalent of putting ten gallons of gasoline in a full tank.

Sometimes the problem can be far more subtle. One man told me how his computer once deleted a whole bunch of sevens from his billing statements. A customer who really owed him $179, for instance, would get a bill for $19. A woman novelist remembered the time her word processor, with a poetic license of its own, duplicated certain sentences and inserted them elsewhere in the manuscript. And there is the classic case, well known in psychological research circles, where a high school's computer printed students' locker numbers in the space where their I.Q. was supposed to go. (The reason it is a classic case is because no one noticed the error at the time, but at the end of the year, the students with the highest locker numbers got the best grades.)

... 85% of the horse-drawn vehicle industry of the country is untouched by the automobile . . . In 1906–1907, and coincident with an enormous demand for automobiles, the demand for buggies reached the highest tide in its history. The man who predicts the downfall of the automobile is a fool; the man who denies its great necessity . . . is a bigger fool; but the man who predicts the general annihilation of the horse and his vehicle is the greatest fool of all.

—Speech at National Association of Carriage Builders, 1907

Price Shock Syndrome

I may have been the first person in all the world to buy a digital watch. As all gadget historians know, they went on sale in the summer of 1973 in selected stores. I got mine at Tiffany's in New York the morning of their first day. It was a Hamilton Pulsar. It cost $350. It displayed the time in red numbers when you pushed a button. And it seemed to weigh about 14 pounds.

It made me very happy.

Within a year, the price had fallen to under $200, and there were some models available that also gave the date. I looked at them wistfully, but without major regrets.

Within three years, the price was down to about $79, including

---

2. If you have a crumb in your mustache *and* your slip is showing, then you've *really* got problems.

a stop watch. With much sadness, I retired the Pulsar to a drawer, where it reposes today, and bought myself one of the new ones. After all, I then thought, how much cheaper, and how much more complicated, could they possibly get?

The answer, of course, lies in the fact that there is an army of at least 40,000 creative engineers at the Casio factory alone, whose only role in life is to figure out how to put more and more stuff into a watch at a lower and lower price. My present watch, two years old and already obsolete, merely has a four function calculator, an alarm, a stop watch, and a Space Invaders game. (It tells the time, too.) It cost $39. But the newer ones have a five-language dictionary, complex mathematical functions, play tunes, and monitor heartbeat and temperature. When the model that stores 100 phone numbers and tells me when the salmon fishing is good off the coast comes along, I'll probably have to buy it. That is, if it's under $20.

The point of all this is that prices are changing in the electronics world at a rate unprecedented in history. Sixty years ago, it cost about 200 days' salary to buy a Model T Ford — and today it costs about 200 days salary to buy a new Ford. In gold rush times, an ounce of gold bought a good new suit. It still does. But less than ten years after the first electronic four-function calculator went on sale for $800, you can walk into any drugstore or supermarket and buy, for under $20, a pocket device that can do more than the huge million-dollar "automatic brains" of the 1940s.

How do people respond to this sort of thing? Some with unbridled joy. Some with annoyance or anger.

Everybody knows someone whose great grandfather traded half of Los Angeles for a half interest in a Chinese laundry, or made some other transaction that, in retrospect, was not a wonderful deal. I had an uncle who rejected a 50-50 partnership offered by an ambitious young chocolate salesman named Milton Hershey and regretted it all his life. And of course there is the standard "I knew it. I just *knew* it" response when a certain stock goes up or the roulette wheel stops on number 21.

Such people are prime candidates for developing ulcers and turning into crotchety old geezers.

It never makes sense to a person who is suffering miserably when someone says, "You'll get over it soon — no one ever died of a broken heart (or a common cold, or whatever)." I *do* remind myself of this whenever I see a new computer product that is

138.

It is unproductive and unhealthy to bemoan price plunges just after you've bought something. It is also very difficult not to so bemoan.

vastly cheaper than what I have. It doesn't stop me from being a little annoyed—but I can generally put it behind me with either or both of these two thoughts:

1. No one forced me to buy what I have already bought. The price must have been satisfactory to me at that time. The stuff is working pretty well. I don't sit and stew if my neighbor gets a car like mine at a better price. I don't fret that I didn't buy IBM stock when it was $10 a share. And I'm *certainly* not the sort of person who checks the sale ads in the newspaper after I've bought something, to see if I could have gotten it cheaper somewhere else.

2. I have not signed any lifetime contracts. I am fully capable of junking, setting aside, or selling any or all of my computer hardware and software. (For me, however, this has been unexpectedly difficult. See page 266 for more on this.)

The most debilitating form of price shock syndrome is to buy nothing, in the certain knowledge that the price will be less in a month or a year. This topic is covered in detail on page 30, "But Wait!" Sufferers never take into account the pleasure they would have gotten *during* that month or year, or even the money they might have saved by using that particular item of hardware or software for a longer time. It is so simple to say, "If you want it, and if you can afford it, then buy it." It is so much harder actually to *do*.

The "Gee Whiz" Syndrome

Nothing I had done in this life prepared me for the feelings I experienced during my first hours at the COMDEX Show in Las Vegas. Walking through the door into the world's largest computer show, I easily could have believed that I had died and gone to gadget heaven.

I knew that I was not immune to the "Gee Whiz" syndrome— the feeling that overcomes many small computer users when they are suddenly exposed to something that is much more desirable than anything they now own. But I was surrounded by more than 10,000 new items, every one (well, at least 90% of them) infinitely superior to all the junk I was forced to use.

The "Gee Whiz" phenomenon has little to do with price (which can cause psychological problems of its own, as just discussed). It is, I think, a regression to the feeling that first occurred in early childhood when the kid next door got a better doll or

AN EXCLUSIVE OFFER
TO READERS OF THIS PUBLICATION

RECENT developments in micro-component technology now permit us to make available an extraordinary precision device—the KL-1000. Weighing less than one ounce, it is no larger than a domestic olive, yet it performs all the photo-graphic, data-processing, and infor-mation-retrieval functions you your-self do—automatically.

The KL-1000 adjusts to available light, sets shutter speed and aperture, then calculates, displays, and prints out on plain paper tape the cube root of your Social Security number. This is photography made so automatic it leaves you completely "out of the pic-ture." The KL-1000 not only flashes "SAY CHEESE" and "STOP MOVING AROUND" on its unique L.E.D. moni-tor screen, it also warns you that you're not taking enough photographs, advances the film after each exposure, then hot-wires your car to rush the completed roll to the drugstore for processing. Don't feel like capturing those personal moments of your life before forgetting them? Relax. It isn't up to you anymore.

A whole world of precision capabil-ity is out there, waiting to enter your home and your life with this fully integrated, so-much-more-than-a-camera device, so much more than a camera. Micro-fiche-and-chips tech-nology makes it a computer, too—performing virtually all functions, in-cluding logarithms, in Roman numer-als. Its binaural jack accommodates two sets of featherweight headphones, so both you and a friend can roller-skate to Coast Guard channel-depth broadcasts. Its light-activated voice simulator tells you to balance the fam-ily budget, chart stocks and bonds, stop smoking, clean your room, and be con-siderate of others. You can talk back, too: the clip-on dynamic microphone instantly triggers a sustained, loud buzzing—enough to wake the sound-est sleeper—if you say anything at all within a fifty-foot radius of the KL-1000.

Yet that is not all, because disc-and-data fineline crosshair-tronics has en-abled us to program the KL-1000 to do *everything*—and more—automati-cally. Consider these exclusive fea-tures:

AT THE OFFICE. Thanks to mini-laser technopathy, the KL-1000 not only copies any-sized document, it ac-tually vaporizes the original's byline without a trace, and substitutes your own name, sex, political affiliation, and yearly income. Its data-network-access function lets you be part of the grid, too, as it narrowcasts product inventory and inflow-outflow figures directly to your digital watch. The KL-1000A word-processing attach-ment assures perfection every time—misspelled words or computational er-rors are immediately obliterated by its built-in document shredder, which also shorts out all electrical power to the entire building and releases a semi-toxic paralyzing gas. Just get it right the first time, and forget it!

WHILE TRAVELLING. Optional carry-strap lets you wear it on your belt, or leave it in your room—the strap extends to a full half mile, and retains enough water in even the lightest drizzles to provide nooselike snugness and hamper torso circulation. Or remain in the room yourself; the unit travels freely on its own, and will simulate your signature on major pur-chases of clothing, art, and real estate without your even knowing. In every major foreign city, the KL-1000 does it all: orders gourmet meals for twenty while you struggle with the menu, loudly contradicts you in museums, and forwards your souvenir purchases to General Delivery, Lima, Peru. All you do is pay freight and handling. And you need never again worry about destroyed traveller's checks, cancelled credit cards, and misplaced passports —the KL-1000 does all these, and more, while you sleep. In the morn-ing, enjoy your own original composi-tions of up to twelve accordionlike

notes in real music, "the international language." The KL-1000 will record and transcribe these melodies automat-ically, then engrave the notes onto an attractive brass pendant, which it will offer for sale to friends and strangers. Do not worry about accidentally switching off the unit, either, because you can't—not even deliberately.

AT HOME. Self-contained forty-eight-hour timer lets it tell itself when forty-eight hours have elapsed, after which timer resets itself automatically. All you do is hide in a closet. Later, use the microwave transponder attach-ment to receive hitherto unavailable signals from turkeys, roasts, and hams. When no one is home, it plays both eight-track and cassette recordings, switches lights and appliances on and off, and displays random words in Italian on its high-resolution screen. The KL-1000 wards off burglars all night long by announcing, in a voice mathematically similar to your own, "We're awake . . . we're awake . . ." Then, in the morning, it counts your pushups, uses all the hot water, and ignores you at the table. Coffee? Of course. There's even some for you. And don't worry about getting dressed —it gets dressed for everyone, then dials ten frequently called telephone numbers and leaves a short inspira-tional message in your name. All you do is stay undressed, watch, and go back to bed.

Advances in macro-waferonics en-able the KL-1000 to use 3-D graphic simulation to transfer black-and-white computerized likenesses of you and your family to T-shirts, dogs, and fro-zen foods. Switch from audio to visual readout for its smoke-detection mode, and receive a hard-copy sheet reading "SMOKE" when your house burns down.

A DEVICE of state-of-the-art convenience, the KL-1000 has already projected your technological needs and, with funds transferred from your checking or savings account, has purchased itself. It has already ex-pedited its own delivery.

Indeed, the KL-1000 is already in your home or office—over there, near that lamp. It is already on line, shred-ding potatoes and complaining about your posture, automatically. All you do is nothing. Just set it at "HIGH" and run away. You'll never have to do anything else for as long as it lives. — ELLIS WEINER

bike or sled. I think I was seven when my best friend, Bobby Rosenbloom, got an incredible toy garage set with a motorized elevator. I still remember it vividly, and I strongly suspect that seeds of our eventual estrangement were planted that day.[3] In fact, that garage probably produced the strongest "I want it" feelings of my life until that morning at COMDEX. As I walked up and down aisle after aisle (the show literature said it would require three miles of walking to see it all, not including diversions to snack bars and hospitality suites), eyes glazing, shopping bags filling with expensively-produced literature, I began to reflect on the nature of the "Gee Whiz" syndrome I was experiencing. What makes the syndrome possible, of course, is the remarkable rate of progress in the computer field. Ten years after Duryea demonstrated the first practical automobile, cars were still primitive, underpowered, uncomfortable, and unreliable. Ten years after the Wright brothers' flight, airplanes were still a novelty, with no practical or commercial use. But ten years after the first primitive electronic adding machine came on the market at $800, it was possible to go to the supermarket or drugstore and buy a far more sophisticated calculator for one percent of that price.

The different ways people respond to their own personal "Gee Whiz" events can be a major factor in whether or not they have a positive computer experience. My talks with people at computer shows convince me there are three typical kinds of responses:

1. *I must have it right now, no matter what.* There are times for some people when reason flies away in the face of an irrational desire to have something (or do something). Quite a few of the people to whom I have talked, some of them using their small computers for little more than expensive paperweights, reported a feeling like that: "When I saw the color patterns the Apple generated, I simply knew I had to have it. Before I knew what I was doing, I had my Visa card in my hand." "The four-color printer was about three times what I had planned to spend, but I wanted it more than I had ever wanted a piece of machinery, so I bought it on the spot." "When I saw my first Osborne in San Francisco at the show, I knew I would never be happy with anything else, so I ordered one there and then."

Some of these people sounded very much like confused de-

139.

Buying expensive equipment on impulse is a surprisingly common behavior, but rarely a wise one.

---

3. Bobby— if you're reading this, I've gotten over it; we can be friends again. Unless you've got an Epson QX-10 computer.

fendants on the witness stand: "Gee, Your Honor, when I came to my senses, I was standing there with the IBM in my hand, and there was my bank account lying dead on the floor . . ."

In one respect, there is really nothing wrong with this behavior in many cases. It is, at the least, the ultimate answer to the "But Wait!" syndrome. However, carried to excess, impulse buying can be debilitating, both to financial well-being as well as to a harmonious computer life. It really *is* desirable to plan purchases in advance, to shop around for the best deal, etc. But this cannot always be, as I said to myself last week, leaving the store with my new Brother portable electronic typewriter under my arm.

2. *I must have it eventually, and because of that I shan't do anything else until I do have it.* I have witnessed more than a few cases of this electronic equivalent of holding your breath until you turn blue. For example, I have spoken to a businessman who has fallen quite irrationally in love with a Seiko computer system, made by the same company that makes watches. His business is small, and cannot afford the $15,000+ for the Seiko just now, so he is doing his accounts receivable, payroll, and general ledger with pencil, paper, and a mechanical Sears adding machine. He is well aware that a $2,000 to $3,000 expenditure for something in the Osborne – Kay-Pro – Apple – Radio Shack line would be immensely valuable to him now—but he sees that as wasted money, since ultimately the precious Seiko will be his.

I found myself in that obsessional boat once. I knew the exact printer I wanted—a $3,000 Qume. I spent about a month with no printer (for me, operating a computer without a printer is like taking a message over the telephone when you can't find a pencil). I was looking for a good used Qume. I was exploring alternative financing. And I eventually overcame my Qume-or-nothing feeling and got a 1/6-the-price Epson, which served me well for a year or so, until I was able to get the Qume.

3. *I admire it, but* . . . There is, thankfully, a wide gap between "Gee Whiz" and "I must have it." For most people in most situations, there is a quite healthy response to a terrific new product: "That is really splendid. I am delighted to know that engineers have been able to come up with a disk drive powered by chipmunks, that plays the Hallelujah Chorus while accessing disks. Someday I may need one. So I shall file the literature or advertisement away in my 'Gee Whiz' file for further reference."

I left the COMDEX show with seventeen shopping bags full of

Electronic calculators can solve problems which the man who made them cannot solve; but no government-subsidized commission of engineers and physicists could create a worm.

—Joseph Wood Krutch

brochures and literature. When I finally got it sorted out into piles, to file away for further reference, the largest by far was the "Gee Whiz" stuff. It's great fun to look at, and to use for amazing and amusing my friends. And it will be especially enlightening to haul it out after the *next* COMDEX show, to see how many of last year's Gee Whizzes are this year's white elephants.

Dealing With Repairs

Find the Right Kind of Friend
or Support Group

Once, in a weak moment, I bought a do-it-yourself spiral staircase kit by mail, from a company in England. What a disaster. The unintelligibility of the instructions was exceeded only by the difficulty of making the parts fit together properly. I remember quite vividly the feeling of utter alone-ness as I fought this particular monster. No one for 2,000 miles in all directions had ever tried to build one of these things.

In a moment of deep despair, I telephoned the supplier in England, and while he couldn't or wouldn't answer my questions,[1] he at least gave me the names of every other American buyer — all two of 'em. So I telephoned the chap in Pennsylvania and the chap in Massachusetts, who had been having no more luck than I, and we formed what is called a Users Group. We gave each other encouragement, we shared our findings, we were able to keep the others from heading down fruitless paths, and eventually we all had quite satisfactory spiral staircases in our respective homes.

The same kind of thing can and should happen with computers' owners.

It is almost impossible to convey the feeling of utter despair when something terrible is happening to your computer at 10 o'clock on a Friday night of a three-day weekend, and you know you can't reach the dealer until Tuesday morning, which seems impossibly far away. It gives new meaning to "the dark night of the soul." Ask my wife.

Salvation comes in having someone to talk to: a knowledge-

140.

The main value of users' groups is in having someone to call for advice when there are terrible problems late Friday night before a three-day weekend.

---

1. He probably hadn't figured out how to build the damn thing himself. If anyone would like approx. 40 lbs. of apparently-spare spiral staircase parts, please apply to author.

205

able friend or a local (or even not local) users' group. Someone who at best can help you work through the problem, because they may have been there before, and at the very least can commiserate, talk you down, or rush over with a bottle of Scotch, a carton of mint chip ice cream, and/or a new Disk Operating System to replace the one you broke when you fell off your chair when you got the electric shock from trying to adjust the cable that was making the TV screen flicker, setting off an epileptic fit in the cat.

I have two very knowledgeable friends that I can call (long distance, but worth it) when all else has failed. They have made my computer life bearable on many occasions. Thank you, Mike and Julie![2] In many larger cities and towns, there are users' groups or support groups for many popular (and some unpopular) computers, often for much the same reasons. There are Apple Corps, North Star Associations, IBM Clubs, and so forth. Many of the groups publish newsletters or magazines, and there are national coordinating offices (sometimes run or sponsored by the manufacturers) to help the groups stay in touch with one another.

In many respects, they are much like the fan clubs extant for Elvis, James Dean, or the Bee Gees. They share information and gossip, and offer commiseration and even maudlin souvenirs when the focus of the club dies. (I understand the Imsai Users' Group actually held a wake when their company went bankrupt.[3]) If I lived in an area with just one or two users' groups, and if I were in the position of trying to decide which computer to buy, this local representation would be an important factor in my decision.

There are users' groups for different software, or programs as well, such as the WordStar Group, the VisiCalc Group, and so forth.

141.

"RYFMs"—people who don't *Read Your F---ing Manual*—are a major annoyance for dealers and repair services. At least give it a try before making the anguished call.

All About "Riffims"

I was talking to the manager of a computer store when his assistant came over and interrupted us:

"You're wanted on the phone," she said to the manager.

---

2. I'll sell you their phone numbers for fifty bucks each!

3. Imsai used to be one of the largest manufacturers of home computers. Have you ever heard of them? End of poignant history lesson.

"Who is it?"

"I'm afraid it's another riffim."

The manager grimaced, and reached for the telephone, whereupon, with seemingly exaggerated politeness, he proceeded to "talk a customer down" from some horrendous problem he or she was suffering.

Of course I had to ask. The manager blushed quite profusely, and informed me that "riffim" was just a little joke of theirs.

Not quite so.

Diligent research has yielded the information that computer store personnel regularly refer to certain customers as "riffims" (or, more accurately, "ryfms.") "RYFM" stands for *Read Your F------ Manual.*" And so, of course, a riffim is someone who calls up or comes in to buttonhole a store employee when the answer to his or her question is clearly stated in the instruction manual.

When not to be a riffim

It really is a kindness to *try* to read the manual first. There is at least a small chance that the answer can quickly and easily be found. There is a large chance that it cannot — but at least you've made the effort, and you can feel good about explaining to the expert that you *did* try.

When it's OK to be a riffim

Most of the time, actually, if you're willing to stand up for your rights — particularly your right *not* to have to be a technical expert in order to use your computer.

When I got a new printer, I was told that I would have to buy an additional gadget called a Super Serial Card, to connect the printer to my Apple. I had expected to plug the gadget into the Apple and the printer into the gadget. No way. The Super Serial Card came with a 137-page spiral-bound instruction manual. Page 1 said, "Please read this manual before attempting to install the Super Serial Card in your Apple. Incorrect installation could cause permanent damage to both the Super Serial Card and the Apple."

That was the last thing I understood. By page 6, we were on baud rates, hardware handshakes, parity bits, and ETX-ACK/XON-XOFF switch settings. I glanced ahead. On page 62, I found "C7AB:BD B8 05 129 PASTATUS2 IDA STSBYTE,X ;GET ERROR FLAGS."

I decided I had no intention of R-ing my F-ing M. In decidedly un-wimp-like behavior, I marched back to the store and said, "Make this work for me." Within half an hour, they did. It has worked satisfactorily ever since, and I have no intention, now or ever, of reading that manual. "Error Flags" indeed.

Don't (Necessarily) Do It Yourself

Since computer repairs can be expensive, time consuming, and unreliable, there is a strong temptation to consider doing your own repairs. A small percentage of the time, this turns out to have been a good thing to do. A lot of the time, more harm than good is done. The real dilemma is knowing when to give it a try.

The best rule of thumb is, unless you have considerable electronics training and expertise, avoid anything electronic, and consider most cautiously certain things mechanical.

As an illustration, this morning, paper stopped moving smoothly through my printer. There are a whole array of electronic reasons why paper stops moving. The portion of the program that tells the printer to click the paper forward a notch might have been erased or altered by a magnet or other mysterious force. The internal logic of the printer itself might have gone blooey.[4] Even if I *could* disassemble the computer or printer down to its electronic components, there is no way in the world I could tell what was wrong. A totally defective electronic chip looks, on the surface, exactly like a perfectly good one.

The beauty of mechanical problems is that they are often visible to the naked and untrained eye. If white smoke is rising from your disk drive, that is probably where the problem lies (unless your disk drive has just elected the new Pope). That, thankfully, is how it was with my printer this morning. I used a behavior technically known as "peering into the works." A gummed label had become detached from a roll of labels we were printing earlier, and was preventing paper from moving through.

Now, there are certain hazards inherent in attempting even simple-appearing mechanical repairs. They include killing your warranty, killing your computer, and killing yourself.

● *Killing your warranty.* Most warranties are automatically voided if it is clear to the manufacturer that you have tampered with the equipment in any way. Some manufacturers actually go as far as placing a non-removable-without-tearing seal over the door to the inner works. Broken seal, no repairs.

This can cause knotty problems. One man I spoke to had a disk drive fail. He removed the outer casing (a simple task involv-

142.

Do-it-yourself repairs can void your warranty and cause physical harm to you or your computer. They can also save lots of time and money. There is no simple way to resolve this.

---

4. This is a highly technical term which I am incapable of explaining.

ing removal of four screws), discovered that a rubber belt had come off its pulley, replaced the belt, replaced the casing, had a disk drive that worked—for about an hour. When it failed again, he could find nothing wrong, but the fact of his first successful repair (and the seal he broke to do it) voided his warranty, and the manufacturer wouldn't fix the second, and (as it turned out) totally unrelated problem until he agreed to pay their usual fees for so doing.

Incidentally, there are quite a few computer add-on gadgets that are sold with the warning, "Caution: use of this product may void your warranty." One example is a device that can be soldered into my Apple that causes the shift key to work like a shift key (a nicety the Apple people neglected to take care of).

THE NIGHTMARE SONG

by John Bear

(with apologies to W.S. Gilbert)

When you try to compute with a disk that won't boot
It is hard to maintain your sobriety.
I conceive you may use any language you choose
To indulge in without impropriety.

In Fortran or Cobol, your miseries snowball,
In Basic things seem just as dreary.
Then your programs abort, and your floppies contort,
And it's time to commit hara kiri.

For your brain is on fire, your disk drives conspire
And blacker than black grows the scenery.
You go deeper in debt, and begin to regret
That dark day when you bought your machinery.

If you'd known that computing could be so uprooting,
You'd never have got your diploma.
Now you break all connections and eat the directions
And sink to the floor in a coma,

Where you get some repose in the form of a doze
With hot eyeballs and head ever aching,
But your slumbering teems with such horrible dreams
That you'd very much better be waking.

For you dream that your Apple is ground up like scrapple
And sprinkled like salt on your dinner,
And your Radio Shack is served up as a snack.
You can't eat then, and start growing thinner.

When you think things can't worsen, along comes a Personal
P.C. from good old I B M.
It's chopped up in your soup, along with a big scoop
Of the guts of your printer from 3M.

You eat disk drives and cables served up on log tables.
You long for a steak from a dear ox.
You eat chips from a tray, and when that's cleared away,
Your dessert is a fudge-covered Xerox.

You get offers to trade disks for plum marmalade,
But you can't face this "Let's Make a Deal" world.
Just when things go well, you awake from your spell
And you find that you're back in the real world.

● *Killing your computer.* One reason manufacturers *do* worry, perhaps overly so, about untrained people plowing around in the works, is that there is ample opportunity to wreak much greater havoc in the act of curing a simple problem.

One computer owner told me how he managed, using some kind of electrical testing tool, to discover a defective plug-in module inside his computer. Such modules, common to all computers, have a large number (24 or more) of tiny pins that must go smoothly into 24 (or more) tiny holes. If one pin gets bent ever-so-slightly out of line, it can set off a chain reaction in which the attempt to straighten one will bend two or three others, and so on. This man finally took his computer to a repair facility and grudgingly paid them $20 for the few seconds it took them to straighten the pins with a small machine designed for that purpose, and plug it back in correctly.

It may well be that the other man, several paragraphs ago, inadvertently caused some unrelated damage to his disk drive while putting the rubber belt back on the pulley. At least it is the *possibility* of such things that causes computer companies to worry about who will be delving around inside their works.

Goodness knows, there is enough opportunity. Even though a computer may have anywhere from zero to a few dozen *moving* parts, it does have an awful lot of stationary parts, and very delicately soldered connections.

- *Killing yourself.* Very unlikely, except through suicide caused by terminal frustration (or disk drive frustration, printer frustration, etc.). In a search through old newspaper files, I found only two cases in which people actually died from electrical shock (or, in one of the cases, shock-induced heart attack) while attempting to repair a computer. But there have certainly been vast numbers of nasty shocks, which can be produced by some equipment even when unplugged.

In summary, then, there are really much better reasons for *not* tinkering with your computer than for trying to solve problems yourself. But faced with a long delay and/or a huge repair bill, the temptation to give it a try is strong. If you proceed very cautiously, the odds are high that you will cause no lasting harm.

(But did I mention that in order to remove that sticky label from my printer, I had to remove the carriage and the tractor feed that pulls paper through the printer? When I removed the carriage, something went "Sprongggg" like one of those old coiled-snake-in-the-peanut-can parlor gags. Got me that time, Qume. Twenty minutes later, I believe I had packed it all back in correctly, and I am now sitting here hoping against hope that the tiny screw I see on the windowsill either (a) was there before, or (b) isn't *really* essential to printer functioning.)

How to Talk to a Repair Person

It has taken automobile mechanics the better part of a century to learn how to deal with the unenlightened public. In the early days of motorcars, all drivers had to be mechanically knowledgeable, and indeed had to make many repairs themselves. When they went into a garage, it was probably because even though they knew what was wrong, they didn't have the time or the tools.

143.

Many computer repairpeople are not good at talking to beginners who are having problems.

Nowadays, when the mechanical wimp drives in to the shop and says, "There's a funny little noise that sounds like a cat snoring coming from the rear end, or perhaps the glove compartment," the mechanics may inwardly smile, but outwardly they are very good about treating the whole thing seriously.

Many computer repair folks haven't reached this stage of development. They don't know how to talk to the total beginner who may only be vaguely aware that "things aren't working right."

Some don't have the time; some don't have the patience or the communication skills. Some may be a whiz at changing a 48-pin

"Surely this is a
one-time-only problem."

chip blindfolded, but they ought to be chained in the back room, and not allowed to deal with the public. Some are just downright weird. (I once carried an ailing computer to a well-recommended man who did repairs in his home. "I'm having trouble with this computer," I said. "Well what did you *expect* with the moon in Libra," he growled.)

While repair people may differ significantly in both repair and communication skills, there are two things you can do to improve the chances of a successful interaction:

1. *Document all your actions.* If the problem is a subtle one, possibly involving some interaction of the hardware and the software, it could be very important for the repairer to know exactly what you tried, and what happened when you tried it.

If you are getting a repeating error—every time you type in something, you get the same response from the machinery—write down exactly what you typed, which buttons you pushed, which items were turned off or on at the time, etc.

Some problems occur at the end of a long sequence of events. For example, I have used a complex name and address sorting program that requires about a dozen disk changes. I type in certain instructions at certain times, and after twenty minutes, the screen would taunt me with "I/O ERROR." I mailed my disks back to the company that sold me the program, which insisted they worked just fine. It was only when they went over my procedures line by line that they discovered that I actually had a defective set of written instructions, and was leaving out one crucial step.

If the problem is not one that is repeatable, or if the whole system has died, it is *still* important to recall as much as possible of what you did just before the failure occurred. Be sure to write it down at the time, rather than try to reminisce in the presence of the repairer ("Well, I think the blue smoke came *after* I closed the disk drive door—no, wait, the monitor exploded *before* the smoke, and the cat died *during* the fire, or was it *after* . . . ").

2. *Bring everything in.* Even if you are confident that the problem is in one particular piece of equipment, or in a particular disk, bring your entire system to the repair depot (unless they have specifically advised you not to). It is important to be able to test each element separately with a system known to be working. Problems can occur in unsuspected places.

One man whose printer was double-spacing when it should have been single-spacing was certain that the problem was either in the word processing disk or in the internal logic of the computer. He didn't even bring the printer along the first time. But everything else checked out. Turned out (Alert: squeamish people turn the page right NOW) that a banana slug had crawled into the printer and died in a hideous manner, short circuiting part of the inner workings to create the problem. For perhaps the first time, the classic mechanic's lament—"I've been working on these for 20 years and I never saw nuttin' like *that*"—really was true.

144.

Keep a precise and detailed diary of all problems that occur, to share with the repair service, the manufacturer, or your lawyer.

IF AT FIRST YOU DON'T SUCCEED TRY AGAIN THEN QUIT. NO SENSE BEING A DAMN FOOL ABOUT IT.

There is a real need for an all-night repair service.

When the Software People Say "It's a Hardware Problem" and the Hardware People Say "It's a Software Problem"

The first time this happened, I couldn't believe that such things were possible. Well, they are, and they are surprisingly common. What happened was this:

Our computer was acting up. We had a fairly simple-to-operate program that was supposed to produce a daily report of business done. It wasn't doing that. It was, instead, producing gibberish. We were 100% certain that we were pushing the right buttons. We telephoned the software company, and their advice was to try the back-up disk in the machine, and if *that* failed, too, then clearly it had to be a machine problem.

We tried, and it failed, so, with great reluctance, we called the dealer for a repair. (The reluctance was because the computer was out of warranty, and we knew the repairman charged $60 an hour, door to door, and his door was a three-hour drive from our door.[5] The repairman arrived, put the computer through a thorough diagnosis, and $480 later announced, "The computer is in perfect condition. The problem is with your software."

How can such a problem happen?

Imagine, if you will, that you are stranded on a desert island, with nothing but a good stereo set, and a single long-playing record. (The island, conveniently, has an electrical outlet.) After years of contentedly listening to your record, one day you lower the tone arm, and the sound comes out all garbled.

What went wrong? Has something happened to the record or to the stereo? If you had a second record, you could play that, and if it sounded good, you'd know the problem is with the record. If you had a second stereo, you could play your record on that, and if it sounded good, you'd know the problem is with the first stereo.

But you've only got one of each, and therefore there is no way to find out. If two repairmen were to float ashore (without their test equipment), there could well be a situation in which one says, "It's a hardware (i.e., the stereo) problem," and the other says, "It's a software (i.e., the record) problem."

---

5. This particular computer, was, alas, much too heavy to carry; see page 40 on why you should never buy anything you can't lift.

With computers, the complexity is compounded by the fact that improperly-working hardware can actually destroy, or worse still, subtly alter the software, so that even if you find an identical machine to try your tape or disks on, it may not work—leading you to think it is a software problem when in fact it is now *both*. Your defective computer has destroyed your programs!

Conversely, although there is disagreement among experts as to whether defective software can actually permanently damage hardware, I have heard enough people say that it can to acknowledge the possibility.

What is the wimp in the middle to do when the hardware people say, "Sorry, you have a software problem," and *vice versa*? It's a lot easier to discuss means of avoiding the situation in the first place, or at least minimizing its likelihood:

- Buy your hardware and your major software (at least) from the same source, with an understanding that they are responsible not just for the separate parts, but for the system working as a whole.

- Buy things that you will have access to duplicates of, to avoid the desert island stereo problem.

If the situation *does* arise, try to get the two contradicting repair people to talk to each other, whether on the telephone or in person. Repair people are generally both honest and helpful, as well as tenacious when it comes to tracking down the source of trouble, and may be glad to cooperate to solve your problem. (Once, when my printer went awry and the printer repairman insisted the fault lay with my label-printing program sending false information to the printer, I paid for the long distance call between the repairman and the company that produced the program, and between them, the problem was isolated and solved. Turned out to be a 30-cent chip that only took three hours to find and two minutes to replace.)

It goes without saying, but use your knowledgeable friend or support group and if you don't have one, now's the time to start looking, in a hurry.

145.
Problems will arise in which the hardware people blame the software and the software people blame the hardware. Best solution: try the software on two identical machines.

Repairs by Telephone

Even if my fantasy 800-number repair service doesn't yet exist (see page 222), it is still possible to solve some quite complex problems by telephone.

146.
Some computer companies encourage telephone repair consultations, some tolerate them, and some refuse them. Potential buyers who live far from dealers or repair depots should take this into account.

A few computer companies (both hardware and software suppliers) and dealers *encourage* telephone repairs. Some *tolerate* it up to a point. And many range from willing-but-ineffective to downright hostile when the user-with-a-problem calls.

1. *Those who encourage.* Some companies have decided that it makes sense to turn their customers into repairers. And the customers don't really seem to mind. Perhaps it is a fortuitous combination of relief (the problem has a good chance of getting fixed right away) and pride (I did it myself! I fixed my own computer!).

The Compugraphic company is a pioneer in this regard. With their computerized equipment, they supply a spare parts kit, containing those parts most likely to fail. There are telephone "hotlines" at several locations around the country. With time zone changes, at least one is open somewhere from early morning to late night. The people on the phones are masterful psychologists, diagnosticians, and teachers. I know, because I made two calls to them myself when the Compugraphic I own a quarter of was acting up, and I was quite astonished by the complexity of things I found myself doing: dismantling half the machine, replacing a defective part, and reassembling it, phone receiver scrunched between ear and shoulder.

Of course I had no idea what I was doing. I felt like the person in that *Reader's Digest* story that runs every month: "My husband died at 16,000 feet and somehow I landed the plane myself." But as long as the man on the other end of the phone line in Renton, Washington knows what *he's* doing, all is likely to be well.

So, *after* reading the manual, but before going to a repair depot, it can do no harm to call the company and ask if they have a "Technical Support" telephone service. In fact, this is not a bad thing to ask when shopping around for a computer in the first place.

2. *Those who tolerate.* Most companies *do* have someone (or a whole bunch of people) who are capable of dispensing wisdom by telephone. But will they? In many cases, yes, if you can get through to them. Sometimes there are quite formidable gatekeepers. But no two situations seem alike.

I've spoken to people who wailed, "Help, I need someone to help me," and were politely turned down. When they called back and said, in a businesslike tone, "Technical support, please," they were put right through.

TECHNICAL SUPPORT HOTLINE

And I've spoken to people who insist that the personal approach—playing on the sympathies of the telephone dragon—has worked for them when a straightforward request was denied.

3. *Those who can't or won't.* Some companies simply do not deal by telephone, and there is really nothing you can do about it.

When my Qume printer had a minor but annoying problem, I telephoned Qume. I was told in no uncertain terms that I had to bring it in. They made it crystal clear that no advice was dispensed by phone.

So I drove the 180 miles to the Qume factory and left it there. Three weeks later, I got a postcard saying it was ready. Can they really be a subsidiary of International Telephone and Telegraph? It was more like going to Sam's Corner Computer and Sewing Machine Repair Works. Small reception room with a matronly lady stapling "Errata" sheets into a huge stack of new catalogues. After a few minutes, a young man lumbered in carrying the printer and plonked it down in the midst of her errata. I wrote out a check for the $298 repair (marked down from $300?), and as I was staggering across the parking lot with it, he came running after. "The bar on the bottom," he puffed. "If you don't remove the bar on the bottom, you'll destroy the print mechanism. I almost forgot to tell you." Errata, indeed.

If the manufacturer can't or won't give telephone advice, it is still worth trying dealers, distributors, clubs, or support groups. There's nothing to lose (except some minor telephone expenses), and if it *does* work, you're ahead of the game.

Problems with Repairs

Every few years, a consumer magazine does the same depressing car repair study. They make some minor and quite obvious (to an expert) adjustment to an otherwise perfectly-running car, and bring it in to a large number of garages. There are always a few who identify the problem at once and fix it at no charge. And there are always some who say, after poking around a bit, "It's bad. We're looking at $400 worth of repairs here." The rest are somewhere in between.

147.

Manufacturing volume has far surpassed repair capability. There are a great many ill-trained or inept repairers. As a result, many repairs are not properly done.

It will be most enlightening when a similar study is done with computer problems. My prediction is that the results will be about the same. There may not be as much *intentional* deceit — but there may be a good deal more of the three kinds of repair-related problems people have been telling me about:

1. *Unsatisfactory or incomplete repairs.* If a car is brought in because it is going klong-klong-klong and emitting flames from the cigarette lighter hole it is going to be pretty obvious whether

or not it was repaired when you come to pick it up. Many computer problems are much more subtle, or at least more complex, so that the repairs cannot be thoroughly checked out at the time you collect it and pay for it.

All too many people are finding, to their dismay, that either the repair was not made correctly at all, or that only *some* of what was wrong was dealt with.

The only certain way to avoid this is to bring the entire system in, either at the time of repair, or at least when picking it up. Insist (if at all feasible) on a demonstration using your own disks and programs. If it works at the repair desk, it has a pretty good chance of working at home or in the office.

2. *Slow turn-around time.* People who depend on their computers in their everyday personal or business lives are often astonished to be told that a certain repair will take two or three or four weeks. Of course the repair it*self* may take three minutes, but it may take a month for them to get to it.

Repair estimate times are not always reliable. It may be that small computers are still too new for repair people to develop a "feel" for the amount of work involved, thus inspiring overly optimistic predictions.

The only solutions are: (a) shop around for shorter estimates — if you have the luxury of more than one nearby facility; (b) find a place (there are some) that have loaners available; or (c) squawk — the squeaky user may get the service — especially if victim one needs the equipment to run a business, and victim two is merely desperate to play Space Invaders.

3. *Inconsistent policies.* People who have had repairs made under warranty have expressed some frustration in the variations in how warranties are enforced. This relates to: (a) what is covered by the warranty, whether user-modified equipment is covered, whether damages allegedly caused by *other* non-warranty defective equipment is covered, etc.; (b) whether repairs made under warranty are them*selves* covered by an extended warranty period (verdict: sometimes yes, sometimes no); (c) whether mixed-breed equipment is handled (e.g., a Radio Shack computer with a non-Radio Shack telephone modem wired into it); (d) whether loaner equipment is available; and (e) whether repairs are made on an hourly basis or a flat rate basis.

The only advice here is to be as clear as possible in advance

148.
Whenever possible, bring the rest of the system in when picking up a repaired item, and see it all work properly in the shop.

149.
Repair policies vary immensely with regard to turn-around time (while-you-wait to 30 days) and whether or not the repairs themselves are warranted. Shop around for repairs.

about what the policies are, so there will be few surprises later—and, of course, when possible, to shop around (preferably in *advance* of need) for the best deal.

How About an 800-Number Repair and Counseling Service

This book is not billed as a "Get Rich Quick" or "How to Start a Business" book. Nonetheless, as a bonus at no extra charge, here is a business plan that will make someone a fortune.

Elsewhere I discuss the feelings of despair, anguish, and frustration that come, once in a while, to every computer user—sometimes every 20 minutes. Most problems seem to occur and questions arise when computer dealers or stores are closed (not that many of them could help much anyway). The feelings of frustration (etc.) grow even more acute when you know that there will be no help for several days, if ever.

And yet, many computer problems *can* be solved over the telephone. But whom do you call?

Consider the following scenario:

It is nine p.m. on a Friday evening. My disk drive has started whirring away, and won't stop. I am afraid to turn it off, for fear of damaging the disk inside. Nothing I can do will make it stop.

I pick up the phone and dial 800-W-I-M-P-A-I-D. A confident-sounding voice answers, "Good evening. What is the nature of your problem?" I explain briefly and the voice says, "Do you have an account with us, or shall we charge your credit card. The rate is one cent per second as long as we are on the phone."

I give them my MasterCard number, and am transferred to a specialist in disk drives. She suggests a succession of things to try (most of which I had not thought of). Finally, she explains how to remove the top from my computer, and flick a tiny switch on the inside, on the disk controller card. The drive stops whirring.

She then says, "Shall we stop here, at 417 seconds, or do you want to see if we can make the repair?" I figure we'll give it another ten minutes. She explains how to run a certain diagnostic program; how to switch one drive for another to determine if the problem is with the computer or the drive itself; and so on. After seven minutes, we discover a loose connection in one of the cable pins. She asks if I have a soldering iron. I do not. She informs me

that my service call is over, and my account will be billed for $7.87. If I wish to purchase a soldering iron, I can call in again and speak to a soldering expert.

I hang up smiling. I'm virtually back in business.

Right now, as far as I know, this is all fantasy. But such a business could come into existence tomorrow, if a few knowledgeable people got together to make it happen. It doesn't even have to be an 800 number. It could have limited hours (evenings and weekends to begin).

The service could be expanded to offer advice and consultation on buying and selling hardware and software, renting, leasing, bartering, etc. It could even be sponsored or underwritten by certain manufacturers ("I'll assist you in a moment, but first please listen to this recorded message from the MegaDisk Corporation . . .").

I don't want any royalties. I just want the number I can call. There's a funny little squeak in my printer, and I need to know if I should clean it, oil it, feed it, pray for it, ignore it, or what?

Two Ultimate Solutions

Computer Consumer Karate

This section is designed for people who are having trouble with their *own* computer hardware and software—but many of the techniques have relevance for people who are being harrassed by *other people's* computers. Consider, for instance, The Case of the Two John Bears.

Many years ago, when living in Chicago, I was using an Amoco gasoline credit card. After dutifully and promptly paying bills that ranged between $20 and $30 each month (I *said* this was long ago), one month I got a bill for over $300. For the first time, I inspected the individual receipts, and discovered that about half of them were signed "John Bear" but not in my handwriting—and that the someone-else had just bought five new tires.

When I telephoned another John Bear whom I found in the phone book, he checked his Amoco receipts and found half of them signed by me. Amoco's computer, unable to comprehend the fact of two John Bears, had given us the same credit card number, and randomly distributed charges between us. For over two years, I had been paying some of his bills and he had been paying some of mine.

I dutifully went through the succession of procedures that are generally recommended for gaining satisfaction in such cases:

1. Polite letter (or two) to company.
2. Less polite letter (or two) to company.
3. Letter to newspaper or radio station "consumer action line" service.
4. Withholding payment, with letter(s) explaining why.
5. Letter to the president of the company.
6. Attempts to telephone the company—first collect, then prepaid.
7. Letter to regulatory and/or consumer protection agencies

150.

When normal procedures fail to get faulty equipment working, the techniques of "consumer karate" often get prompt, satisfactory results.

(Better Business Bureau, Federal Trade Commission, Chamber of Commerce, etc.).

8. Letter to my congressman and senators.

All of the above failed. The only response from Amoco was computer-printed threats to pay up or else.

That was when I invented (or perhaps discovered) the approach that ranks in the top four consumer karate techniques.[1]

Consumer Karate Method #1:
THE SHOTGUN TECHNIQUE

Business executives love to get listed in various "Who's Who" directories, from *Who's Who in America* to *Who's Who in the Midwest* to *Who's Who in the Petroleum Industry*. Significantly, most listings include family information and a home address.

From the *Standard and Poor* and the *Dun and Bradstreet* directories, I learned the names of two dozen top Amoco executives, their law firm, and their advertising agents. Then from the other directories, I secured the home address and wife's name of nearly all of them.

Next I wrote personal letters to all of these blokes *at home* giving a short history of my case and begging for action. I *also* wrote personal letters to each of the wives, at home, on this theme: "Your husband's company is driving me crazy. He doesn't answer my letters. *Please* see if you can get him to help me."

Three things happened.

1. The computer mess was cleared up within three days.

2. For the next three *months* I was getting letters from various Amoco executives (and a few of their wives) assuring me that matters would be taken care of soon, not to worry.

3. I received a "corrected" bill for $119.07. (Turned out John Bear #2 had paid more of my bills than I had paid of his). I wrote out an invoice to Amoco for my time and expenses in fighting them. It came, remarkably, to $119.05. I mailed in my check for two cents with a copy of their bill and mine marked "Paid in Full" — and I never heard from them again.

Consumer Karate Method #2
SEND IT BACK

Most manufacturers of computer hard- and software, as well as

---

1. I can say this with authority because I later wrote the first Ph.D. dissertation ever on how corporations are influenced by consumers.

other consumer products, expect their customers to behave in certain well-established ways. One of these expectations is that when a customer has an unsatisfactory product, he or she will deal with the retail outlet or a factory-approved repair facility.

When customers break the mold, companies large and small often are at a loss as to how to respond.

One simple example. I bought a small Sears tape recorder to use with my Radio Shack computer. After about four months, it stopped working. The warranty had expired, and my local Sears store told me it would cost more to fix it than it would cost to buy a brand new one (abut $30), so I should junk it.

Neither junking it nor Sears' policy of selling unrepairable hardware was acceptable to me. I went through the initial complaint letter stages described above. I *did* receive a few patient and friendly explanations of why I was not going to get satisfaction. I decided not to spend the time needed for the "shotgun approach" over a mere $30.

So I looked up the name of the president of Sears in the *World Almanac* and I mailed him the tape recorder with a brief explanatory note asking him to fix it and send it back to me. (I sent it insured, with a return receipt requested.)

Now letters are small and ignorable or throw-outable, but here's this actual *object* sitting on his (or someone's) desk, and it won't go away. It can't easily be tossed in the trash. ("Please *do* something with that *object* Miss Finsterwald," I imagined the president of Sears saying.)

Anyway, I received a working tape recorder (whether repaired or new I cannot say) in about two weeks.

I have since talked to half a dozen people who have sent computer products back to the manufacturer unsolicitedly, and all but one got prompt satisfaction. (I also read about a man who crated up his Lincoln and shipped it back to Henry Ford II.)

This technique will probably *not* work for software, since software is contained on a tape or disk, which *is* possible to ignore or lose back at the factory.

Consumer Karate Method #3
USE INFLUENCE

If you were having trouble with your Rosenkrantz Mark IV computer — *and* having trouble getting them to deal with your trouble — and if you could write to them thus: "My uncle, Sam

Automation: a phenomenon which causes long lines to form at unemployment offices, the unions to rant, pink slips to rain — all for the good of the country.

— Irwin Van Grove

Rosenkrantz, largest investor in your company, hopes that you'll deal with my problem really soon" — the probability is high that they would deal with your problem really soon.

But what if you don't know any officers or investors in the company? No problem. You don't even have to lie; just *imply*. Simply get a name — an officer, as listed in one of the business directories, or better still a major shareholder (check with a stockbroker, who may have filings from any public offerings the company may have made). Let's say there is a major stockholder named James R. Hardesty, Jr.

Your letter, probably to a vice president (the president is more likely to know Mr. Hardesty personally) might say, "Before I take this relatively minor problem to Jim Hardesty, I thought I would try one last time to see if we can get it cleared up without bothering him."

Unless good ol' Jim died last week or is now in prison, the probability is high that they'll go ahead and try to satisfy you without checking the nature of the implied relationship.

I have only used this method once, when Northstar told me it would take 30 days to get my computer repaired. With a magic name invoked, they actually fixed it while I waited.

Consumer Karate Method #4
PUBLIC EMBARRASSMENT

Outside a computer show once, I saw an earnest young couple passing out leaflets that said, "Please don't buy such-and-such brand disks." The leaflet explained that they had bought a box of defective disks, and the company was refusing to make good on it.

Well, as soon as word of their demonstration reached the company's booth inside, someone was dispatched to negotiate with them. They accepted an offer of *two* boxes of disks if only they would stop.

This kind of "informational picketing" is a tried and true technique of consumer action groups. It has been used successfully at automobile dealerships, appliance stores, and computer retailers, with anywhere from one to dozens of people marching back and forth with signs or leaflets.

One of the main reasons this works is that they don't know, can't know, how far you are willing to go. Will you be there all day? All week? For the rest of your life? With a dozen friends?

Better far (in most cases) to make peace and stop this embarrassing show, which could do far more harm than the modest request being made by the demonstrators.

This may be one of the best "last resort" methods for getting back at a software vendor who has wronged you. The amount involved isn't large enough for the shotgun or personal influence approach, and sending the product back is not likely to be noticed.

There are other possible methods — some of them quite drastic indeed. Someday I shall make public how I singlehandedly put the British Leyland automobile company into bankruptcy because of what they did to my Land Rover. But that's enough for now. I hope you won't stoop to considering petty and irrelevant revenge, like having 40 tons of manure dumped on the company president's lawn, or putting sleazy sex books on the public library shelves in the president's home town, with bookplates saying "Gift of (president's name)" in them. Such acts may be temporarily satisfying, but they are unlikely to get your *own* problem solved.

Two more points.

When I talk about these consumer karate methods to people, a common response is, "But what if *every*body did these things?" The only suitable answer is the one Yossarian gave to the same question in *Catch-22*: "Then I'd be crazy not to."

Finally, what about the *company's* side of things. The customer is most emphatically *not* always right. True enough. But they *usually* are. I have run both retail and mail order businesses, and I learned early on that it is far better to treat all complaints sensibly (and perhaps be nice to a phony or two who didn't deserve it) than to investigate and contest virtually every complaint (and irritate practically everybody).

You Can Change Horses in Midstream

An American who speaks perfect, accentless Japanese was once talking to a business acquaintance in Tokyo. "What a shame," the Japanese was saying, "that you Americans do not take the time to learn to speak Japanese." "But honored sir," replied the American, "we are *speaking* Japanese." And so they were, and had been for an hour.

It is permitted to dispose of
an unfriendly computer.

There are none so blind as those who cannot see. Or hear. Or compute. I think about this often when I am communicating with someone who has been having devastating long-term problems with his or her computer. "But honored victim," I think of saying, "have you noticed that it is permitted to dispose of an unfriendly computer?"

Well, that kind of statement can be a real knee-slapper. For whatever reason, so many people have the feeling that they are *wedded* to their computer, for better or worse, until death do them part. It somehow simply never occurred to them that there was such a (relatively) simple way out of their problem.

Until that realization, their only reaction to continuing computer problems was to keep on trying; to dig themselves in deeper; to throw good money after bad.

So the only purpose of this little section is to tap you gently on the shoulder and remind you that it *is* entirely possible, and often quite reasonable to change horses in midstream. If you are having terrible computer miseries, give very serious thought to indulging in one of the following three:

1. *Change horses.* Switch over to a comparable computer system that can run the same program and use the same files and records you have. Even get another of the same make and model, if you are satisfied that your lemon is a rare event.

2. *Start over.* If you're still sold on the *idea* of computers— not just the stuff you're presently stuck with, go back and begin from scratch, utilizing all you have learned from your experience (and mine), which should make round two a far happier experience than your first one.

3. *Give up entirely.* Thousands upon thousands of people have relinquished their computers and lived to tell the tale. More often than not, their mental health improved, their social standing did not suffer, and their bank account grew healthier.[2]

151.

Many people with terrible problems never seriously consider changing computers or giving up entirely, even though those alternatives might be economically or psychologically best.

---

2. I wonder if people who have given up computers repose in the same social niche as people who have voluntarily given up telephones. The only person I've known to live an urbane life without telephones—the attorney Dinty Warmington Whiting—claimed never to have had regrets—other than that he was generally known as Dinty-Whiting-the-lawyer-without-a-telephone.

PART FIVE

THE DARK UNDERBELLY OF THE COMPUTER WORLD

1,000,000 mistakes per second. Fear of computers. Health hazards of computers. Deciding whether or not to be a pirate. Stealing computers and computer time. Computer sabotage. Computer crime. Computers and privacy.

1,000,000 Mistakes
Per Second

Let's say you're driving down a suburban street at 10 miles an hour. Suddenly the entire Rotary Club steps out in front of your car. At that speed, you have no problem gently braking to a stop. But what if you had been traveling 50 miles an hour? No matter how good a driver you are, the very *fact* of the high speed means that when you *do* make a mistake, it's going to be a doozy.

The worst shortstop in baseball history once made five errors in one inning. A really bad accountant might, if left unchecked, make a few dozen blunders a day. But even a small computer is fully capable of making 1 million mistakes per second.

Dreadful computer problems will happen because computers are faster, dumber and/or bigger than (most) human beings. Let's look briefly at each factor.

1. *Faster.* Because computers are *so* fast, many people find it hard to adapt their slow lives to the lightning output. As the *New York Times* reported, "a business can become so dependent on them for billing and accounting that a faulty computer could bankrupt a firm before its human officers realized that anything was wrong."

This has, in fact, happened—very likely many, many times. For example, an insurance company called Triangle Industries claimed, in its suit against a computer company, that the business' cash flow was destroyed when the computer paid money out, but did not bill clients. By the time humans got wind of this, the $20 million business was forced into liquidation.

The Wheeling Heating Company of West Virginia had accounting software that "constantly spewed forth incorrect invoices and payroll checks." After sales had fallen by half, the company president "pulled the plug. We went back to a pencil and paper, and we're doing much better," he said.

Not all disasters caused by computer speed are quite so devastating. My label-printing program once jammed, and before I

152.

Because computers are so fast and humans are so slow, faulty computers have ruined businesses and other enterprises before anyone knew something was wrong.

The computer can, in a fraction of a second, work out the shortest of 10,000 alternate routes between Windsor Castle and St. Paul's, but it can never say that if a detour is made through a garden in the spring, this is one of the things that make a journey *seem* shorter.

—John Hargreaves

caught it, it had printed out 4,000 labels for the same person. Quite possibly if I had *also* had a computerized mailroom, I might have mailed 4,000 books to that poor lady in New Hampshire. Fortunately, a human instantly noticed what had happened, and destroyed 3,999 labels. Not so lucky was a national magazine that *did* in fact once send 30,000 copies of the same issue to one subscriber.

2. *Dumber.* Computer people are fond of saying that computers are really just big dumb adding machines—it is the *programmers* who are smart. Or should be smart. The problem is that it is often either impossible, or not worth the bother, to anticipate and deal with all the errors that might occur.

One community decided to use their computer to match census-type data with school data, to locate any children over six years old who were not in school. The programmer left two columns to record the ages of people. And that's why a 107-year-old lady whose age was recorded as "07" received a visit from the truant officer.

> What it is possible for technology to do, technology will have done . . . Regardless, regardless of anything.
>
> — Archibald MacLeish

A programmer could have anticipated that one. An error that *is* acknowledged, then ignored, occurs in the business of "personal" computer-produced letters. You know the sort: "Dear Mr. Pottle; The Pottle family can be the envy of Greenville with a brand new Ford parked outside 456 Ferndale Lane . . ."

Now everybody has funny stories about letters to the Dept. of Acctg. addressed, "Dear Mr. Acctg." And how about some spiffy new aluminum siding on P.O. Box 1412. And the Dept. of Gynecology being offered the opportunity to purchase the "Gynecology Family Crest."

As annoying or amusing as this stuff may be, the fact is that many businesses *are* making money with such approaches. But they would *not* make money if they had to hire human beings to go through their mailings and extract all the errors. It is worth it to them to send out mailings with 2% or 3% or 5% errors.

Problems often arise when human beings defer to the wisdom of the computer. If the computer says so, it must be true. Critic Rex Reed writes of the time he was arrested by store detectives for using a stolen credit card (his own). When Reed convinced them of his identity, they still tore up his credit card. Why? "Our computer has been told that you are dead, and we cannot change this," they said.

3. *Bigger.* The more parts something has, the greater the likelihood that at least some of them will fail. A small computer has thousands of times as many parts as a simple calculator (if we consider each of the microscopically small components of a chip as a part). A small calculator has vastly more parts than an abacus, and an abacus has about ten times the number of parts as the typical human has digital counting wands (fingers).

Computer philosophers argue over whether increasing the size of a system increases the likelihood of errors *arithmetically* or *geometrically*. In other words, if I have one item (a computer) and add a second item (a disk drive), will I have *twice* as many errors or *four* times as many? If I add a second disk drive, is it going to be *three* times or *eight* times as many?

153.

There is a tendency in many people to accept the word of a computer as the gospel truth. If the computer said it, it must be correct. Not so.

A good argument can be made for the geometrical theory. Not only does each expansion offer the opportunity for more errors in that unit itself, but since it will interact with each other unit, the opportunities for failure are multiplied.

If we are to believe recent published reports, the biggest computer system in the world may well be among the least reliable of all.

As *The Washington Monthly* says, "What if the Pentagon spent $10 billion on the computer that is the nerve center of the entire U.S. military apparatus, and then botched up the job so completely that the system didn't work at all almost 70% of the time, and was pitifully inadequate the other 30%?... Well, it's happened." They go on to explain how the "WIMEX" (Worldwide Military Command and Control System) failed in 247 of 290 tests.

Newsweek pointed with alarm in early 1983 at the system that "can be aggravating when a mistake involves a paycheck, but disastrous if it triggers the early-warning system." They suggest concern that the new system could "create a nuclear catastrophe on its own." Oxford University computer scientist Charles Hoare reminds us that "the next rocket to go astray as a result of a programming language error may not be . . . on a harmless trip to Venus: it may be a nuclear warhead exploding over one of our own cities."

What can we do?

Worry. Healthy concern offers the best hope of avoiding or forestalling small problems in the home and office, and even massive problems on a global scale. If only everyone who deals with computers would remember, always and everywhere, that they *are* in fact big, dumb, fast machines that do not dispense the Holy Writ (unless, of course, they have been programmed to do so).

Published accounts of computer-related disasters, from the recipe program that said "2 c. pepper" instead of "2 t. pepper" to Three Mile Island are replete with "If only . . ." and "We should have . . ." and "Next time we'll know that . . ."

Something to keep in mind. Whether you are barrelling along at 50 miles an hour or a million calculations per second, the potential for disaster is immense. There's nothing inherently *wrong* with those speeds. You just want to stay extra alert, and keep your seatbelt — physical or electronic — buckled.

154.
As computer systems grow in size, the potential for errors and breakdowns grows even greater.

Maybe I Could Just Die Early:
Fear of Computers

It was a 51-year-old vice president of a medium-sized company who voiced the plaintive lament. He had been informed that his department was being "computerized." He tried to cope. He bought (but could not read) computer books. He hung around computer stores, but could not confess his fear. Finally, in desperation, he went to the counselor that his company had sensibly provided during the transition. Too young to retire, too old to start over, he wailed, "Maybe I could just die early."

How widespread is this kind of fear?

Very. A recent major survey by the management consulting firm of Booz, Allen & Hamilton found that about one-third of all professionals are "not receptive" to the idea of computers — but that with training and counseling, about 90% eventually "come around."

Even if that 90% figure, which my hunch tells me is very high, is accurate, that *still* means that there are millions of people out there who may *never* "come around."

As one would logically predict, the level of fear is greatest among older people, but it is quite prevalent in the 20s and 30s as well. (A 1983 Booz, Allen report stated that roughly 90% of the top 10 million executives and managers in America are computer illiterates!) Of course as "computer literate" children move into the workplace, the percentages will decline, but it is clear that "computerphobia" is a problem that will be with us for many years to come.

What is the nature of the fear?

I've identified eight different reasons people are afraid of computers. Some people have one; some may have them all.

1. *Fear of losing job.* As *Business Week* puts it, "You can resist it, or you can embrace it. You can submit to its discipline or you can bend it to your own ends. And how you respond is likely to affect your career, not to mention your peace of mind."

Richard Byrne, a fear-of-computers counselor reports that "I experience a lot of executives who are nervous about 17-year-old kids taking their jobs away from them . . ."

2. *Loss of status.* A Harvard Business School professor says

155.

Millions of intelligent people are simply incapable of dealing with computers. Some can overcome their feelings with counseling or training; some never will.

A Florida bank president refuses to read anything printed on paper with little holes along the sides.

that the more foolproof computers become, the more people using them begin to feel "insignificant and overwhelmed." Morale and motivation plummet.

Time puts it this way: "Having built careers on intangibles like personality and leadership, executives may fear that a computer, with its unshakable command of facts and figures, will erode their authority." And a *Wall Street Journal* editor writes, "Computer enthusiasts overlook . . . emotional snarls. As a result, managerial egos are bruised and minor matters bloom into major stumbling blocks." The *Journal* also reports that women executives who can skillfully type into their office computers are "constantly needled by other managers asking if 'they take dictation too.' "

3. *Can't type.* It's surprising how common a fear this is. Typing is something secretaries and clerks do, not higher-ups. For example, a vice president of a big chemical company who resisted computers "wondered if it is an efficient use of . . . time searching for a 'p' on the keyboard."

4. *Fear of math.* Seymour Papert, an expert in teaching programming to children, says that "most people who are not mathematicians view the computer field as incomprehensible, even threatening. This 'mathophobia' . . . will inhibit large segments of society from achieving fluency in a computerized world."

5. *Fear of instant rebuke.* Much of society is built on a certain level of courtesy and gentility in dealing with others' errors: "Say, Jenkins, don't you think it might have been better if . . ." The computer is intolerant, and comes back with an instant flashing "ERROR" message, which some find most unsettling.

6. *Too late to start.* While some people aren't sure the revolution has started, others fear that it is over and all the booty has been shared. Not all are as snide as Charlie Haas, who writes, "Some people . . . believe they will be excluded from the bonanza of opportunities to which the digital era is giving rise. They may feel that all the good slots in 'puterland have been filled. Perhaps they failed to develop an adequate background in the sciences because they were able to get dates in high school."

7. *Fear of becoming too dependent on it.* Some people worry that they will grow to like their computer *too* much — and then live in fear of power outages and breakdowns.

8. *Fear of never being good enough.* This is mine. I never learned to play bridge because my father was a Grand Master and I knew I'd never have the time to get that good. Same for me with

156.

Inability to type (or to type well) is a major cause of computer fear or problems. (But there are some outstanding learn-to-type computer programs.)

There is no more need to learn computer terminology to use a computer than there is to learn the names of your digestive enzymes in order to enjoy a good meal.

—Michael Rothenberg

programming. I'd rather not start than be a duffer. Or, as *Business Week* put it, computers "are like grand pianos — you can become a virtuoso, or you can play 'Chopsticks' all your life."

What do people do about computer fear?

Either they fight the fear or they fight the computer.

1. *Fighting the fear.* Some enlightened companies offer counseling, advice, and hands-on experience — often with small computers that can be borrowed and taken home, to make a friend out of the perceived foe.

Some people take classes specifically designed for people who are afraid of computers. The American Management Association, for instance, offers three-day seminars via a slick brochure called *Computer Phobia*? "Register today and leave your computer phobia behind you." You'll also leave $800 behind you. A company called Springboard! offers "to help people jump into the deep end of the computer revolution, enjoy the ride, and come out surfing the third wave."

2. *Fighting the computer.* Quite a few people enjoy (and may even contribute to) computer breakdowns. As Shoshanah Zuboff of the Harvard Business School puts it, "The resulting fear of impotence and concomitant loss of status leads sometimes to retaliation."

157.
Special courses and counseling services are widely available to help people overcome fear of computers.

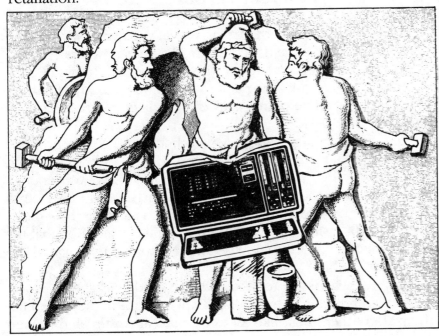

Although computer sabotage is a significant problem (see page 252), most people don't go as far as putting sugar in the computer's gas tank; they are more subtle. Here is just one example of a subtle rebellion.

At great expense a major bank installed an "executive information system" to send memos and other information back and forth. The top management couldn't see the benefit of using it, since their secretaries did all the work anyway. And lower executives saw it as losing control: they couldn't avoid messages and claim they had never gotten them.

In an attempt to make the system more acceptable, the designers added an "executive daily calendar." Each employee could inspect each others' calendar electronically to learn where he or she was, and when they would be available for appointments. Nobody wants to admit to a sparse calendar. So, to regain control of their lives, most employees spontaneously began filling their electronic calendars with fictitious appointments. Eventually the system was discontinued. But, significantly, the computers remained in place. They almost always do.

Computers May Be
Hazardous to Our Health

In the 1930s and 1940s, there was a great vogue for watches with dials that glowed in the dark. What made them glow was a radium compound, applied by hand to the numbers on the watch face. The unfortunate souls who painted the numbers used to lick their brushes to get a fine point. Many of them later contracted cancer and died.

In our eagerness to adopt new technologies, we are prone to rush ahead and buy or use the latest thing—only to discover, years or decades later, that we should have left well enough alone. People over 40 will remember that shoe stores used to fluoroscope children's feet to show worried mommas how nicely the bones fit inside the shoe. Then came the realization that the X-rays used might also be *destroying* the bones. Away with those particular machines.

An essential issue to acknowledge, and perhaps to worry about with regard to computers, is whether or not there is something about them that, like asbestos, nuclear wastes, and radium dials, will come back to haunt us years from now. Are there any "If only I had known . . ." situations that *can* actually be known now?

Perhaps. There are people who worry about three different kinds of problems that small computers may be causing — both now, and for our future.

1. Physical problems

Historians may find it curious, perhaps incomprehensible that in the latter years of the 20th century, millions of people chose to sit virtually still (except for their fingers), hour after hour, in an uncomfortable chair, staring at little white letters and numbers on a flickering screen.

I spent a day doing research in a law library, and discovered that there already have been dozens of lawsuits filed by, or on behalf of, computer entry operators, claiming disability due to bad back, headaches and dizziness, and other infirmities allegedly caused by sitting at a computer. (There was also one case of a broken foot caused by dropping a computer on it, and one child who lost the tip of a finger by sticking it into a whirling disk drive, but those are not likely to become major recurring problems.)

There are some neurologists who believe that constant staring at the subliminally flickering screen and the flashing cursor on the screen may trigger epileptic fits, minor strokes, and other neurological disorders in some regular computer users.

Industrial designers and psychologists have been devoting more and more attention to these matters, as have union contract negotiators. There is some evidence that the simplest immediate step that can be taken is to put an orange or a green filter over the television monitor. Add to that a high quality chair and a realistic work schedule that does not require long hours of data entry, and there are likely to be fewer lawsuits at least. Steel boots to minimize the hazards of computers dropped on feet are not a high priority item.

2. Psychological problems

Some of the psychological problems that can be caused by computers have been discussed. But there may be much more to it than that. According to an article in *Omni* magazine, "Computer scientists at the Massachusetts Institute of Technology have given an alarming analysis of the computer threat to human society . . . [They] stated that computers were engulfing almost all functions of human society."

According to Dr. Joseph Weizenbaum, a well-known computer scientist, "We are rapidly losing, have perhaps already lost, physical and mental control of our society."

The concern is that computers are perceived as so powerful, they destroy people's self image, the urge to be creative. Just as our Jehovah's Witness friend says, "Why bother to diet; the world is going to end soon anyway, and I'll get a perfect body in the next world," so, presumably, are people saying, "Why bother to learn skills and try to solve problems; the computers will always be able to do it better and faster."

The point is *not* whether these people are right, but whether enough people will come to *believe* in this point of view to have a noticeable negative effect on society.

3. Spiritual problems

This is a much harder area to get a handle on, but there are certainly a lot of persuasive people who are worried about computers simply because they are somehow *wrong,* or inappropriate for this day and age.

For one thing, there is the matter of positive ions. Computer systems give off positively-charged particles. In recent years, there have been increasing numbers of advertisements for negative ion generators. The claim is made that when there are too many positive ions in an area, people suffer. They develop a feeling of being ill at ease without knowing exactly why; they grow irritable and crotchety. When the ion balance is restored, matters improve. Negative ion generators produce huge numbers of negative ions, which balance the positive ions, and allegedly create feelings of well-being.

This is not an all-or-nothing, black or white situation. It is a matter of tiny degrees. When there are too many positive ions, the quality of life just isn't quite as satisfactory, somehow, as before. Some computer users feel it is quite important to have a negative ion generator operating in the immediate vicinity of the computer.

Even more esoteric is the notion of geomancy — the science or study of how man lives on earth in relation to natural lines of force, gravity, magnetic poles, and so forth. In its most common manifestation, there are quite a few people who believe it is important to sleep positioned in a north-south direction. Some prominent geomancers have gone much further, and expressed the view that computers somehow do not fit into the natural

> Our cathedrals are like abandoned computers now, but they used to be prayer factories once.
>
> —Lawrence Durrell

> The real danger is not that computers will begin to think like men, but that men will begin to think like computers.
>
> —Sydney J. Harris

harmony of the earth; that where there are computers, there will inevitably be increased unrest, turmoil, and distress, both among individual users, and in society as a whole.

These matters interest and concern me. Not enough, surely, to dispose of my computer in order to please Mother Earth. But I do have a negative ion generator; after all, it appears that it can do no harm, and may do much good.

I tend to think of it like this: Suppose in the year 1900, someone had said:

"I have a terrific new invention. It will enable you to get from one place to another four times faster than with your horse. Its only drawback is that within 85 years, it will be killing 200,000 people a year in accidents, and untold more from respiratory disease because of the way it will pollute the atmosphere. Shall I go forth, or shall I destroy the plans?" When put in that way, most people probably would have voted to outlaw the automobile.

Now, suppose in the year 1983, someone said, "I have a terrific new invention. It will enable you to calculate your income taxes and write reports four times faster than before. It will play wonderful games, and help the military design amazing new weapons. Its only drawback is that, as a result of positive ions, flickering screens, and violation of natural laws, it will be causing the deaths of 200,000 people a year by the year 2068. Shall I go forth, or shall I destroy the plans?"

Without benefit of such foresight, of course we are plowing madly onward. We can only hope that we all are not the radium watch dial painters of today.

Dealing with the Decision Whether or Not to Be a Pirate

Let us say that someone came along and offered you a machine that could make absolutely perfect copies of a $20 bill. You put a $20 bill in the slot, and out came two $20 bills. You were told that using this machine was illegal, and would subject you to a large fine or a jail term, but at the same time, it was clear to you that there was literally zero chance that you would ever be caught. Would you use the machine?

Let's carry this one step further, before getting to the point. What if you were *also* told that every time you made a perfect copy of a $20 bill, $5 was deducted from the bank account of a

Modern man is the victim of the very instruments he values most. Every gain in power, every mastery of natural forces, every scientific addition to knowledge has proved potentially dangerous, because it has not been accompanied by equal gains in self understanding and self discipline.

—Lewis Mumford

158.

Many expensive computer programs can easily and cheaply be copied. Huge numbers of people become software "pirates" with scarcely a thought for the ethics of their acts.

man you did not know, and never *would* know. Now, do you use the machine?

It is the case that most computer programs can be automatically copied using the computer itself. This is an extremely desirable feature, because if a disk or a tape is damaged or lost, you will have replacement, or back-up copies of your programs. Copying a program or an entire disk full of programs is fast and simple, and the only cost to you is the few dollars for a second disk or cassette tape.

It is *also* the case that many programs are copyrighted, and making copies, except possibly for your own use as a spare, is strictly forbidden.

Fig. 2

Look at it this way: the word processing program I am using now retails for $150. Physically, it consists of one disk (worth about $2), and an instruction manual (maybe $3 more). *And* it consists of at least $145 worth of skill and creativity and cleverness on the part of the people who devised the program who deserve to be rewarded for their abilities.

Now let's say a good friend of mine, who has the same model computer, wants to get into word processing. Why should he buy a $2 disk for $150, when I can whip off a copy for him. No one would ever know. No alarms go off at the manufacturer's offices when an illegal copy is being made. Sure, the disk has a stern warning on it ("Unauthorized copying is a violation of Federal Law, and may carry a fine of up to $50,000 or imprisonment or both.") But no individual user is ever going to be caught or prosecuted for this, any more than for taping music off the radio.

Well, my personal answer to the dilemma is simple, but it isn't the common one. You see, I earn my living from royalties on the sale of things I create. I believe I *do* have an internal alarm that goes off in my gut every time someone, anywhere in the world, copies a book of mine on the company's Xerox machine, thereby depriving me of my rightful royalty. And I'm not about to do that to anyone else, either.

But for most people, it's just like having that $20 bill machine. No one can possibly know, so why not go ahead and do it.[1]

Some manufacturers of computer programs attempt to take

---

1. What they *don't* know is that there is a special circle of Hell reserved for flagrant copyright violators. How would *you* like to spend all eternity standing up to your waist in ice-cold oatmeal, scratching the complete works of Barbara Cartland onto an infinitely-long screeching blackboard with your fingernails?

temptation from your hands by making their disks electronically uncopyable. They have cleverly figured out how to put an instruction on the disk short-circuiting standard copying procedure.

Then along came several other companies selling special disk-copying programs which, they claim, will enable you to copy almost any "uncopyable" program. Of course they were being piously sold as devices to enable you to make back-up copies of your programs, but you must never, never use them to violate anyone's copyright, you naughty boy, you. (This is the marketing equivalent of the people who run ads in scummy tabloids offering a book on "How Dishonest People Tamper With Their Electric Meters," and a "Complete set of master keys to open and start any car, so you'll never get locked out of your car." Suuuuure.)

This created a big flap in the Ethics Departments of the many computer magazines. Some refused to run the ads. Some refused even to comment on the matter, presumably believing that if their readers learned about these "unlocking" programs, they would all rush out to buy them. Others accepted the ads, and reviewed the programs, just as if they were another space game or mailing label program.

Poetic Justice Department: The first copy-anything-uncopyable program, called Locksmith, was itself uncopyable. In other words, they had made a program that could copy anything in the world but itself. At a recent computer show, there was a booth selling a new copying program, guaranteed to copy everything *including* Locksmith. Heh heh.

159.

Some programs are made to be electronically uncopyable, but you can buy, at otherwise reputable dealers, programs designed to make copies of uncopyable programs.

The legitimate program developers' and sellers' response to all of this has been generally reasonable. Undoubtedly they are hard at work to develop uncopyable disk technology. But they also supply (in most cases) one back-up copy of a program, either at the time you buy, or, commonly, they mail you one when you send in your warranty card—either free, or for a $5 payment. Then, if something ever goes wrong with a disk, so that it needs repair or replacement, if anyone other than the registered owner sends it in, there may be trouble.

(One program I have requires, in its first use, that the owner type his or her name in. They don't tell you why at the time, but the result is that the owner's name is permanently on the disk—and, thus, on any copies that are made. Another program permits one and only one copy to be made. In the process of making that one copy, the program becomes electronically uncopyable.)

Lots of clever stuff going on in what will probably be an eternal battle between the manufacturers and the pirates. You'll have to decide for yourself what to do—but please don't forget those of us who live on royalties. Thank you.

On Stealing Computers (and Computer Time)

It hadn't occurred to me that people actually steal computers until mine was stolen. And it hadn't occurred to me that people steal time on other people's small computers until I saw all the protective gadgets sold at computer shows.

Theft prevention

At Thief School, I imagine one of the things taught is to pay attention to the price/weight ratio of stealable goods. Better to steal a ten diamond rings worth $1,000 each than a grand piano worth $10,000. Here is how computers rank in a rather arbitrary price per pound list:

Stamp collection	$10,000/lb
Gold	$5,000/lb
Silver	$150/lb
Computers	$50/lb
Typewriters	$25/lb
Pianos	$20/lb
Stereos	$10/lb
Books	$5/lb
Sofas	$2/lb
Chickens	$1/lb

In other words, computers rank fairly high on the desirability

160.

Small computers are major targets of home and office thieves, making relatively inexpensive burglary-prevention devices worth considering.

Computer Protection Unit

index for thieves, and indeed a great many small computers *are* stolen.[2]

In addition to all the standard things people do to protect their premises (locks on doors, remembering to use locks on doors,[3] alarm systems, guard dogs, land mines, etc.), there are two

2. The question arises, what else is done in thief school. An insider, Mr. Y., reports an amazing electronic breakthrough to counterattack those anti-theft barking dog tapes now on sale: a tape recording of meat.

3. This one was my problem. I had assumed my remote rural location was protection enough. The stolen Northstar did turn up nearly a year later, but by then I had used the insurance money to buy an Apple and a TRS-80. Thank you, thief.

kinds of gadgets sold specifically to keep people from stealing small computers:

One category are devices that fasten permanently (with super glue, I believe) to your desk or table, and to which the computer can be locked. This presumably discourages all but the most persistent thieves — or furniture thieves, who will inadvertently take your computer along with them as they make off with your table.

The other category are alarm devices, which fasten to a wall plug, and into which you plug the computer. When someone unplugs it, either because they are stealing it, or because they are moving it so they can vacuum behind your desk, a shrill alarm goes off, deafening the thief (or the maid), and perhaps causing either to drop the computer to the floor and run.

The value of either depends, of course, on your own personal situation. Your homeowner's or business insurance policy may cover computers now (and can surely cover them with a special rider or endorsement), and may provide just as much peace of mind.

Preventing theft of time

This can be a major problem with large computers that are on most of the time, and have telephone line connections. The literature of computer anecdotes is full of stories of teenagers from Iowa City (or somewhere) who use their school computer and telephone to double the size of the payroll checks of a company in Tennessee, to send 10,000 telegrams to their favorite teacher, or to launch a missile attack against Ecuador.

This is of little relevance to the small computer user, whose main concern may be that unauthorized business colleagues, fellow students, family members, or pets may use his or her machine after hours. Presumably this is something of a problem, because quite a few manufacturers make gadgets to prevent its happening. These take the form of plastic devices that cover the keys (or the whole computer) and lock into place, or electrical locks that keep power from reaching the computer until a key is turned.

If I lived in a big city and/or worked in a big office, I probably would worry about some of the above matters, and would be glad to know that the necessary equipment is available, at modest prices, to protect my equipment.

The Sledgehammers of the Night: Computer Sabotage

A newspaper reporter from Colorado responded to my "tell me your problems" letter to the editor that was printed in his paper. He started out almost enthusiastically, telling me how easy it was to write and edit on the computer terminals that had been installed at his paper a few years ago. He really didn't miss his old Remington Standard typewriter at all.

So why was he calling? Well, it turned out he *did* have a problem or two. Or 20. Just yesterday, in fact, a major story, written under pressure of a tight deadline, was totally lost somewhere in the bowels of the computer system. And there's no carbon copy, as on the old Remington. This was by no means the first time that had happened. Oh, and the flickering green screen gave him an almost constant headache.

Now his voice took on a conspiratorial tone. He asked for and I gave assurance that I would not mention his name or city.

"You know what I'd do," he asked, "if the doctor told me I had incurable cancer, and had only six months to live? I'd go to the hardware store and buy the biggest sledgehammer they had. Then I'd go to the newspaper office in the middle of the night, and I'd smash every one of the 30 computer terminals there into smithereens. *That's* what I'd do."

He probably would, too.

And not everyone waits for a terminal cancer diagnosis, either. Computer sabotage is a significant problem in the nation's offices and factories. Even the home computer is not safe — although the problem there is more often an impulsive act, rather than planned mayhem.

Leaving out, as irrelevant to this book, cases in which people sabotage computers in order to get revenge on their employer, their company, or the world, we are left with two kinds of situations in our casebook: people who want to kill their computer because it doesn't work correctly, and people who want to kill their computer because they think it is trying to kill them.

Sabotaging a poorly-working machine

The literature and lore of computers are replete with tales of people getting so fed up with malfunctioning machinery that they try to put it out of its misery. Sometimes they are the owners of the machines; sometimes, like the fantasizing Colorado reporter, they are the innocent victims of someone else's equipment.

A man in Washington murdered his home computer with a shotgun. Two blasts right between the disk drives. "I had taken all I was gonna take from that little bastard," he told the sheriff. A woman in Illinois set her Apple carefully in her driveway, and drove back and forth over it half a dozen times. Someone (never identified in the press) in a Texas office building threw a TRS-80 computer from a sixth-floor office window to the street below. An architectural firm in Massachusetts held a funeral for its computer system, then buried it beneath six feet of dirt. (What do you suppose these folks told the insurance investigators?)

Since these, and many more like them, are stories that actually made the newspapers, one cannot but wonder how many more tales there are, either secretly carried out, or simply not deemed sufficiently newsworthy for the major papers.

(Happily, not all destructive fantasies are carried out. A disgruntled Northstar owner who is also a private pilot told me of his secret plan to drop his computer onto the Northstar building from a height of 5,000 feet. He said that the only reason he hasn't is his inability to drop it directly onto the head of the person who designed the disk drives.)

Killing the machine before it kills you

Physical and psychological hazards involved in using a computer are discussed on page 242. Most victims (or people who feel victimized) deal with perceived problems in what might be called a socially acceptable manner: they take whatever is dished out; they try to make changes; or they sue the pants off their employers or the computer company.

But some people perceive a great evil in the machine, and feel they are doing mankind a favor by eliminating it from the face of the earth. A New York woman who believed she was losing her eyesight from watching a computer screen for years, sprayed black paint on the screen, the insides of the computer, and, apparently, her desk. A man who came to believe that his programs were being altered just a little every day, set fire to 50 floppy disks in the company restroom. A Canadian wife who felt that her husband's home computer was breaking up their marriage weighted it (the computer, not the husband) with rocks and drowned it in a nearby lake. And when virtually all the employees of an Ohio

161.
Computer sabotage is a significant problem in offices and factories. In the home, sabotage is perpetrated mostly by jealous spouses, since computers cannot be sued for alienation of affection.

I begin to believe that the computer is not the great god we have been led to believe, but a hollow idol, manipulated by crafty priests.

—Bernard Levin

carpet warehouse threatened to quit soon after a new computer system was installed, claiming it was destroying the quality of life there, the management not only removed the offending system, but called in a priest to exorcise the evil electronic spirits that might remain.

Dealing with the urge to kill

Unless one has irrefutable evidence that one's computer is trying to kill someone (e.g., HAL in the movie 2001), it is probably much healthier (and generally more economical) not to murder your computer. However, there are indisputably times when *something* has to be done for your own mental health.

My daughter Mariah found considerable satisfaction in destroying just one floppy disk—one that had been causing her problems. Disks burn very nicely, with a multi-colored flame, and little flaming "buzz bombs" of particles that whiz to the ground. Of course this needs to be done carefully, perhaps with an environmental impact report, lest you set your carpet ablaze or loose a flood of vile particles on the nearby populace. I have burned only two disks in my first eight years as a computer owner. Since the same $5 expenditure would have bought me only four minutes with a psychiatrist, I consider it an excellent investment in mental health.

Computer Crime

This is not the place for a definitive survey of computer crime (Thomas Whiteside has already done that in his splendid book, *Computer Capers: Tales of Electronic Thievery, Embezzlement, and Fraud*). Nor is it the place for a "how to" manual, either on perpetrating or detecting computer crime. But I think it is important to point out how easy the former is, and how difficult the latter is.

We are *all* victims of computer crimes (except for the computer criminals), if only in that we pay higher fees for bank, credit card, insurance, and other services, because *someone* has to pay back the $5 billion or more that is stolen through computer crime each year.

Some industry spokesmen deny the figure is even one tenth this high. But some insiders believe it could be a great deal higher than $5 billion. The reason for the huge discrepancy is that by its very nature, computer crime is almost impossible to detect.

162.
Setting fire to one disk is a satisfying way of overcoming temporary computer hostility.

163.
We are all victims of computer crime, whether we know it or not. An enlightened public offers the one faint hope of dealing with the problem.

If a robber points a gun at a bank teller, fills a sack, and roars off, no one will dispute that the bank has been robbed. But when a computer criminal makes a minor adjustment in the bank's computer and transfers one dollar from each of 100,000 accounts into his own account, it may be years before anyone notices, if ever.

With telephone computer links, such crimes can be committed without ever setting foot in the bank. There are hundreds of published accounts of people — often teenagers using their school computer — who tap into someone else's computer, and wreak havoc. Sometimes they just leave amusing messages; sometimes they do a great deal more. For instance, four 13-year-olds at a fancy New York private school tapped into the computer of several banks and corporations, juggling accounts, and erasing millions of bits of information.

How computer crime goes undetected

If you left a $20 bill on your dresser at night and it was gone in the morning, you would begin to suspect a crime. But let's say you left a $20 bill on your dresser, another in your car, and a third in your office. Along comes a clever thief. He breaks in and steals the $20 from your dresser. But then, just before you get up, he steals the $20 from your car and leaves it on your dresser. Just before you go to your car, he steals the $20 from your office and puts it in your car. Before you arrive at the office, he has gone back and re-stolen the $20 from your dresser and put it in your office. Since you can only be in one place at a time, as far as you know, you have three $20 bills. But in fact, you only have two; the thief has stolen one-third of your assets.

Using this strategy, computer thieves have set up incredibly elaborate electronic systems to cover up their crimes. They rig a bank's computer to take money out of accounts, but to transfer it back in from someone else's account just before the auditor comes through.

I visited one of the most successful computer criminals of all time at a California state prison, where he was serving a two-year sentence for stealing millions of dollars from a bank.[4] He told me

I fear none of the existing machines; what I fear is the extraordinary rapidity with which they are becoming something very different to what they are at present . . . Should not that movement be jealously watched and checked while we can still check it?

—Samuel Butler, 1872

---

4. Even when caught, which is rare, computer criminals rarely get long sentences. Judges and juries both have trouble understanding the nature of the crime. While a typical armed bank robber nets $2,500 and serves 11 years if caught, the typical computer bank robber nets over $100,000, and serves less than 3 years.

that he was aware of dozens and dozens of crimes currently being committed — some of them having been in progress for several years — and most of which, he predicted, would never be detected because of ingenious track-covering programs.

Various kinds of computer crimes

One doesn't have to be a programming genius to commit computer crime. In fact, some people argue that if you notice the telephone company's computer has undercharged you by a dollar, and you don't report it, you are, in effect, a computer criminal.

- A bookkeeper for a 50-employee company was shown how to enter payroll data in the computer. Although she knew nothing about programming or computers, she quickly figured out that she could deduct $4 each week from each other employee's withholding and add it to hers, thereby producing a huge tax refund for herself each year.

- A clerk in a doctor's office noticed that when a patient had a very rare operation, the insurance company paid for it, but due to a programming flaw, the payment information was not listed on the account summary. She tentatively put through another patient with that rare operation added to his other treatments, and again payment was made. And so every patient of this doctor, whether they came in for an annual physical or a wart removal, was "given" this rare operation. The insurance company kept on paying, and there was no evidence, written or electronic.

A penny here, a penny there, it adds up

Many computer crimes are as close to victimless as any crime can be.

- Once, when bank interest rates were 5-1/3%, a programmer noticed that the bank was paying 5.3333% to two account-holders and, randomly, 5.3334% to a third (so it would all come out even). He rigged things so *all* customers got 5.3333%, and *he* got the remaining .0001% added into his account. That's only a penny a year for each $30,000 — but with "50 billion a day flushing back and forth across America in the form of electrons" (as Joseph Coates puts it), those tiny bits added up to many thousands of dollars a year.

- A man rigged the computer at a dog racing track to figure the payoffs on one race per day as *if* there had been three additional winners. So each of thousands of real winners would get a dollar or two less, and this chap, with his winning tickets issued by an accomplice *after* the race, was netting a couple of thousand dollars a day.

- A bank employee adjusted a program to add 15 cents a month to thousands of checking account service charges. Since no one understands those charges anyway, no one noticed — and $10,000 a month was skimmed off, ending up (electronically, of course) in a Swiss bank.

Other popular forms of computer crime

- Stealing information. One company taps into another company's computer, to learn about their sales, pricing changes, etc.
- Changing information. Students enter their school's computer and change their grades. This is almost impossible to discover. A school like the University of California issues over a million grades a year, and to cross-check each one with the professor's grade cards would cost a fortune.
- Stealing merchandise. A college student worked at a telephone company warehouse during the summer, and learned that branches would order merchandise by tapping in information on touch-tone phones. Over the next few years, he ordered over a million dollars in parts, which he sold through his "cover" company, Creative Telephone.
- Creating people. If a computer says someone is real, they are real. The billion-dollar Equity Funding scandal involved inventing thousands of non-existent people, by computer, giving them life insurance policies, and then selling those policies to other companies. That's the grand scale. There are many, many cases where companies bought non-existent goods from non-existent suppliers with real money; had a few phantom people on the payroll, etc.

What can be done?

Not a whole lot. Awareness is part of it, of course. One computer detective says that most companies protect the change in the soft drink machine more carefully than access to their computer. Most banks spend more on video cameras and armed guards than on seeking out electronic fraud. But it seems clear that whatever system an honest expert can invent, a dishonest expert can solve and defeat. Elaborate systems of encryption, passwords, and other controls are regularly broken almost as soon as they are installed.

Some people lobby for mandatory ethics study in computer classes. That should work at least as well as the 55-miles-an-hour speed limit.

An enlightened public offers another faint hope. That crook who was extracting 15 cents from each checking account was caught only because one bank customer fought through the bank's supercilious "We can't be wrong" attitude and finally got through to someone willing to check out that 15-cent overcharge.

But that's a rare event. It is almost certainly the case that the computer boom is destined to grow hand in hand with the electronic crime boom.

The Jangling Can:
How Computers Destroy Privacy

Every American president since Dwight Eisenhower has been intrigued with the idea of a National Data Bank. If *all* the information the government has collected at various times on each individual were combined in a single giant computer, would there not be wonderful benefits (to the government)?

By matching census with draft data, all unregistered persons over 18 could be identified. By matching driver's licenses with people who get aid to the blind, frauds could be uncovered. By comparing income tax forms with real estate records, people who failed to declare capital gains might be found. And so on.

There are only two problems with all of this: errors and Hitlers.

1. *Errors.* Computers *do* make mistakes. If they attempted to cross-check and correlate a dozen factors for a quarter of a billion Americans, and if the machinery operated at a 99.999% accuracy, then there would only be a few *billion* errors made. When author Charles Reich testified before the U.S. Congress in opposition to the National Data Bank idea, he likened such errors to a jangling can. "All the rest of his life, wherever he (the innocent victim) went, he would have a tin can jangling along behind him."

2. *Hitlers.* Civil libertarians point out that if Germany had had a National Data Bank in 1939, Hitler's extermination of the Jews would have happened much faster and more efficiently. It seems amazing to me that the same people who oppose gun registration because then the Commies would know where to come and get their guns, generally support the National Data Bank idea. How

do we know that the next Hitler to come down the pike won't have it in for Catholics or old people or Masons or veterans or truck drivers or Jewish dentists who drive Volvos?

But how much do computers *really* know about us now? You want a list of Jewish dentists who drive Volvos? A man in Ohio got such a list by using a computer to cross-check computerized lists of Jews, dentists, and Volvo owners, all of which appear on various computer records.

Sometime in a library, for a good scare, look up the *Standard Rate and Data Mailing List Directory.* It describes thousands and thousands of computer mailing lists that almost anyone can rent for about five cents a name. Subscribers to most magazines. Bald people. People who have more than $10,000 in their checking account. Stamp collectors. People who buy X-rated video-cassettes. Tall people. Black people. People with more than three children. One-legged people.

Every time you use your name in public, whether to get a driver's license, buy by mail, use a credit card, sign a guest book, give to a charity, write to a senator, enter a hospital, rent a car, join a union or a club, etc. etc., you end up in someone's computer, and your name becomes a rentable or saleable commodity.

The thought of combining all these computer records into a single National Computer is terrifying. Consider, as Joel Chaseman, president of Post-Newsweek Stations puts it, what will happen "when the computers of cable companies and charge card companies speak to AT&T's computer, and together discuss what you've watched, where you've gone, what you've read, the source and size of your income, and what calls you have made. The computers know and they will tell, unless Congress decides that they should not. . . ."

What can we do?

Oppose the National Data Bank (76% of Americans do, according to the Harris Poll).

Support the American Civil Liberties Union's battle against the National Data Bank.

Consider the Swedish approach, where the Data Inspection Board regulates every computer data bank in the country that keeps personal records. They license data keepers, check out security systems, and investigate and prosecute violations.

If you use your small computer in business or any public-related way, use it responsibly.

Track the computerization of your own life by using different names or middle initials in harmless public situations. We once took out a magazine subscription in the name of my daughter's pet rat, Sean Lord Derryberry. If that rat had a mailbox, it would never be empty. Offers, catalogues, Easter seals, charity requests, even a chance to buy his personal family coat of arms.

The law now requires that you can demand to have your name removed from a mailing list—but it may have been rented to 17 other organizations before it is deleted, and each of those 17 will use it and rent it, and the tin can goes jangling along.

Spanish Ladies on Bicycles: Computers and the Economy

"Electronic Brain To Replace Million Workers," screamed the headline in a 1953 science magazine. Throughout the 1950s, many philosophers devoted much time and many square inches of text to the matter of how computers would affect the economy.

Remarkably, well into the third decade of the computer age, we're still not sure what the effect has been, or what it will be. As Jon Stewart wrote in *Saturday Review* a few years ago, "The United States government is notable for its lack of initiative in calculating the job impact of the new technology . . ."

It seems easier for critics to investigate, and to point with alarm (or pride) at individual cases, rather than at society as a whole. For example: Business A "hires" a computer and fires two bookkeepers and an accountant as a result; Factory B installs computers along its assembly line and lets seven hourly workers and one foreman go; Newspaper C proposes computerizing its pressroom, whereupon the union announces that this will eliminate 64 jobs, and calls a strike.

It would certainly *appear* that some of the early "electronic brain" fears were correct. And yet, when we look more closely at individual cases, we often see that things are far more complex than they appeared on the surface.

Business A may have fired three pencil-pushers, but they had to hire a higher-salaried programmer, take out an expensive service contract, and retrain various other employees. Things got shuffled around, but the bottom line—company profits—didn't improve at all.

Factory B had so many problems getting their computers up and running, and learning to live with them, that they actually *lost* money for the first two years of computerization, but are hoping to show a profit in the third.

And Newspaper C negotiated an arrangement with the union whereby no one will be fired, but the work force will be reduced by attrition over the years. So five people operate the addressing and labeling department, just as before, even though one person plus the computer could do it just as well.

The one thing that seems clear to everyone is that a great many "traditional" jobs *are* going to be lost. A report on the effect of computerizing French industry was so devastating, the reigning government suppressed it until after a forthcoming election. (It predicted that 30% of the people in labor-intensive industries — banking, insurance, etc. — would lose their jobs within ten years.)

In America, the Service Employees International Union (which used to represent elevator operators and bowling alley pin spotters, so they *know* what automation can do) worries that the jobs of 40% of all office workers may be eliminated by 1990.

Another thing that most people agree on is that the computer industry *is* creating a large number of new jobs. These new jobs fall into three categories: programmers, attendants, and Spanish ladies on bicycles.

1. *Programmers.* The smallest category is computer programmers. We have a few hundred thousand now, and ultimately we'll need somewhere between one and five million, depending on whose predictions you read. (The way young people, and unemployed older people are rushing into programming classes, we may have more unemployed programmers in the '90s than we had unemployed space scientists in the '70s or teachers in the '60s — to name two other fields people were once advised to rush into.)

2. *Attendants.* Computers require a great deal of attention, from when a business first considers one (planners, salespeople, etc.), to the installation (architects, designers, movers, electricians, heating and ventilation people, etc.), to its operation (data entry clerks, paper movers, etc.) to its upkeep (repair people, cleaners, adjusters, etc.)

For instance, one large refrigerated packing plant installed computer-controlled thermostats to replace the old mechanical

165.

Three decades into the computer age, there is still much disagreement on whether computers are good or bad for the economy and employment.

166.

People who computerize often seem surprised by the amount of routine clerical behaviors *someone* must do to keep it running.

ones. The old ones clicked off or on every 10 or 15 minutes, and turned the air conditioning off or on as a result. The new ones monitored the temperature 60 times a second, and turned the compressors off and on so often that two people had to be hired just to repair or replace switches, relays, and wiring that wore out. Their salaries nearly equalled the savings from the more precisely controlled atmosphere.

3. *Spanish ladies on bicycles.* Robert Hutchins used to tell the story of the huge bakery in Germany that computerized its operation. Dozens of highly-trained bakers were dismissed. The computerized ovens had error-detection systems which turned on a little red light when something was going wrong. In order to monitor the red lights, the bakery hired a platoon of Spanish ladies (the cheapest available labor) to ride up and down the aisles on bicycles. When they saw a red light, they reported it to a foreman who sent out a technician.

In other words, the computer appears to be bringing about a major reshuffling of job behaviors. As Peter Drucker puts it, "The main impact of the computer has been the providing of unlimited jobs for clerks."

Computers are undoubtedly having a major effect on the way much of the world operates — but whether they are good, bad, or indifferent for the economy is still a matter of much speculation and dispute.

PART SIX

REFERENCE, ETC.

My computer autobiography. Books you
may wish to read. Glossary of relevant
terms. Index.

My Computer
Autobiography

The original title of this book was going to have been, "How I went from a $35,000 Digital computer to a $15,000 Micromation computer to a $10,000 Northstar computer to a $3,000 Apple computer to a $600 Radio Shack computer to a 10¢ Eberhard Faber pencil."

A little hard to remember, albeit reasonably accurate.

The purpose of this section, then, is to establish my credentials for writing a book of this sort. There is nothing really wrong with those scores of people who spend a few months (or even a few years) with a certain computer, and then write the "definitive text" on What It All Means.

Often, a certain perspective, gained only through having a wide range of experience, is missing. People have actually written guidebooks to faraway lands based on a three-week trip. Their sweeping generalizations ("It almost always rains in Macho Grande, and the women do not take kindly to strangers") are often not utterly reliable.

I bought my first computer in 1975. My mail order business had about 80,000 names and addresses on an antiquated mechanical system designed for 5,000 names at best. My then-partner and I decided we would get the best computer we could afford. We went to the then-largest manufacturer of small ("small" in 1975 meant under $100,000) computers, Digital Equipment Corporation, and bought their model 310, which, with software, accessories, and all, came to about $35,000. Four 8″ double-sided double-density disk drives.

It never worked well. The manufacturer claimed it was delivered and installed improperly (by the dealer), and that there were major software flaws. The software company always claimed it was a hardware problem, and that their programs were perfect. However, from delivery day to the day we sent it away, more than 400 hours of repair and service time were logged. (After 18 months, we actually moved our business 150 miles, solely to be nearer to a DEC repairman, so we wouldn't be paying $60 an hour, door to door, for him to make a three-hour drive each way.)

When my partner and I split up, he kept the DEC. I got two chairs, a table, and the fire extinguisher.

Computer number two was a Micromation, bought largely because it was one of the very few machines that came with a one-year instead of the standard 90-day warranty. Two 8″ double-sided double-density drives, a Texas Instruments printer, and a lot of software — some "off the shelf," some specially written, and a total bill around $15,000.

The first major lesson learned was that a one-year warranty saves some money, but if the machine has to be hand-carried in to the company (including taking it up a long flight of stairs), and the company is 150 miles away, there is a certain lessening of the convenience factor, especially since major repairs were required every couple of months.

Having speedily developed the axiom "Never buy anything you can't lift," when an opportunity arose to trade the Micromation system even-Steven for a smaller Northstar Horizon computer (two 5-1/4″ double-sided double-density drives, and a system price around $10,000), I leaped at it.

The first need was to convert all our records from the Micromation's 8″ disks to the Northstar's 5-1/4″ disks. While theoretically, this is no more complex than, say, converting your record collection to cassette tapes, in practice it was my first awareness of the deadly "99% factor." If you capture 99% of the notes when you re-record your phonograph records, no one will ever know. But when you lose 1% of your numerical data, you're in big trouble.

Add to this disk drives that just didn't work well (a Northstar service executive admitted that the company may have been "premature" in releasing the double-sided double-density version; other versions apparently worked just fine), and the Northstar experience was far from enjoyable.

A glimmer of light was just visible at the end of my Northstar tunnel, but then thieves turned off the light. The Northstar computer was stolen over the New Year's weekend of 1981. There was some joy in my tears of sorrow. There was some sorrow in my tears of joy.

When the insurance check finally came, I bought the *only* computer that was then locally sold, locally serviced, and allegedly locally supported (help, information, advice): an Apple II+, with two single-sided single-density disk drives. I have used this machine with considerable happiness for more than two years. There were a few minor problems while it was under warranty; there have been none since. I am aware that it is said to be slow and old-fashioned in ways I cannot really understand; I realize that newer machines can do lots more, and in jig time as well; yet I have seen nothing so radically different *and* so readily affordable that I am ready to give up the old Apple yet. Someday, I surely will. Perhaps next Tuesday.

Computers number 5 and 6 are a couple of Radio Shack TRS-80 Model 1s. These were required because they are the only computers that can "drive" the old-fashioned Compugraphic phototypesetter of which I am part owner. The fantasy has been that I could write books into a computer, and the words would ultimately end up in typesetting, without having to be typed again.

The Radio Shack experience has, to date, not been a lot of fun. There have been problems with both computers and all four disk drives. To their credit, Radio Shack has been prompt and not too expensive in fixing things. But there have surely been a lot of things in need of fixing.

Some people swear by Radio Shack; others swear at them. I am locked into using them for my typesetting ventures, but I wish I didn't have to. Many people have told me they have had very positive TRS experiences. I wish I could join them.

What I am going to do next

Gee, I don't know. Buy another computer, I suppose — either because the Apple wears out, or because something new comes along that I cannot live without. So far (knock on silicon) neither has happened.

Actually, I *do* know exactly what I want. Instead of looking at what the various manufacturers were offering *me,* I carefully analyzed my own needs, and determined the features that I require from them. The only problem is that such a machine does not yet exist. But I have good reason to believe it will, and when that happens, if the funds are available, I will buy.

I can describe my personal "dream" computer. It will be quite different from many other people's dream computer. (We all use them in different, personal ways.) All I want is this:

- a 10-pound-or-less battery-powered (50-hour batteries) computer
- an 80-column eight-line-or-more screen
- ability to store data on microcassettes or mini-disks
- silent operation
- a good word processing program
- full compatibility with a larger office computer, which will accept the same disks or tapes, or otherwise permit transfer of data
- cost of under $5,000 for the entire system — the portable and the office equipment

You see, what I want is to be able to carry the little battery-powered unit around with me, so I can do my usual stuff (writing, correspondence, note-taking, etc.) in libraries, on airplanes, on vacation, whatever, and then send or carry the disks or tapes back to my office, where someone (generally me) edits them, prints them out, and dispatches them to the waiting world.

We're almost there, Santa. Maybe this year. Teleram is close. Epson is close. Radio Shack is close. Apple and IBM are doubtless feverishly working to please me. How many days 'til Christmas?

Books You May Wish to Read

Then again, you may not wish to read them. There never should be any *need* to read a book about computers (except perhaps the instruction manual, and not even all of that) in order to use computers successfully.

There are several thousand books about computers now on the market, and a dozen or two new ones appearing each week! Even if I *wanted* to offer a list of recommended books, it would be quite out of date by the time it reached print. Nearly all of the books pretty well fit into one of four categories:

1. What does it all mean?

Philosophical books on the meaning, nature, and import of the computer revolution we may be experiencing.

2. How to get started

A remarkable number of nearly identical books, albeit with different titles, on how to buy your first computer.

3. How to get more out of your whatever

Hundreds of books geared to specific models of computers: how to write programs for the ZX-80; how to play games with the QX-10; how to use the B747; etc.

4. Books for experts

Well over a thousand books presumably for advanced programmers and other experts; most of the time, I don't even understand the titles (e.g., *Optimization of Error Recovery in Syntax-Directed Parsing Algorithms*).

Over the years, reading computer books has not been a major pastime of mine. However I *have* bought eight books that I liked — in part because they didn't fit into any of the above cate-

IMPORTANT RULE:

Beware of any computer book using

THIS TYPE FACE

just as you should beware of any Chinese restaurant using

gories. I've read all of one, most of some, and some of most. For whatever it may be worth, then, they are, alphabetically:

Computer Choices: Beware of Conspicuous Computing by H. Dominic Covvey and Neil McAlister (Addison-Wesley, 1982). "Conspicuous computing" is defined as "an irrational lust for the aura of sophistication and progress that a person, department, or institution can acquire by becoming computerized." A delightful potpourri of philosophy, common sense advice on whether or not to buy a computer, and some horrendous case histories and anecdotes.

Computer Consciousness: Surviving the Automated 80s by H. Dominic Covvey and Neil McAlister (Addison-Wesley, 1980). This is essentially quite a technical book, explaining a great deal about how computers work, but it is written in comprehensible English—quite a rarity for this kind of book. Some interesting philosophy on man-machine systems.

Mindstorms: Children, Computers and Powerful Ideas by Seymour Papert (Basic Books, 1980). Professor Papert is a leading educational theorist, and at the forefront in the field of computers and education. This book talks a lot about some potentially vast changes computers can make in how people think as well as how they live. A lot of semi-technical stuff on Papert's LOGO program for teaching programming to young children.

An Introduction to Microcomputers, Volume 0 by Adam Osborne (Osborne/McGraw-Hill, 1980). When Osborne (later to market the Osborne computer) published Volumes 1, 2, and 3 of his series, readers cried out for a simpler volume for people who knew almost nothing. The result, Volume 0, provides detailed and quite comprehensible explanations of all those things you don't *need* to know but might *want* to know: how information is physically stored on tape and disks; how the binary number system operates; what semiconductors do; etc.

The Personal Computer Book by Peter A. McWilliams (Prelude/ Ballantine, 1982). Quite a delightful book, with useful information on how computers work, how they are used, and how to buy one, with a heavily-opinionated brand-name buying guide. More than

100 pages of sometimes amusing but totally irrelevant illustrations.[1] Deservedly one of the best-selling computer books around.

The Psychology of Computer Programming by Gerald M. Weinberg (Van Nostrand Reinhold, 1971). A most intriguing book, often technical but even more often comprehensible, dealing with the behaviors and thought processes of programmers; how programs can reflect the personality of the programmer, etc. It was this book more than anything else that showed me why I should never learn programming, for which I am grateful.

The Soul of a New Machine by Tracy Kidder (Little, Brown, 1981). A best-seller and a Pulitzer Prize winner, this fascinating book ostensibly describes the designing of a new computer at the Data General Corporation, but it says a great deal more about the computer industry and the people who make it run.

The Word Processing Book: A Short Course in Computer Literacy by Peter A. McWilliams (Prelude/Ballantine, 1982). A useful and amusing book that tells everything a beginner could possibly want to know about word processing. Not a specific "how to do it" book, but especially useful for people considering getting involved with word processing, yet uncertain as to just what is involved.

The following two reference books, referred to in the main text, are useful for people who may wish to learn more about computers by correspondence study, or to parlay their computer knowhow into a college degree.

How to Get the Degree You Want by John Bear (Ten Speed Press, 1982). The only reason for mentioning another book by the author of *Computer Wimp* (other than an attempt to sell more books) is that, as explained on page 126, it is actually possible to earn college credit (and even degrees) based on credit for computer experience. The key concept is *life experience learning*. If you can demonstrate to the school that you have the knowledge, they'll give you the same credit (or degrees) as residential stu-

---

1. "You should talk." — P.A.M.

dents with equivalent knowledge. My book explains how to do this, and describes all the schools offering Bachelor's, Master's and Doctorates by this method.

Guide to Independent Study Through Correspondence Instruction (Peterson's Guides, Princeton, NJ, revised every few years). This book is like a master catalogue of those 68 colleges and universities offering correspondence study. All courses (by course title only) at all schools are listed. By using the barely-satisfactory index, you can locate the scores of computer classes (and, indeed, classes on any subject) available from among the several thousand separate offerings. Three of the schools offering a variety of correspondence courses in computers and computer programming are:

Graduate School of the U.S. Department of Agriculture
Correspondence Study Program
600 Maryland Ave. S.W., Room 133
Washington, DC 20024

Oregon State System of Higher Education
Office of Independent Study
P.O. Box 1491
Portland, OR 97207

University of California
Independent Study, Dept. NN
2223 Fulton St.
Berkeley, CA 94720

Glossary

There are computer dictionaries on the market with thousands and thousands of definitions. The few definitions that follow are those that are most likely to be needed by the relative beginner. It is useful to know the words "hardware" and "software." Beyond that, nothing is essential. There will be no quiz at the end.

alphanumeric
Characters including both letters and numbers (and, usually, punctuation marks and other symbols). Typewriters and most printers are alphanumeric. Small calculators are numeric only.

assembly language
A programming language permitting advanced programmers to write complex or sophisticated programs. No one who understands assembly language would be likely to read this book.

back-up
A copy of important files. One should always make back-up copies of programs, data, and other records. Sensible people store the back-up in another location.

BASIC
One of the most common and simplest programming languages, developed for beginners at Dartmouth many years ago.

baud rate
The rate at which data is sent, or transmitted, from one place to another. One baud (rhymes with "flawed") is one bit per second. Many computers transmit at 300 to 1200 baud. Humans talk to each other at about 10 baud.

binary
The number system all computers use. All numbers are expressed using only 1's and 0's.

bit

The basic unit of information or data used by computers. A bit is represented by a 1 or a 0, corresponding to a computer switch being on or off. A string of 8 bits makes 1 byte.

boot up

The act of electronically transferring a program from a tape or disk into the temporary memory of a computer, so that it can be used, is called "booting up" the disk or the program. "Why don't you boot up that disk and we'll see what we've got."

buffer

A part of the computer where information can be stored temporarily. For instance, there might be an "edit buffer" into which a chapter of a book can be electronically dumped, edited, and then returned to permanent storage. The footnotes might be kept in a "footnote buffer" until needed.

byte

A string of 8 bits. A byte is equivalent to a single character: a letter, number, or other symbol. 1,024 bytes makes 1 kilobyte, or 1K.

character

Generally the same as byte: a single letter, number, or other symbol. The word "byte" was probably invented because "a 64 kilo-character" computer sounds funny.

chip

A hunk of silicon about the size of your little fingernail, on which are etched thousands of tiny electronic circuits. One chip can hold as much stuff as a room full of 1960 machinery.

compatible

Two pieces of hardware are compatible if they can work with each other. Thus two computers are compatible when they run the same programs and their disks or tapes are interchangeable. A computer may or may not be compatible with a given printer, disk drive, telephone modem, etc.

compiler

A special program that takes instructions written in a programming language and translates them into the machine language the computer understands. Sort of the equivalent of the waitress who hears "Two poached eggs on toast, please" (input) and shouts to the chef, "Adam and Eve on a raft" (output).

computer

An extremely fast and complex adding machine.

configuration

The layout or design of a computer system, often used as a verb: "We'll configure a system to meet your needs."

CP/M

An operating system used in many popular small computers. Programs designed to be run on a "CP/M machine" will not run on computers without CP/M.

CPS

Characters per second, as in the speed of a printer. Printers can range from 10 cps to several hundred.

CPU

The central processing unit, or CPU, is the actual core of the computer—the logic and circuits where data is processed. In modular computers, where there is a printer, disk drives, a monitor, etc., the element with the keyboard is sometimes called the CPU.

CRT

Cathode ray tube: the "picture tube" in a television monitor or computer terminal. Computer descriptions might refer, for instance, to a 9″ CRT.

daisy wheel

The small round device used on "typewriter quality" printers to print characters onto paper. The letters are at the tips of the "petals" of the daisy.

descenders

The parts of lower case letters such as g, j, p, q, and y that descend below the line. Some dot matrix printers cannot print descenders, and some people think that makes their printout look funny.

diagnostics

Tests used to determine whether a computer, printer, or other hardware is working properly. Some pieces of hardware have "built-in diagnostics."

disk

Computer purists insist a disk is the big metal thing used in big computers, while the small plastic things used in small computers are "diskettes." Most people who use diskettes call them "disks" or "floppies" (from "floppy disk" because they are flexible). Information is stored magnetically on disks in the same way it is stored on audio or video tapes. Floppy disks come in sizes from 2" to 8" in diameter, with 5-1/2" and 8" being the most common.

disk drive

A unit that "plays" a disk in much the same way a phonograph plays a record.

diskette

See disk.

double-density

A disk and disk drive that squeezes twice as much information into the same space as a single-density system. Single-density disks will normally work on a double-density system, but not vice versa. Also called "dual density."

double-sided

A disk and disk drive system in which information can be stored and extracted from both sides of a disk. If, for instance, a single-sided single-density 5-1/4" disk can hold 90,000 bytes of information ("90K"), then a double-sided *or* a double-density disk will hold 180K, and a double-sided double-density disk would hold 360K.

dot matrix

A printing system in which each letter is formed out of an array, or matrix, of tiny dots, as with letters on scoreboards.

downtime

The time a computer is out of service, or "down." People talk about the "downtime record" of a computer.

8-bit processor

A computer that can "swallow" 8 bits, or 1 byte at a time. This is the smallest size in common use, and is about one-fourth as fast as a 16-bit processor.

end user

Computer companies and dealers refer to the customer — you and me — as the end user.

file

A collection of specific information stored in a given place in a computer's memory, not unlike a file stored in a filing cabinet. The things in a file are often called "records."

floppy disk

See disk.

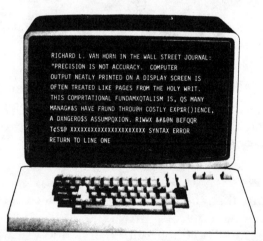

```
RICHARD L. VAN HORN IN THE WALL STREET JOURNAL:
"PRECISION IS NOT ACCURACY.  COMPUTER
OUTPUT NEATLY PRINTED ON A DISPLAY SCREEN IS
OFTEN TREATED LIKE PAGES FROM THE HOLY WRIT.
THIS COMPRTATIONAL FUNDAMXQTALISM IS, QS MANY
MANAG#&S HAVE FRUND THROU@H COSTLY EXP%R()IENCE,
A DXNGERO$S ASSUMPQXION. RIWWX &#&@N BEFQQR
T¢S%@ XXXXXXXXXXXXXXXXXXXXXX SYNTAX ERROR
RETURN TO LINE ONE
```

If you put tomfoolery into a computer, nothing comes out but tomfoolery. But this tomfoolery, having passed through a very expensive machine, is somehow ennobled and no one dares criticize it.

—Pierre Gallois

GIGO

"Garbage In, Garbage Out." In other words, a computer is no better than what you put into it. In some circles, however, this is known as "Garbage In, Gospel Out." In other words, whatever a computer says must be right.

hard copy

The same as "printout"—the actual paper that comes out of the printer, as contrasted with words and numbers appearing temporarily on the monitor screen.

hard disk

A sealed storage unit with a much higher capacity than floppy disks, often from 1 to 10 megabytes (1 to 10 million bytes).

hardware

The actual physical equipment in a system: the computer, disk drives, printer, etc. Contrasted with the software, which is the changeable stuff—the programs that drive the equipment. A good analogy: stereo system is hardware; records and cassette tapes are software.

input

As a noun, that which is entered into a computer. "The input consists of monthly sales figures. The computer's output will be annual sales comparisons." Alas, seems to be becoming a verb, too: "Jones here will input the latest figures."

interactive

A program that, in effect, carries on a conversation with the human at the controls, providing instructions, prompting for responses, and pointing out errors. "Incorrect entry. ZIP codes must have five digits." Interactive programs are often helpful at the start but grow tedious when one has learned what to do. (In some programs, the prompting can be turned off.)

interface

Technically the connection between two parts of a computer system, by cable, plug and socket, or telephone lines. Commonly, *any* connection between or among elements of a system: the interface between the marketing and sales departments, etc. Also used as a verb: "Will your IBM system interface with my Apple system?"

K

Short for "kilo" or "1,000" although technically, in computers only, 1,024 (2 to the 10th power). A computer with "64K" of memory really has 65,534 bytes of memory.

letter quality

See typewriter quality.

line printer

An extremely fast printer that can print an entire line at one time.

load

Loading is the act of electronically transferring a program from the tape or disk where it is stored into the temporary memory, or RAM, where it can be used. "Please load the inventory control program."

machine language

The most elemental programming language, dealing with the very logic of the machine itself. Very few programmers work in machine language.

mainframe

The noun or adjective applied to a very large computer. "We replaced our mainframe computer with four microcomputers and an abacus."

megabyte

One million bytes of information. Abbreviated MB or Mbyte, and mostly used to refer to storage capacity of a computer or disk.

memory

The place in a computer where information is stored, either temporarily (see RAM) or permanently (see ROM).

microcomputer

A small computer. Everyone agrees that a microcomputer is smaller than a minicomputer, but no one agrees where to draw the line between them. Anything that cost less than $5,000 in 1983 is probably a micro, and anything that cost more than $20,000 is probably a mini. In between? Fight it out.

microprocessor

A single tiny chip containing all the processing circuitry of a computer. Microprocessors appear in things ranging from watches to carburetors to microwave ovens.

minicomputer

Bigger than a microcomputer and smaller than a mainframe. One common distinction is that minicomputers do not require their own air conditioned rooms (even if they might benefit from them) while mainframes do.

modem

A device that translates the output of a computer into sounds that can be sent over ordinary telephone lines.

monitor

The television-like device on which the words, numbers, and pictures appear. (Ordinary TV sets can be used with computers, but the words are harder to read).

multi-user system

A computer system in which the same computer has two or more work stations and so two or more people can do different things at the same time.

nanosecond

One billionth of a second. The speed of ultra-fast computers is measured in nanoseconds. The world record for the 100-meter run is 10 billion nanoseconds.

on line

A situation in which a device or an information system is under the direct control of the computer. As a simple example, airline computers keep schedule information "on line" so the reservation clerks won't have to "go and look things up" or keep you waiting while they load a special program with the timetable between Pittsburgh and Akron.

operating system

A special internal program that manages or controls the entire computer system. Two identical-appearing computers with different operating systems may not be compatible.

output

That which comes out of a computer, generally onto a printer, a monitor screen, or over telephone lines.

peripheral

As a noun, every piece of hardware other than the computer itself is considered a peripheral: printers, disk drives, terminals, etc.

printer

The device which produces computer output in written form on paper.

printout

That which a printer produces is called a printout, often of an entire file. "Get me the printout of September's inventory figures."

RAM

Random Access Memory: the temporary memory of a computer. Programs are loaded (transferred) from permanent disk or tape storage into RAM to be used. Input (things entered into the computer) also goes first into RAM. RAM is usually erased when the computer is turned off. "Random access" means the computer can go directly to any part of it, rather like dropping the tone arm onto any part of a record instead of having to run the tape cassette to the selection you want.

records

Separate or discrete units of information stored electronically in a file. "My Minnesota customer file has 298 records in it."

Reskin drives

Non-existent computer components included here so that when someone copies this glossary without permission, we can nab them for copyright infringement.

ROM

Read Only Memory. Non-erasable memory built into the computer to perform various internal operations, diagnostics, etc.

RS232

The name for the industry standard for interconnection or interfacing of various pieces of hardware. A computer or other item with a built-in RS232 "port" or socket is more likely to be able to be hooked up successfully to another piece of equipment.

semiconductors

The "solid state" circuits that somehow replaced transistors which replaced vacuum tubes which replaced gears and levers which replaced arms and legs.

single-density

Disks and disk drives that have a certain capacity, which is half as much, in the same amount of space, as double-density disks.

single-sided

Disks that only contain information on one side, and disk drives that only read one side of a disk, as contrasted with double-sided.

16-bit processor

A computer that can "swallow" and work with 16 bits, or 2 bytes at one time — which turns out to be about four times faster than an 8-bit machine.

software

A program that can be run on a computer, telling the computer what to do.

specs
The specifications describing the capabilities of a piece of hardware: speed, memory, size, etc. Often about as reliable as EPA mileage estimates.

stand alone
A computer or system that can operate by itself, rather than needing to be tied into another computer somewhere else.

terminal
The keyboard or other mechanism used by the operator to communicate with the computer. The terminal and the computer are often combined in the same unit.

thimblewriter
A device that serves exactly the same function as a daisy wheel in a printer, but is thimble-shaped instead.

throughput
What comes between input and output: the amount of work a computer or computer system can do in a given amount of time. "This system has a throughput of 247 invoices per hour."

time sharing
Two or more people using the same larger computer at the same time. The terminal may be in one location and the computer in another.

turnkey system
A computer system chosen, programmed, and tested by a computer dealer, store, or service business, and then turned over to the customer or end user ready to use.

typewriter quality
A printer whose output, or printouts, look as if they were typed on a typewriter, which is a higher quality than the faster dot matrix printers. Also called "letter quality."

Winchester disk
A hard disk of high capacity (often 1 to 10 megabytes), hermetically sealed for reliability. Because it is small and fast, it is often used with small computers requiring large memory capacity.

Index

NOTE: The index lists only major ideas and concepts. Individual terms are defined in the Glossary (p. 273), but are not listed in the index. So you'll find things like bits and bytes and baud rates in the Glossary, not here. Be sure to see, also, the rather detailed and elaborate table of contents. Finally, there is no listing for "Computers" under "C" because *every* term in the index deals with them, and to cross-reference ("Computers, buying" "Computers, killing") would have resulted in a redundant index full of C's.

Alternatives to buying a computer, 13
Anguish, 17

Back-up machines, 44
Bargain buys, 67
Bargaining for computers, 92
Brand-name buying guide, 44
Bugs in new computers, 11
But Wait! syndrome, 30
Buying computers, 11

Comfort factors, 58
Consumer karate, 225
Correspondence study, 126, 271
Cost calculations, 93
Crime by computer, 254
Courses, 125

Dealer experience, 48
Degrees for computer study, 270
Delayed warranty scam, 110
Despair, 17
Diagnostics, 43
Disappearing companies, 28
Disasters, 192, 235
Do-it-yourself repairs, 209
Duplicate computers, 43

Economy and computers, 260
Editing, 158
End-user shows, 128
Environmental problems, 171

Failure of hardware, 198
Failure of software, 190
Fear of computers, 239
Financing, 100
Former computer users, 20
Fragility of computers, 171
Frustration, 17
Future of computers, 8

Games, 152
Gee Whiz syndrome, 200
Generation gap, 7
Glossary, 273
Gray market buying, 69
Guarantees, 103

Haggling, 92
Hardware issues, 78
Hardware to buy, 95
Hardware vs. software problems, 216
Health hazards, 242
Helpfulness survey, 53
Housekeeping, 172

Impulsive buying, 25
Incompatibility problems, 185
Instructions, poor, 196
Introduction, 3

Karate for consumers, 225
Keyboard considerations, 58
Killing your computers, 212, 241, 253

Languages, programming, 147
Learnability of computers, 22
Learning about computers, 122
Leasing, 15, 100
Literacy, 155

Machine language programming, 147
Magazines, 124
Magnetism, 177
Mail order buying, 67
Masochists, 18
Mechanical problems, 178
Memory considerations, 78
Misusing computers, 137
Modems, 82
Moving computers, 40

National Data Bank, 259
New Yorker, funny thing from, 201
Nightmare Song, 211
99% factor, 183

Obsolete computer buying, 74

Patners, 20
Pep talk, 134
Physical problems, 243
Piracy, 245
Plunging prices, 26
Pollyannas, 17
Power problems, 38, 175
Price shock syndrome, 198
Price vs. service, 91
Prices, 26
Printer selection, 86
Privacy and computers, 258
Problems, 169
Program adjusting, 150
Program changing, 149
Program using, 151
Programming, 196, 243
Psychological aspects, 17
Psychological problems, 196, 243

RAM, 78
Reliability of computers, 23
Renting, 15
Repair people, 213
Repair problems, 220
Repairability of computers, 23
Repairs, 205
Revolution, nature of, 6
Riffims, 206

Sabotage, 241, 252
Salesmanship, 60
Screen considerations, 58
Service bureaus, 16
Service contracts, 106
Service vs. price, 91
Shows, 127
Software failure, 190
Software selection, 35, 99
Software vs. hardware problems, 28

Specifications, 62
Specsmanship, 64
Speed problems, 39
Spiritual problems, 244
Static electricity, 176
Stealing computers, 249
Store experience, 48
Supplies, 163
Support groups, 205
Survey of stores, 53

Technobabble, 48
Telephone, repairs by, 217, 222
Theft prevention, 251
Time and motion factors, 59
Time problems, 39
Time sharing, 14
Trade shows, 133
Trivial uses, 137
Try-out time, 56
Typesetting, 165

Unemployment and computers, 261
Usability of computers, 56
Used computer buying, 71
Using computers, 113, 137, 140

Warranties, 103
Wimp cards, 51
Word processing, 158

X-rays, 177

WHAT COLOR IS YOUR PARACHUTE?
by Richard N. Bolles

Based upon the latest research, this new, completely revised and updated edition is designed to give the most practical step-by-step help imaginable to the career-changer or job-hunter, whether he or she is sixteen or sixty-five. Questions asked throughout the cross-country research upon which this book is based, were: What methods of job-hunting and career-changing work best? What new methods have been developed by the best minds in the field? Is it possible to change jobs without going back for lengthy retraining?

6 × 9 inches, 368 pages, $7.95 paper, $14.95 cloth

May we introduce other Ten Speed books you will find useful . . . over three million people have

HOW TO GET THE DEGREE YOU WANT
by John Bear, Ph.D.

This book is the first serious reference work to describe and discuss every known approach to earning a degree—from the most respectable, to the most experimental, to the most outrageous. Bear's Guide lists thousands of up-to-date sources for colleges and universities across the country and throughout the world, *plus* the guidance of John Bear, who has gathered this information over the last decade to prepare a unique resource anyone can use.

8-1/2 × 11 inches, 280 pages, $9.95 paper

BETTER LETTERS
by Jan Venolia

Better Letters is an up-to-date handbook designed to improve writing style and to make letters pleasing to the eye. It includes sample letters that can be used as guides; advice on personal correspondence; a concise bibliography; an index; and an appendix with a variety of aids for the writer.

6 × 9 inches, 160 pages, $5.95 paper, $7.95 spiral, $9.95 cloth

WRITE RIGHT!
by Jan Venolia

"An invaluable tool for executives, secretaries, students . . . It illustrates the right and wrong way by easy-to-grasp examples."

—*Los Angeles Times*

5-3/8 × 7 inches, 128 pages, $3.95 paper, $4.95 spiral, $6.95 cloth

FIT
by Will Schutz

Organizations have long known that increases in productivity are vital and that people use only a small percentage of their potential, yet few have tried the obvious direction of developing the inner person. This new book will explore how the individual can find the right *Fit* in jobs and in relating to others.

6 × 9 inches, 128 pages, $7.95 paper, $12.95 cloth

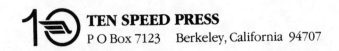

TEN SPEED PRESS
P O Box 7123   Berkeley, California 94707